The Princeton Review

Cracking the
TOEFL® CBT

GEORGE S. MILLER, UPDATED BY TIMOTHY R. WHEELER

2003 EDITION

RANDOM HOUSE, INC.
NEW YORK

www.PrincetonReview.com

Princeton Review Publishing, L.L.C.
2315 Broadway
New York, NY 10024
E-mail: booksupport@review.com

ISBN 0-375-76275-2

Editor: Maria Dente
Production Editor: Maria Dente
Production Coordinator: Jennifer Arias

TOEFL is a registered trademark of the Educational Testing Service, which does not endorse this book.

Manufactured in the United States of America.

9 8 7 6 5 4 3 2 1

2003 Edition

ACKNOWLEDGMENTS

Many thanks to Maria Dente, Jennifer Arias, Tim Dougherty, Tommy Furuhata, David Kelley, Jacqueline Jendras, Matthew Reilly, Alex Weiner, Chris Warnasch, and Iam Williams.

A special thanks to Adam Robinson, who conceived of and perfected the Joe Bloggs approach to standardized tests, and many of the other successful techniques used by The Princeton Review.

CONTENTS

Get More from *Cracking the TOEFL CBT* by Using Our Free Online Tools

Buyers of this book receive access to the latest in online interactive tools for test preparation. Go to www.princetonreview.com/cracking to register for all the free services we offer to help you improve your test score and find the right college or graduate school. Once you've logged on, you'll be able to:

- **Take Extra TOEFL Diagnostic Exams.** You can get even more TOEFL practice by taking full-length TOEFL tests online. After each test, you'll receive a personalized score report showing your strengths and weaknesses. You'll know exactly where you should be concentrating your preparation efforts.

- **Research and Apply to the Best Colleges and Graduate Schools for You.** Through our award-winning college search site, you can access our complete library of information about US colleges and graduate schools, manage your application process, and even apply electronically to colleges, law schools, and business schools.

Reading Your Score Report

After you take a test, you'll receive a score report that looks like this:

Score Report						Subject: Reading

Date: 05/02/01   Listening: 4 Structure: 8-27 Reading: 14 TOTAL : 87-150

[Main Menu] [Essay] [Section 1] [Section 2] [Section 3] [Section 4]

Section 4:

Q#	R W B	Q#	R W B	Q#	R W B	Q#	R W B	Q#	R W B	Q#	R W B
1	✗	11	✓	21	✗	31	✗	41	✗	51	✓
2	✓	12	✗	22	✓	32	✗	42	✓	52	✗
3	✗	13	✓	23	✗	33	✓	43	✓	53	✓
4	✗	14	✓	24	✓	34	✗	44	✓	54	✓
5	✗	15	✓	25	✗	35	✓	45	✗	55	✗
6	✓	16	✗	26	✓	36	✗	46	✓		
7	✓	17	✓	27	✓	37	✓	47	✓	57	
8	✓	18	✓	28	✗	38	✓	48	✓		
9	✗	19	✓	29	✗	39	✗	49	✓		
10	✗	20	✓	30	✓	40	✓	50	✓		

*Click on the question ● to review each question.

On the screen you'll see a chart showing each problem and whether you answered it correctly, incorrectly, or left it blank. If you want to return to that question and check your work, click on the question number. If you want to see the explanation for an incorrect answer choice, click on the corresponding question mark.

Performance Summary:
R = Right
W = Wrong
U = Unanswered

TOTAL	R	W	U	% Correct	% Unanswered
Total	52	48	0	52%	0%

Here you'll see a breakdown of how many questions you answered correctly, incorrectly, or left unanswered.

CATEGORY	R	W	B	0 - 100 %
Reading	31	24	0	56%

Here you'll see how well you did on the various kinds of problems. If your number of wrong answers is high in a certain category, this means that you should spend a little extra time working on that type of problem.

Foreword

No other educational system in the world offers the degree of diversity and flexibility of that found in the United States. A vast array of educational opportunities is offered among both public and private institutions, allowing each student to pursue his or her particular academic and social goals in the environment that best suits that individual.

Students in the United States typically begin school at around six years of age and study for six years in elementary (primary) school, three years in junior high (middle) school, and three years in senior high (secondary) school. It takes a total of twelve years for students to complete both their primary and secondary education, after which they may go on to a college or university for postsecondary study.

POSTSECONDARY EDUCATION: AN OVERVIEW

Postsecondary education in the United States is unique. In most countries of the world, higher education is operated or controlled by one central ministry of education or some other centralized government agency. In the United States, each individual state regulates those institutions within its borders. The federal government has no direct control. Quality and uniformity of degrees and programs are achieved through private, nongovernmental accrediting agencies that tie the state systems together.

In each state there are both public (state-run) and private colleges and universities. Private institutions may either be independent or have a specific religious affiliation. The degree of influence such affiliation has on the academic program and student life varies from one college to another. Most colleges in the United States are coeducational, meaning that they accept both men and women students; however, a small number of institutions accept only men or only women.

There is no direct relationship between public and private schools and cost. Some private institutions cost more than public institutions, and vice versa. Costs vary tremendously from school to school. For example, tuition at Harvard—a private university—is around $25,000 per year, not including living expenses. On the other hand, it is possible to study at a junior (two-year) college for as little as $5,000 per year plus living expenses.

Most public institutions have two rate structures: one for students who are legal residents of the state, and another for students from other states or countries. Private institutions charge the same tuition for all students.

DEGREES

Postsecondary education in the United States is provided by two-year junior or community colleges and four-year colleges and universities. Universities offer more postgraduate courses than colleges, including the doctorate degree. There are four basic degrees offered by United States colleges and universities:

1. The **associate's** degree is usually an Associate of Arts (A.A.) or an Associate of Science (A.S.), and is offered primarily by junior or community colleges. This degree requires two academic years of full-time study to complete. Students can pursue either a technical or an academic course of study. Technical programs are considered "terminal" (they end after two years of study), and they typically prepare individuals for a trade or profession. Students pursuing an academic program will usually transfer to a four-year college or university after receiving their associate degree.

2. The **bachelor's** degree is the first degree earned at a four-year United States college or university; it generally requires four years of full-time academic study.

3. The **master's** degree is the first postgraduate degree earned at a college or university. Depending on the field of study, this degree requires one to two years of academic study beyond the bachelor's degree.

4. The **doctorate** is the highest degree offered at universities. It requires two years of full-time study beyond the master's degree, plus a dissertation based on original research.

The first two years of a bachelor's degree program consist of general education courses. During the final two years, students specialize in their chosen major field of study. Most institutions recognize that students' interests may change as they expand their academic horizons, so they allow individuals to change their majors at any time without losing credit for courses already completed. It may be necessary for a student to complete a few extra courses to satisfy the requirements of a new major, but credit for all courses successfully completed is never lost.

Students may also transfer (or change) institutions during their postsecondary studies, usually without loss of credit for courses previously taken. Transfer credit, however, is not automatic. Whether or not a college or university allows credit for prior study at a different institution is at the discretion of the particular school.

ACADEMIC CALENDARS

The academic year in the United States is approximately nine months long, beginning in September and ending in June of the following year. Most colleges and universities also have short-term summer programs during which students can complete one or two courses toward their degree.

There are four basic academic calendar systems:

1. **Semester** calendar of two terms in the academic year (fall and spring semesters), each consisting of approximately fifteen weeks of classroom instruction. There may also be an optional summer session offering a limited selection of courses.

2. **Trimester** calendar of three ten-week terms (fall, winter, and spring) in the nine-month academic year. An optional summer session offering a limited course selection may also be offered.

3. **Quarter** calendar of four ten-week terms year-round (fall, winter, spring, and summer); students generally attend three of the four sessions, but have the option of attending all four if they wish to expedite their academic program.

4. **4-1-4** calendar of two four-month terms with a one-month "intersession," during which students generally concentrate on a specialized project. There are several variations on this calendar, including 4-4-1 and 5-1-5.

When selecting an institution for study in the United States, you should consider nine basic factors:

1. **Your financial resources**—How much money do you have per year for your education? The yearly costs vary greatly from state to state and from school to school.

2. **Your academic record**—Each college or university has its own requirements for admission. Universities such as Harvard, M.I.T., and Stanford are highly selective and accept only the top students from the best schools. Be sure to select an institution that accepts students within the range of your academic achievements. However, be assured that if you have successfully completed secondary school, you will find an institution in the United States that will accept you as a student for postsecondary studies.

3. **Your major field of study**—No single school offers all the fields of study that are available in the United States. Be sure the college or university to which you apply offers the program you wish to pursue.

4. **Location of the institution**—Physical and social conditions vary greatly from one region to another in the United States. There are large, mid-size, and small colleges in both major urban areas and in smaller towns. Life in a large city is very different from that in a small town. Colder climates in winter are found in the north and east of the country, while the southern portions are more temperate. Every prospective student should have an idea of what kind of setting to expect when arriving in the United States to begin studies.

5. **Size of the institution**—The student population at colleges and universities can vary from as little as 500 to more than 10,000. The size of an institution influences its social and educational atmosphere.

6. **Accreditation**—Is the institution accredited? *Accreditation* means that a given institution has been investigated by a team of experts and found to meet the minimum requirements of the accrediting agency. It is not recommended that international students attend a nonaccredited school, for several reasons. First, students should be sure they are getting the best possible quality education for the investment of time and money. Second, if a student initially enrolls in a nonaccredited school and later wishes to transfer to an accredited institution, the new school may not allow credit for past studies. And finally, many countries will not recognize degrees from nonaccredited institutions for purposes of employment or professional licensing.

7. **Applicability**—Will the degree earned at a particular college or university be recognized by employers, educational institutions, and/or the government in your home country?

8. **Living facilities**—Does the institution offer dormitory facilities? Living in an on-campus residence hall can be more convenient, reduce the stress of cultural adjustment, and make finding friends easier than if you live off campus in an apartment. Apartment accommodations, on the other hand, allow a greater degree of independence.

9. **Type of institution**—The last factor to consider is the type of institution you wish to attend. There are both private and public colleges and universities. Some institutions accept only men or only women, but the vast majority are coeducational. Some private schools are operated by, or affiliated with, religious organizations. Is attending a university with high "prestige" important to you, or will a lesser-known institution that provides a solid education be acceptable? Do you want a college that emphasizes academics, one that affords an active social life, or a school that falls somewhere in between?

THE APPLICATION PROCESS

Once you have decided which institution you would like to attend, the next step is to obtain an application and apply for admission. You may contact the school directly and request an application for enrollment, or you may visit our website at www.PrincetonReview.com.

It is important that you begin the application process far in advance of the term you wish to attend. Many universities have deadlines after which they will not accept applications for that semester or year. Sometimes it takes several months for an admissions officer to process an application; applications for postgraduate study can take as long as six to nine months to process.

Although the forms from different schools may appear to differ greatly, the documents necessary to complete an application are much the same regardless of the college or university. All institutions require the following:

1. An application form. Be sure to answer all questions thoroughly; an incomplete application could delay the entire admissions process.

2. Transcripts of all academic work you have completed, showing courses taken and grades received. An original official copy and a certified English translation are required.

3. A financial statement demonstrating that you have sufficient funds at your disposal to support your study and living expenses in the United States.

4. An autobiography of yourself, in English, with a statement of your educational goals in the United States.

5. Many institutions require a statement of good health from a physician, in English or with an official English translation.

6. Demonstrated proficiency in English. This requirement may be fulfilled in several ways. The TOEFL (Test of English as a Foreign Language) is the most widely accepted test of proficiency; it is a standardized test that is administered worldwide. An alternative to taking the TOEFL is first to enroll in an English as a Second Language (ESL) program. There are numerous such programs in the United States, many situated on college campuses.

A student who has been accepted to a college or university or to an intensive English program will receive two documents: A letter of acceptance and a Form I-20. The Form I-20 is a United States government form filled out by the accepting institution, which gives a student the right to go to the nearest United States Embassy or Consulate and request an F-1 student visa. The visa officer has the sole authority either to grant or deny the visa.

In making a decision, there are two main things a visa officer considers. First, applicants must prove that they have sufficient financial resources to live and study in the United States without working, at least for their first academic year. Second, the visa officer must be convinced that the students will return to their home countries upon completion of their degree programs.

THE CHOICE IS YOURS!

As you can see, the educational alternatives in the United States are many and perhaps even overwhelming. However, the great variety of programs and institutions means you can receive as much education as you want if you work for it and can figure out how to pay for it.

The United States has a long tradition of welcoming international students into its colleges and universities. Most institutions, both large and small, have services in place to assist international students in making the transition—whether academic, cultural, or social—as smooth as possible.

—Nora Saidi

PART I

Orientation

What Is the TOEFL CBT?

The computer-based Test of English as a Foreign Language (TOEFL CBT) is a standardized test administered by the Educational Testing Service (ETS), a huge, tax-exempt private company located in New Jersey. ETS is the same testing organization that administers the GRE, SAT, LSAT, and a bunch of tests in other fields, including hair styling, plumbing, and golf. The TOEFL CBT is supposedly designed to test a non-native English speaker's proficiency in American English. For that reason, all the expressions, idioms, and grammar tested in the TOEFL CBT are those most common in America, *not* in England or other English-speaking countries.

What Does the TOEFL CBT Measure?

It is unclear exactly what the computer-based Test of English as a Foreign Language measures. Clearly, a person fluent in English will perform better on the test than would a person only somewhat familiar with the language. However, how well you speak and understand English is not the only factor that determines your TOEFL CBT score. Some people get very nervous when taking a test and don't get the score they deserve. Others always do well on tests even when they don't study. Standardized tests aren't the most reliable measure of proficiency in *any* subject. So what is *really* tested by the TOEFL CBT? Well, one might say, the main thing that TOEFL CBT scores represent is your ability to take the TOEFL CBT; not necessarily your fluency in American English.

This book will help improve your TOEFL CBT score by showing you how to look for shortcuts, avoid common mistakes, and practice taking the test. These skills are just as important to your TOEFL CBT score as studying English.

For many of you, taking a computer-based test is a new experience. Fortunately, you have this book to help you prepare.

How Important Is the TOEFL CBT?

The importance given to your TOEFL CBT score varies greatly from school to school. Although ETS does not intend (or at least that's what they claim) for TOEFL CBT scores to be used by universities as cutoffs (for example, rejecting all applicants with scores below 250), usually that is exactly what happens. Another result of a low TOEFL CBT score might be that a college will admit you but not allow you to register until you have taken a semester or two of English courses. If you're taking the TOEFL CBT in order to apply to a college or university, find out how your scores will be evaluated and used. The majority of colleges and universities in the United States, and many in Canada, require TOEFL CBT scores from all international applicants. Each year, approximately 800,000 students worldwide take the TOEFL CBT as part of the application process for everything from undergraduate, masters, and doctoral programs, to professional licensing, governmental employment, and various scholarship programs.

WHY IS THE TEST GIVEN ON A COMPUTER?

Until 1998, the TOEFL was only available as a paper-and-pencil test. Sometimes problems arose because those persons administering the test often were unfamiliar with the TOEFL, and, at best, could barely answer any question posed. Furthermore, ETS realized the enormous financial benefits they could reap from transforming the paper-and-pencil TOEFL test into the Computer-Based Test (CBT). It now saves money on printing test materials, renting facilities, and processing answer sheets. It also doubled the test fee from $55 to $110.

Honestly, ETS doesn't really care about evaluating or improving your English, they are more interested in business efficiency and convenience. When the paper-and-pencil test was still offered, you had the option to review the material after taking the test. Now, with the TOEFL CBT, ETS makes it impossible for you to:

- Know which answers you got wrong

- See the test or questions again

- Learn from your mistakes

- Be sure the computer accurately determined your score

However, there's not much to be gained from bemoaning the fact that the TOEFL is given on computer, because with limited exceptions, there is no other way to take it.

HOW DOES THE TOEFL CBT WORK?

Cracking the TOEFL CBT is a great tool to help you prepare for the TOEFL CBT. However, since the Listening and Structure sections of the TOEFL CBT are adaptive, you will have to overcome some of the instincts you have developed in school for taking a linear pencil-and-paper test when you are completing those sections. You cannot simply turn back the page and revisit questions you skipped when the answers suddenly pop into your head, or save all of the hardest questions for last. In an adaptive section, once you have clicked on an answer choice and confirmed your decision, you will never see that question again. Furthermore, you cannot move to the next question until you answer the current question.

Computer adaptive tests measure your performance based upon various factors including:

- The number of questions you answer in the time given

- The number of questions you answer correctly

- The relative difficulty of the questions you answer correctly

- The location (beginning, middle, end of section) of the questions you answered correctly

An adaptive section will always start with a medium level question and ETS will assume that the test taker deserves a medium level score. Each subsequent question is chosen from a pool of available questions based upon the test taker's performance up to that point in the section. In other words, the difficulty of question number 2 will be based on your performance on, and the difficulty of question number 1. Similarly, in selecting question number 10, the computer will consider your performance on, and the difficulty of questions 1–9. In general, if you answer a question correctly, the computer adjusts your score upwardly and then serves you a more difficult question. If you answer incorrectly, the computer adjusts your score downwardly and serves you an easier question. The process continues until the computer zeroes in on what it thinks is the perfect score for you. Since the computer doesn't know you very well at the beginning of the test, the score adjustments at that point are greater. These adjustments become smaller throughout the test, until, at the very end, a correct or incorrect answer may change your score only slightly or not at all.

This knowledge will be very valuable when considering how to pace yourself through an adaptive section. Simply put, because the score adjustments are greater earlier in the section, your responses then will have a greater impact on your final score than will your responses to questions later in the section. So take extra care when answering the first five or so questions in any adaptive section, even if it means spending slightly more time on those early questions. But remember, these tips only apply to the Listening and Structure sections of the test, not the Reading section, and obviously, not the Writing section.

Never try to figure out how difficult a question is; rather, concentrate on working carefully on each question that you get. You'll learn a lot more about pacing, as well as general TOEFL CBT strategies and techniques, in the following chapters.

THE BAD NEWS FIRST

There are several disadvantages to the TOEFL CBT.

- The cost rises from $55 to $110.

- The test is longer, and therefore more exhausting.

- Testing appointments are limited.

- Some question types are more difficult.

- A 30-minute essay (the Writing section) is mandatory.

Now The Good News

- You have more time to answer the questions! There is no longer a 12-second interval between the Listening section questions that there was for the paper-and-pencil test. You get to work at your own pace!

- You can take the TOEFL CBT any time a testing center is open. There is no deadline for registration. However, since the seats fill up quickly, we recommend that you register at least one or two weeks before you want to take the TOEFL CBT.

- The atmosphere is quiet and comfortable, and you can actually hear the speakers in the Listening section.

- You can receive your scores faster, and ETS will send them to up to four academic institutions, rather than just three. (You can always pay for additional score reports.)

- Selecting an answer is easier on the computer. No more annoying ovals to fill in with a number 2 pencil.

How Is the TOEFL CBT Structured?

The TOEFL CBT is divided into four sections and lasts approximately four and one-half hours. Although each test taker's score is based on the same number of questions, the actual number of questions you will see in any section may vary within a specific range. This is true because ETS sometimes inserts extra "pretest" or experimental questions into the various sections of the test. Your responses to these extra questions will not affect your score. You are merely providing ETS with some free statistical research on questions that they may use in future tests. However, you will be told at the beginning of each section how many questions will be given and how much time you will have to answer them. You can expect your test to look something like the chart on the following page.

Section 1: Listening	
Part A (short conversations)	approx.1/3 of Listening questions
Part B (6 to 9 lectures and long conversations)	approx. 1/3 of Listening questions
Total: 30–49 questions	
Time: 15–25 minutes	
Section 2: Structure	
Sentence Completion and Error Identification	20–25 questions
Total: 20–25 questions	
Time: 15–20 minutes	
Break Time: 10 minutes	
Section 3: Reading	
4 to 5 passages	10–13 questions per passage
Total: 44–55 questions	
Time: 70–90 minutes	
Section 4: Writing	
1 typed or hand-written essay	
Time: 30 minutes	
Approximate number of questions: 94–129	
Total Time: Approximately 4 and one-half hours	

You will be given 15–25 minutes to finish the Listening section. However, since the clock only runs while you are answering questions (or adjusting the volume), the section will take 40–60 minutes to complete.

Keep in mind that the total time takes into account the mandatory tutorials that explain the computer, question types, and all other procedures. Even though your performance on the tutorials has *no* impact on your final score, they are tiring and time consuming. You should move through them as quickly as possible in order to save energy for the actual test questions and to avoid test fatigue.

How Is the TOEFL CBT Scored?

The TOEFL CBT score report you receive from ETS will contain five different scores. First, you will see separate sub-scores for Listening, Structure/Writing, and Reading. Each of these scores is based on a scale of 0–30. The Structure/Writing sub-score represents a combination of your performance on the Structure section and the score you received on the 30-minute essay. Next, you will see a composite or total score within a range of 0–300. ETS computes this score by adding the 3 sub-scores together, multiplying that number by 10, and then dividing the total by 3. Generally, schools are most interested in your composite score.

Finally, you will receive an essay score on a scale of 0–6 in half-point increments. Unlike the other scores, this one is not generated directly by the computer. The reported score is the average of two separate ratings assigned by two different readers. In the event that there is a discrepancy of more than one point in the two ratings, a third reader is brought in to independently grade the essay.

Upon completion of the TOEFL CBT, an unofficial score report will appear on the computer screen. The Listening and Reading scores will be accurate and final. The Structure/Writing score will be given as a range of scores due to the fact that your essay will not yet have been rated. For example, a score of 5–25 means that if you did very poorly on the essay; you will receive a score of about 5 in this category, while if you did very well on the essay, your score will be closer to 25. Because the Structure/Writing score can not be computed on test day, your total score will also be given as a range. Just as in the Structure/Writing score, the lower end of the range represents a total score with a poor essay while the upper end of the range represents a total score with an excellent essay. At this point, you will be given the option to either report or cancel your scores. Should you decide to cancel your scores, they do not become part of your record unless you request reinstatement (with an extra fee, of course), in writing, within 60 days. Should you decide to report your scores, you will be given the opportunity to select up to four institutions or agencies to receive official score reports. Remember, even though you are allowed to see your scores on test day, you will not be given a written report. Therefore, be sure to write down your scores as soon as you leave the testing room.

When Will I Receive My Scores?

ETS sends your official scores to your address and the academic institutions/agencies you select, approximately two weeks after your test if you type your essay, or five weeks after your test if you hand-write your essay. Additional score reports (beyond the four free reports you may select on test day) cost $11 US each, and may be ordered with a special form found in the back of the TOEFL CBT Bulletin; or you may call 1-888-863-3544 (all major credit cards accepted). ETS stores your scores for a period of two years. Therefore, if more than two years have elapsed since you last took the TOEFL, you will need to take the test again. Although your scores are confidential, ETS reserves the right to use your performance anonymously for research purposes.

Where Do I Take the TOEFL CBT?

The actual names and locations of TOEFL CBT testing centers vary from country to country. Most tests are administered by a company call Prometric at their own permanent testing centers. All available testing centers are listed in the TOEFL CBT Bulletin. Generally, the test is given at individual computer testing stations similar to study areas you might find at a library. The testing rooms are under camera surveillance to discourage cheating; security is tight!

How Do I Register For the TOEFL CBT?

By Phone:

The easiest way to register is by phone. You must have a valid Visa, Master Card, or American Express card.

Step 1: Get a TOEFL CBT Bulletin. You may call ETS at 1-609-771-7100 to request a bulletin. Or, simply go online to www.toefl.org and order the bulletin electronically or download the bulletin and CBT voucher request form from the website. You may also pick up a bulletin at most colleges and universities or at your local testing center.

Step 2: Fill out the CBT Voucher in the center of the bulletin. This is the information you will need to supply over the phone. The test will cost $110 US.

Step 3: Call the Regional Registration Center (RRC) that covers the location where you want to take the test and supply them with the information on your CBT Voucher Request Form and your credit card number. The RRCs, phone numbers, and test center locations are all listed in the TOEFL CBT Bulletin. If you wish to take the test in the United States, call the test center directly. Or, call 1-800-468-6335 from within the US, or 1-443-751-4862 from outside of the US, to reach Prometric Candidate Services for help in selecting a testing site. The operator will give you a confirmation number, test date, the time you must report to the test center, address, and identification requirements. *Do not lose your confirmation number!*

By Mail:

Paying by check is a little more complicated.

Step 1: See Step 1 above. You may also write for a bulletin at the following address:
TOEFL Office
P.O. Box 6151
Princeton, NJ 08541-6151

Step 2: Complete the CBT Voucher located in the center of the bulletin and mail it to the appropriate address. (Look inside the envelope for the mailing labels.) Be sure to enclose your check or money order payable to TOEFL.

Many testing sites fill up very quickly, so register as soon as possible.

Step 3: In approximately four weeks, ETS will send you a TOEFL CBT voucher with a confirmation number. *Do not lose your confirmation number.*

Step 4: Call the Regional Registration Center (RRC) that covers the location where you want to take the test and supply them with your Voucher Number so they know you have paid. The RRCs, phone numbers, and test center locations are all listed in the TOEFL CBT Bulletin. If you wish to take the test in the United States, call the test center directly and give them your Voucher Number. Or, call 1-800-468-6335 from within the US, or 1-443-751-4862 from outside of the US, to reach Prometric Candidate Services for help in selecting a testing site. The operator will give you a confirmation number, test date, the time you must report to the test center, address, and identification requirements. *Do not lose your confirmation number!*

You should also make sure to visit the TOEFL website at www.toefl.org for additional information.

CAN I RESCHEDULE MY TEST DATE?

Yes, but you must contact the RRC, testing center, or candidate services at least three business days (five business days for supplemental test centers) before your appointment. You will need to provide your name and confirmation number, and pay a rescheduling fee of $40 US.

CAN I TAKE THE TOEFL CBT MORE THAN ONCE?

Definitely—but only once per month. If you take the TOEFL CBT more than once per month, the second test will *not* count, you will *not* be able to see your score, and you will *not* get a refund. Don't despair if you have to retake the test. Since ETS only reports the scores you want them to, it is to your advantage to take the test more than once and then submit your best scores to the schools or institutions to which you are applying.

CAN I STILL TAKE THE PAPER-AND-PENCIL TEST?

Probably not. Although ETS has announced that it will phase out a number of test centers in 2002–2003 and offer the pencil-and-paper test in some of the affected areas, the overwhelming majority of test takers will be required to take the test on the computer. Check the TOEFL website at www.toefl.org for more information and to find out if your area will be affected by the phase-out. In general, once the TOEFL CBT becomes available in a country, the paper-and-pencil test is eliminated.

WHAT IS THE PRINCETON REVIEW?

The Princeton Review is a test-preparation company based in New York City. We have offices in more than fifty cities across the country and the world. We've developed the techniques found in our books and courses by analyzing actual exams and testing their effectiveness with our students. We don't want to waste your time with a lot of unnecessary information. It would be foolish for us to try to teach you every rule of English grammar or every subtlety of spoken English. Those things aren't necessarily what will raise your score.

What we will teach you is how to approach the test. Once you learn to think like the people who write the test, you'll learn what sorts of questions come up most often and what a right answer looks like. You'll learn to use your time effectively, avoid problems along the way, and find answers to questions you may be unsure of.

You need to do only two things: Trust the techniques, and *practice*.

ARE THERE ANY OTHER WAYS TO PRACTICE FOR THE TOEFL CBT?

If you feel that you have adequately covered all the information in the book and could use more practice, ETS offers practice paper-and-pencil TOEFL tests, practice questions, and practice CBT tests on CD-ROM. You may order these materials on-line at www.toefl.org or by calling ETS directly at 1-609-771-7243. An order form is located in the TOEFL CBT Bulletin.

The Princeton Review also offers a highly successful TOEFL CBT preparation course at many of its sites. The course is famous for its small classes, personal attention, and most importantly, excellent results. For information about course offerings in the United States, call 1-800-2Review.

For course information in the following countries, call The Princeton Review in:

Hong Kong	(011) 85-2-507-9323
Mexico	(011) 52-5-564-9468
Montreal, Canada	(514) 499-0870
Japan	(011) 81-3-3463-1343
Korea	(011) 82-2-554-7762
Saudi Arabia	Call in the U.S. at (413) 584-6849
Singapore	(011) 65-6-835-0355
Spain	(341) 571-3849
Taiwan	(011) 88-6-2751-1293
Thailand	(011) 66-256-7080
Toronto, Canada	(800) 495-7737
Turkey	(011) 90-212-265-2468

The Basics

WHY PRACTICE FOR THE TOEFL CBT?

ETS will tell you that it is not possible to learn English in a short period of time. While this is true, what you *can* learn in a short period of time is how to take an exam.

Would you rather take the test in *this* situation:

You wake up tomorrow morning to discover that the test is being given in an hour. You rush to the test center, unprepared, upset, and out of sorts. You arrive at the test center nervous and unsure of what to expect. You begin the test, misread the instructions, and make time-consuming mistakes. Unfamiliar with the computer-based TOEFL, you make more silly mistakes, which continue to lower your score.

Or this one?

After preparing for the test, you arrive at the test center on time, confident and relaxed. You know what to bring with you. You know how long the test will take. There are no surprises. You don't waste your time or your brainpower trying to familiarize yourself with the TOEFL CBT test. You are completely used to all question types and are not intimidated by the changes ETS has made. Your score reflects your confidence.

There is no reason to panic over the TOEFL CBT. Nothing can alleviate your stress more than knowing what to expect. Don't let your score be affected by the unknown! Prepare and get ready to improve your score.

How To Use This Book

What this book sets out to do is to train you for the TOEFL CBT in the most efficient way. There is not a lot of memorizing, but as with any study aid, it is best to allot a few hours each day for a few weeks before the test. You'll want time to find your strengths and weaknesses. You'll want to practice the techniques and do the drills a little at a time. Do not try to finish everything in a weekend!

In addition to the information in the book, here are a couple of general pointers to help you become as familiar as possible with spoken and written English:

- **SPEAK!** Don't be intimidated by English. Try to converse with native English speakers as much as possible. If you have a friend or teacher who is an English speaker, practice with that person. Have conversations on the telephone. Learn the idiomatic expressions, feel the rhythm of the language, and get to know how Americans express themselves. Nothing can improve your English more than speaking with real people in real situations. The most important thing you can do is *speak, speak, speak!* Got it?

- **LISTEN!** Turn on the radio and television. This is a fun way to improve listening comprehension! Try to understand what is being implied in a conversation or discussion. Talk shows can be great sources of conversation.

- **READ!** Buy newspapers and magazines. Get used to skimming articles to find the main ideas. Pay attention to captions under pictures. The longest passage you will encounter on the TOEFL CBT is about 350 words, so look for short articles that are factually dense such as those found in the Op/Ed section of most newspapers.

- **BE POSITIVE!** Set reasonable goals and stick to them. Your English *will* improve if you believe. Eliminate your fear.

These are some of the most interesting and natural ways to practice. Make it your goal for the next few weeks to spend as much time as possible *speaking*, *listening* to, and *reading* English.

CAN I REALLY IMPROVE MY SCORE?

Yes, you can. ETS likes to say that the advice provided by preparation books and courses does not yield consistent results. However, if you check the TOEFL CBT Bulletin and the TOEFL website you will see that they offer plenty of vague advice themselves. Also, if you think about it, ETS would prefer that you do poorly on the TOEFL CBT, that way you'll have to come back in a month or two and pay them another $110. Although native English speakers will out-perform non-native English speakers on the TOEFL, learning more American English is not the only factor involved in raising your score. The more familiar any test taker is with the structure of the test, the types of questions presented, and the reoccurring content, the better that test taker will score on the TOEFL CBT. Quite simply, anyone can learn how to take a standardized test.

The Princeton Review method includes familiarization with the test and its content, techniques, and strategies for each individual section, and an overall approach to achieving the best score possible. We will start with the basics in terms of content and technique and quickly move you through more complex, advanced strategies. We have devoted millions of dollars and thousands of man-hours to perfecting our unique plan for attacking the TOEFL CBT that really works.

Let's start with some general strategies for attacking the TOEFL CBT.

POE (PROCESS OF ELIMINATION)

Perhaps the best thing about ETS's standardized TOEFL CBT is that the correct answer is always in front of you, right? You never have to fill in a blank, or come up with the answer on your own. Furthermore, because there are usually three times as many wrong answers as there are right answers, it's often easier to eliminate the wrong answers than to pick the correct one. Thus, by identifying and eliminating the incorrect answers you may increase your chances of selecting the "credited response" or correct answer.

WRONG ANSWERS

Eliminate wrong answers to find the correct answer.

ETS has labeled the wrong answers as "distractors." The definition of "distract" is to draw attention away from one object, and focus it on another. This is exactly ETS's goal: *to draw your attention away from the correct answer, and focus it on a wrong one.* This ETS strategy keeps you from earning points accidentally. Once you are able to recognize ETS's distractors, your score will greatly improve! It makes sense!

Improve Your Odds

Use POE to improve your chances of clicking on the best answer.

Every time you are able to eliminate an incorrect choice on the TOEFL CBT, you improve your chances of clicking on the best answer. The more you use POE, the better your odds. Think about it. If you guess on any question, you have a one-in-four chance of getting the best answer. When you eliminate just one choice, you are now down to one-in-three. Eliminate just two answers and you now have a 50/50 chance of guessing the best answer. In the Listening and Structure sections, you have to click on an answer before the next one appears. If you don't know the answer, you'll have to guess, so guess intelligently. This indirect way of finding the correct answer helps you avoid the traps that ETS wants you to fall in. POE is a powerful testing tool!

In the Reading section, every question is worth the same. Logically, you will want to learn how to skip the more difficult questions and leave them for last. However, you must answer every question by the end of the Reading section. It is very important to know that you are **not** penalized for guessing. Use POE and make your best guess.

Pacing

Be extra careful at the beginning of the Listening and Structure sections.

In the last chapter, you learned a little about the way an adaptive test operates. On the TOEFL CBT, only the Listening and Structure sections are computer adaptive. As you recall, this means that in these sections each subsequent question is selected and served based on your responses to all of the previous questions in the section. In general, if you get a question wrong, the next one will be easier; if you get a question right, the next one you see will be a little harder. Also recall that the jumps in difficulty that the computer makes at the beginning of the test are larger than those it makes at the end of the test. Why is this important? Quite simply, if the jumps in difficulty are greater in the beginning of the test, you must be extra careful there because those questions will have a greater impact on your score. Because of the way adaptive tests work, you must remember to pace yourself accordingly. On adaptive sections:

- Spend a little more time on the first 1/3 of the questions than you do on the middle third or the last 1/3. How much is a little more? Enough extra time so that you may get most of the first 1/3 or so correct. But, be careful not to take this to the extreme. If you have to guess on half of the test, your score will not improve.

- Do your best to answer all of the questions in the section, even if you have to guess at the very end.

- Don't get hung up and spend too much time on any one question. If you are truly unsure, use POE to eliminate incorrect answer choices, take your best guess, and move on. You should never spend more than two minutes or so on a single question.

Pacing in the Reading section is quite different because that section is linear, not adaptive. The questions are all selected in advance and do not come in any set order of difficulty. You may answer the questions in any order you wish. But remember, unlike in Listening or Structure where the questions at the beginning of the test will affect your score the most, all of the questions in Reading have the same impact on your score. Since the choice is yours, which questions do you want to answer first? Why the easiest ones of course! In the Reading section:

- Answer all of the questions in any single passage before moving on to another passage. We'll talk later about which passages to do first.

- Answer the easiest questions first (more on this later too).

- Always answer all of the questions in the section, even if you have to guess on some of them as time runs out.

As you may have noticed from the chart in chapter 1, you have around 4 and 1/2 hours to complete:

- Several tutorials describing the computer, the different sections, and question types

- Approximately 94 to 129 questions

- A 30-minute mandatory written essay

That's a lot to accomplish. You will be mentally and physically exhausted by the time you get to the last section. Don't give in to fatigue. Prepare to reward yourself when you finish. Stick with it. Never just answer a question to "get through" and "get it over with."

Practice Using a Computer

A major obstacle facing many students taking the TOEFL CBT is their fear of computers. Take heart in the fact that ETS has made it impossible for you to accidentally erase your score, crash the computer, or delete any information. In fact, they make a great effort to explain how to move, point, and click a mouse. Mandatory computer tutorials explain the different question types that will appear on the TOEFL CBT and how to properly enter your answers. Although prior computer skills are not required to be able to take the TOEFL CBT, familiarizing yourself with a computer before signing up for the TOEFL CBT will greatly increase your confidence. Furthermore, here at The Princeton Review, we've done our best to make it easy for you. Some of the very best practice you can get is waiting for you at www.review.com/cracking/toefl.cfm. There you will find drills, practice tips, and best of all, full-length adaptive TOEFL exams. These resources are designed to not only familiarize you with the test and its content, but also to allow you to become comfortable taking tests on a computer. Be sure to include them in your study plan.

> Try to familiarize yourself with the computer.

The Week of the Test

By the week of the test you should be confident in your test-taking abilities. Keep in mind that you are not really memorizing specific information, such as algebraic formulas or the state capitals for this exam. It's more about practicing techniques and strategies until they become so natural to you that you don't have to think about what to do next, you just do it. By the week of the test you should have reviewed most of the information in this book. If possible, it's a good idea to save some practice test material for the last week. If you haven't managed to save anything, redo some of the first drills and tests you did in order to refresh your skills. When you work on drills, test sections, or complete tests during the final week, be sure to time yourself and try to complete entire sections or entire tests in one sitting. It's important to simulate the test taking experience as closely as possible, so that on test day, there are no surprises.

Don't cram a great deal of studying into the last week. Consider yourself an athlete in training for a big race. Most of your training should be done weeks or even months before the big event, not just a few days before it. The last week should be reserved for fine-tuning, reviewing, and running through a test or two to bring everything together. You don't want to feel exhausted and sick of test questions, you want to feel confident and prepared. The last week you should try to stay healthy and well rested. Plan to practice TOEFL materials just enough to finish up and keep your level of confidence high.

The night before the exam, plan to eat a light meal and maybe see a movie. *Don't study.* All you will learn that last night is how to be nervous. You're well prepared, so relax and get a good night's sleep.

The Day of the Exam

Be sure to bring:

- **Photo identification**—This basically means your passport. However, if your passport picture doesn't resemble your current look, expect some trouble. There are no exceptions. The administrators at the test centers are no-nonsense and will not hesitate to throw you out if they suspect something is wrong.

- **Confirmation number**—The confirmation number was given to you by the friendly operator if you registered by phone, or is listed on your CBT Voucher if you registered by mail.

- **A watch**—The time remaining for each section is always in the upper left corner of the screen. However, it isn't a bad idea to bring your own time source.

- **A positive attitude**—This is perhaps your biggest advantage to cracking the TOEFL CBT.

You are not allowed to bring anything into the testing rooms. No food, drinks, tobacco, paper, pencils, beepers, cellular phones, pagers, pens, calculators, books, pamphlets, dictionaries, and so forth are allowed. Only during the Writing section will you be given paper. At some test centers, lockers are available to store your stuff in, but they are *small*—only big enough for a small purse! You have one official 10-minute break between the Structure and Reading sections; however, you can leave at any time provided that you sign in and out. Time will still run if you are in the middle of a test section. If you must, take a break during the tutorials. It is important that you eat before you start the test. Being hungry or tired in the middle of the exam will likely affect your score. Even though you cannot bring food into the room, you may want to bring a snack to eat during your break.

Before each section of the TOEFL CBT, you will go through a tutorial, which basically teaches you about the computer and the different test questions you will encounter. Move through them quickly so that you do not waste your energy and brainpower. The test centers are also monitored by closed-circuit television cameras. Ignore them. You won't be doing anything wrong, so block them out.

Now relax and feel confident. You are well prepared and will do your best. *Think positively!*

PART II

Listening

THE BASICS

In the Listening section of the TOEFL CBT, you will have to answer between 30 and 49 questions in 15 to 25 minutes. You will be told at the beginning of the section exactly how many questions you will see and exactly how much time you will be given to answer them. You will be given a set of headphones to wear while audio passages play on your computer. Remember that the clock does not run during the audio passages, only while you are answering the questions that follow each passage. Also, for some reason, if you adjust the volume during a passage, the clock runs then too. So be sure to adjust the volume properly in advance. Even though you are given 15 to 25 minutes to answer the questions, because of the audio passages the section will take 40 to 60 minutes to complete. There are two separate parts in the Listening section:

Part A: In this part you will hear short conversations between two speakers. A third speaker will then ask you a single question about what was said. About 1/3 of the questions in the section will be in Part A.

Part B: In this part you will hear either a long conversation between two to four speakers, or a lecture given by one person. In both cases, another speaker will ask you a series of questions about what was said. Expect to see 6 to 9 passages.

WHAT IS IT SUPPOSED TO TEST?

ETS claims that this part of the test offers you "an opportunity to demonstrate your ability to understand spoken English." According to ETS, the information it obtains from your performance on this section is supposed to help a school determine if your English is good enough to understand what is going on in your classes.

WHAT DOES IT *REALLY* TEST?

Before you feel too grateful for the opportunity to demonstrate your English skills, think for a minute about what this section really measures. If you wanted someone to "demonstrate his ability to comprehend" any spoken language, what would you do? You would probably try to have a conversation with that person.

What you probably *wouldn't* do is make him wear headphones and sit in a room full of computers with 15 other people and answer a bunch of multiple-choice questions that have little relevance to anything. That kind of test measures:

- How well you hear
- The ability to comprehend idioms and non sequiturs
- The ability to stay calm under pressure

But does it measure your ability to understand spoken English? Not very well. The one thing the TOEFL CBT Listening section does with total accuracy is measure how well you do on the TOEFL CBT Listening section.

How to Tackle the Listening Section

This chapter will teach you how to use some of the weaknesses of the Listening section to help you rather than hurt you. We'll also show you how to use Process of Elimination (POE) to find the right answers, *even if you didn't understand what you heard.*

How Much Will Your Scores Improve?

That depends on how much you practice and *how* you practice. If you use the techniques, your scores will improve, but remember:

- It's easier to improve starting with a medium or low score than it is to improve with a high score. The Listening section, like Reading and Structure, is scored on a scale of 0 to 30. If you are already scoring somewhere between 25 and 30, there is not much room for improvement. On the other hand, if you're doing that well, your scores don't need to improve very much to satisfy the requirements of just about any institution.

- If you improve your listening abilities, *and* learn the techniques, your score will improve even more.

If you have planned well in advance, you may have a few months to prepare for this test. In the Conversational English chapter, we've included some suggestions for ways to work on your listening skills. Get started as soon as possible!

> Start practicing your conversational English today!

Conversational English

PRACTICING LISTENING TO ENGLISH

As we often say in English, "practice makes perfect." In other words, if you want to learn to do something well, you should do it over and over again until you have mastered it. If you wanted to, say, learn to play the piano, or learn to play basketball, you would probably put in several hours of practice per week. The same goes for learning a new language. Here are a few activities you can practice to help prepare you for the Listening section of the TOEFL CBT.

- Talk on the telephone (in English, of course). Speaking on the phone eliminates facial expressions, gestures, and any other clues as to what the person on the other end of the line is saying. The same is true for the Listening section; you can rely only on the speakers' voices to answer the questions.

- Listen to talk shows and news reports on the radio. Like the telephone, the radio eliminates physical clues that help you determine what the speaker is saying.

- Practice speaking English where it is difficult to hear. If you have friends with whom you can practice speaking English, go to noisy places to do it, such as restaurants or nightclubs or even train stations.

VOICE EMPHASIS

When speaking to people face to face, visual clues help you understand not only the words they use, but also the meanings of those words. Facial expressions, hand gestures, and body posture can all help you understand what a person is saying. However, in the TOEFL CBT Listening section, you can't see the speaker, so you are forced to rely solely on vocal cues.

In spoken English, people place emphasis on certain words in a given sentence to convey additional meaning beyond their dictionary definitions. The most common way to place emphasis on a word is raising or lowering the pitch or volume of one's voice. This will enable that word to stand out from the rest of the sentence. One of the things that vocal emphasis can tell you is which information in the sentence is most important.

WHAT'S IMPORTANT?

In the following sentence, every word is stressed equally.

Jane's red bag is on the table.

However, when emphasis is placed on specific words in the sentence, the intention of the speaker changes slightly.

Jane's red bag is on the table.

When the sentence is spoken with emphasis placed on the word *Jane's*, that word becomes the most important in the sentence. In other words, the primary goal of the speaker is to communicate the ownership of the bag. The person the speaker is talking to probably thought the bag belonged to someone else, and the speaker wants to clear up the misunderstanding.

Jane's *red* bag is on the table.

When the emphasis is on *red*, the color of the bag is what's important. The other person likely thought that a different bag was being discussed, probably of another color.

Jane's red *bag* is on the table.

Now the emphasis is on the actual item. The other person may have thought that something else belonging to Jane was on the table, such as a red book or a red sweater.

Jane's red bag *is* on the table.

The emphasis is on *where*. The other person may have just said, implied, or thought that the bag was not on the table.

Jane's red bag is *on* the table.

The speaker wants to make clear that the bag is on—not under, next to, in front of, or behind—the table. The other person probably misunderstood the location of the bag.

Jane's red bag is on the *table*.

Again, the speaker clarifies the location of the bag for the other person. In this case the other person was probably confused about *what* the bag was on. He or she might have thought that the bag was on something else, such as the cabinet, the stairs, or the bed.

Voice Emphasis Drill

Directions: For the following drill, play Track 1 of the CD that came with this book. You will hear the sentences printed below read with emphasis on different words. Imagine that each statement you hear on the CD is a reply or response to something that some other person has said. Your job is to listen to the speaker on the CD and try to figure out what she or he implies about what the original speaker said. Remember, implications are often indicated through emphasis of certain words. For each sentence, circle the word or words that were stressed; then, on the line below the sentence, jot down a couple of words to express the implied meaning of what the speaker said. (You will have about ten seconds to do this, so don't worry about writing complete sentences.) If the drill moves too quickly for you, you also have the option of pausing the disk between sentences. When you're done, check your answers against the answer key on pages 52–53. Pay special attention to the ones you got wrong. Try to figure why you got them wrong so that you may avoid a similar error in the future.

1. Louis always recycles his newspapers.

   _____

2. Louis always recycles his newspapers.

   _____

3. Louis always recycles his newspapers.

   _____

4. Louis always recycles his newspapers.

   _____

5. Louis always recycles his newspapers.

   _____

6. Diane will arrive at three o'clock on Tuesday.

   _____

7. Diane will arrive at three o'clock on Tuesday.

   _____

8. Diane will arrive at three o'clock on Tuesday.

   _____

9. Diane will arrive at three o'clock on Tuesday.

   _____

10. Diane will arrive at three o'clock on Tuesday.

    _____

11. What do you want?

    _____

12. What do you want?

    _____

13. What do you want?

    _____

14. This test is pretty easy.

    _____

15. This test is pretty easy.

    _____

16. This test is pretty easy.

    _____

17. This test is pretty easy.

    _____

What's Understood?

In spoken English, it's sometimes acceptable to speak in ways that violate the rules of written grammar. One of the most common violations is speaking in incomplete sentences. This is possible because one speaker can use the context supplied by the other speaker without having to repeat it.

There's an elephant at our front door.

What's at our front door?

An *elephant!*

It's *where?*

At the *front door!*

At *whose* front door?

Ours!

If you looked at any of these "sentences" by themselves, they wouldn't make any sense, but since you know what the first speaker said, the meaning is clear.

WHAT'S IMPLIED?

Many words in English take on additional meaning when spoken aloud. You can often recognize these constructions because if you took their meaning literally, the sentence wouldn't seem to mean anything. Many of these expressions use exaggeration or sarcasm to make the point.

You *could* help me with the dishes.

The speaker doesn't mean that the other person "has the ability" to help with the dishes. The emphasis on *could* carries with it the implication that the speaker believes the other person *should* help with the dishes. The speaker is being sarcastic. The other person would probably respond by apologizing and would immediately start to help.

You can say *that* again.

Again, the speaker uses a form of *can,* but not in the sense "have the ability to." That meaning would make the sentence illogical. Here the meaning of the sentence is that the speaker agrees strongly.

It *can't* be eleven o'clock already!

Another use for *can.* The speaker doesn't mean that it's impossible for it to be eleven o'clock. Rather, the speaker knows it is eleven o'clock and is very surprised by how quickly time has passed. Depending on the context, the speaker is either happily or unhappily surprised by the time.

Do you need a little help?

Help? I need a ***miracle!***

Are you hungry?

Hungry? I'm ***starving!***

In each case, the person answering the question uses exaggeration to mean: Yes, I certainly do! or I certainly am . . . but much more than you can imagine!

EMPHASIZED EXPRESSIONS

Following are some expressions you might find on the TOEFL CBT that have special meanings *only when they are emphasized.*

We'll be lucky if . . .

> *We'll be lucky if* we get there by the year 2018!

This means: We're encountering so many obstacles that whatever we're doing may take a very long time.

> *You'll be lucky if* you get out of here alive!

> *He'll be lucky if* he has two cents left to his name.

We might as well . . .

> *We might as well* be in Timbuktu.

This means that we are in such a remote place, it's as if we were many miles away in Timbuktu.

> *We might as well* walk to New York from Kansas!

This means that our means of transportation is so bad that it would be the same if we walked an impossibly long distance. This statement makes clear it is an impractical scheme.

Only . . .

The word "only," when emphasized, answers the question, "Yes," "Of course," or "Yes, a lot!"

> Did you have fun at the dance?
> I *only* danced my feet off!

> Did you really want to spend time with me?
> I *only* drove a whole hour to see you!

> Does Sam know anything about American politics?
> He's *only* read everything that's ever been published about it!

If only . . .

If only means "I really wish."

> *If only* I had known before now!

> *If only* I had a million dollars!

Did/was/is

When the second speaker emphasizes the auxiliaries *did, was,* or *is* in response to the first speaker, the second speaker is expressing surprise.

> I just got home from the concert.
> So you *did* go.

> David really enjoys his new car.
> So he *did* buy a new one.

Professor Wheeler really helped me with those math problems.
Oh, so he *did* help you.

Don't you love Michael's new musical arrangements?
So, those *are* his arrangements.

Did you see Andrew and his new girlfriend at the hockey game?
So, they *were* there.

We all noticed that you weren't in class on Monday.
So, it *wasn't* cancelled.

Can always . . .

The speaker uses *can always* to remind you that you still have another alternative.

If you don't like the party, you *can always* go home.

You *can always* change your mind.

Can't . . .

Can't is emphasized to indicate the speaker's surprise in a particular situation. The speaker means: I know that it *is* true, but I can't believe it!

It *can't* be eight o'clock already!

This *can't* be my last dollar!

That *can't* be our bus pulling out of the station!

CLICHÉS

All of the following are clichés (a phrase or expression that has become overly familiar or commonplace) that appear on the TOEFL CBT and are used to express simple ideas. We've grouped them by meaning in order to make them easier to learn.

I don't know.

I couldn't tell you.

I wouldn't know.

I haven't the vaguest.

I haven't the foggiest.

I haven't any idea.

Who knows?

It's a mystery to me.

Don't look at me.

Don't ask me.

It's over my head.

You got me.

Beats me.

Don't do it!

I wouldn't if I were you.

Oh no you don't!

Cut it out!

Not here you don't.

Better leave well enough alone.

Forget it!

Don't bother.

You can't be too careful.

Question/Suggestion

How about . . . ?

Why not . . . ?

What about . . . ?

What would you say to . . . ?

What do you think about . . . ?

Would you mind if . . . ?

Shouldn't you . . . ?

Agreement

To say the least.

That's putting it mildly.

You can say that again.

That's for sure.

Don't I know it.

Now, that's an idea.

There you go!

Now you've said something (. . . I agree with, whereas you didn't before.)

I'll say.

I couldn't agree with you more.

Count me in.

Why not!

Do I ever!

You bet!

Disagreement

I doubt it.

Probably not.

Not likely.

I wouldn't say that.

Don't bet on it.

Don't count on it.

Don't be too sure.

I don't think so.

No way.

Never.

Not in a million years.

Thank you!

Thanks!

I appreciate it.

Thanks a lot.

I don't know how to thank you.

You're a lifesaver.

I'll never be able to repay you.

I'm grateful.

You're welcome!

It's the least I can do.

Forget it.

Don't mention it.

Never mind.

It doesn't matter.

No problem.

What did you say?

Pardon me?

Excuse me?

Sorry?

What?

Isn't that something!

I can't believe that . . .

My goodness!

How about that!

It/He/She's too good to be true!

We made it!

You're kidding!

You're joking!

Come on!

It can't be!

Who says?

To think I . . . !

No! You don't say!

No way!

Get out!

HOMONYMS

Another trap you need to know about when listening is homonyms—words that are spelled differently, but sound alike. These are used to fool you. Write a short sentence or phrase after each one to familiarize yourself with the differences. Because your sentences will vary, ask an English speaker to check them for you to make sure that you got them right.

This is by no means a complete list. We have not included every definition for each word—just the most common definition. Remember, when you come across a homonym the most important thing to do is to put the word into context.

new: not used. "I bought this *new* dress today with the money I earned."

Your sentence _____

knew: past tense of know. "I *knew* that you were going to show up at the party!"

Your sentence _____

flower: daisy, tulip, rose. "I love to grow *flowers* in my garden."

Your sentence _____

flour: ingredient in baking. "I need two cups of *flour* for the cake."

Your sentence _____

sew: use a needle and thread. "I want to *sew* the rip on these jeans."

Your sentence_____

so: who cares? "*So* what? I really have no interest in what you are saying."

Your sentence_____

won: defeated an opponent. "We *won* the game by 2 to 1."

Your sentence_____

one: the number 1, or alone. "There is only *one* girl on the softball team."

Your sentence_____

plain: simple, unadorned. "This dress is too *plain*—there are no designs on it."

Your sentence_____

plane: airplane, for flying. "We flew to Europe in that new *plane*."

Your sentence_____

sea: ocean. "We swam in the *sea* today."

Your sentence_____

see: to view, use your eyes. "I *see* that you are wearing the sweater I gave you for your birthday."

Your sentence_____

wood: material from a tree. "The furniture is made out of *wood*."

Your sentence_____

would: subjunctive or conditional mood of "will". "I *would* like a new table."

Your sentence_____

hour: a sixty-minute time period. "This class is one *hour* long."

Your sentence_____

our: possessive form of we. "We like *our* new teacher."

Your sentence_____

red: the color. "Stop at a *red* light."

Your sentence _____

read: finished reading. "I *read* a whole book last night."

Your sentence_____

wait: to pause, stop. "*Wait* for me—I'll be right there."

Your sentence _____

weight: heaviness. "The *weight* of this package is three pounds."

Your sentence _____

maid: someone who cleans. "The *maid* will clean your room."

Your sentence _____

made: past tense of *make*. "I *made* the bed myself."

Your sentence _____

way: direction. "Which *way* should we go?"

Your sentence _____

weigh: to figure out how heavy something is. "Did you *weigh* these vegetables?"

Your sentence _____

hole: an empty space. "Last week, I dug a big *hole* to plant those seeds."

Your sentence _____

whole: entire "He ate the *whole* pie before anyone else could even have a piece."

Your sentence _____

by: near "Her house is *by* the sh   opping mall."

Your sentence _____

buy: to purchase. "I want to *buy* a new car."

Your sentence_____

sail: on a boat. "The *sail* catches wind and pushes the boat."

Your sentence _____

sale: a discount, bargain. "I bought this coat on *sale* and saved a lot of money."

Your sentence _____

sense: as in common sense. "That advice makes good *sense*."

Your sentence _____

cents: pennies, money. "The phone call cost twenty-five *cents*."

Your sentence _____

reflex: unconscious movement. "I pulled my hand out of the water as a *reflex*."

Your sentence _____

reflects: casts back an image. "The lake *reflects* the trees perfectly."

Your sentence _____

soul: spirit. "The Buddhists believe the *soul* is reincarnated."

Your sentence _____

sole: only. "He was the *sole* survivor of the train accident."

Your sentence _____

son: male child. "She has one *son* and two daughters."

Your sentence _____

sun: the earth revolves around it. "The *sun* is very hot today!"

Your sentence _____

I: me, myself. "*I* am taking a vacation next month."

Your sentence _____

eye: what you see with. "My *eyes* are bothered by cigarette smoke."

Your sentence _____

banned: not allowed. "Short skirts are *banned* at her school."

Your sentence _____

band: a music group. "The *band* at the party played only the most popular songs."

Your sentence _____

hire: to employ someone. "I need to *hire* a tutor to help me with my studies."

Your sentence _____

higher: more elevated. "Put the books on a *higher* shelf."

Your sentence _____

worn: past tense of *wear*. "Have you *worn* those shoes yet?"

Your sentence _____

warn: to caution. "I *warn* you—he's a tough teacher."

Your sentence _____

jeans: denim pants. "Levi's are my favorite *jeans*."

Your sentence _____

genes: units of inheritance. "He inherited blue eyes from his mother's *genes*."

Your sentence _____

cell: the smallest unit of living matter. "The amoeba consists of a single *cell*."

Your sentence _____

sell: to make a sale. "I want to *sell* this old car and buy a new one."

Your sentence _____

pale: light in color. "Jane is *pale*—she hasn't been to the beach."

Your sentence _____

pail: a container. "She carried two *pails* of milk from the barn."

Your sentence _____

tale: story. "That was some *tale* Jack told us."

Your sentence _____

tail: at the end of an animal. "Don't pull the cat's *tail!*"

Your sentence _____

scene: where something takes place. "That *scene* in the movie was filmed in New York City."

Your sentence _____

seen: past tense of *see*. "I've *seen* that movie three times!"

Your sentence _____

fair: festival, carnival. "The town *fair* is held every summer."

Your sentence _____

fare: cost. "The round trip *fare* by airplane is $200."

Your sentence _____

here: this place. "Come *here* right now!"

Your sentence _____

hear: listen. "Did you *hear* what I said?"

Your sentence _____

principal: the head of a school. "*Principal* Jones supervises the whole school."

Your sentence _____

principle: belief. "Stand by your *principles*."

Your sentence _____

weather: what it's like outside. "The *weather* report calls for rain."

Your sentence _____

whether: if. "I need to know *whether* you will go."

Your sentence _____

die: to become dead or expire. "The man will likely *die* from his severe injuries."

Your sentence _____

dye: used to color things. "What *dye* did you use to get that interesting purple color?"

Your sentence _____

Idioms

Idioms are words or phrases that do not translate literally. For example, "break down" may not mean to break something in a downward motion, but to lose control. Luckily, idioms occur infrequently on current TOEFL exams, but that doesn't mean you shouldn't review them. Make a list of those you have trouble with and practice using them.

Of course, nothing beats practicing conversation with native English speakers—it's the easiest and most natural way to learn English idioms. But for now, we've divided the list of the most commonly tested idioms into three sections. Work on a section at a time and test yourself on each set after you've finished going over them.

Section 1

break down—a collapse of physical and/or mental health; failing to work:

> When she heard that her pet iguana had escaped, Mary Lou *suffered a break down* and cried in front of the whole class.

> After their car *broke down*, Marty and James had to walk five miles to the nearest service station.

break in—to enter forcibly; with an item of clothing, it can mean to wear in and make comfortable:

> I must *break in* these new shoes, they are giving me blisters.

> The thief *broke* into the museum and stole all the artwork.

breakthrough—a sudden achievement:

> The new vaccine represented a significant *breakthrough* in the battle against the virus.

break up—to separate or collapse; to divide and disperse:

> In 1969, the Beatles officially *broke up* after playing together as a band for more than a decade.

clear away—to free from something:

> When all this trouble *clears away*, he'll be able to go back to school.

> If you *clear away* the dishes, I'll wash them.

clear out—to leave a place, usually quickly:

> The fire marshal ordered the people to *clear out* of their homes due to the possibility that the brush fires would spread.

come about—to happen:

> The train wreck *came about* as a result of the engineer's negligence.

come across—to find or meet by chance:

> We *came across* my grandmother's old diary while cleaning out the attic.

come down with—to get sick:

> When she *came down with* a terrible case of laryngitis, Kathy Lou Kelly wasn't able to perform at the benefit concert.

come up with—to produce something or have an idea:

> It was Juan who *came up with* the scheme to trick Mrs. Huxtable.

come from—to derive or originate from:

> The English language *comes from* many sources, such as Greek and Latin.

come of—to result from:

> "Nothing good will *come of* that sort of behavior," my mother always said.

come out—to disclose:

> The news finally *came out*—cholesterol is not as bad for you as scientists originally believed.

come through with—to succeed in doing:

> The union finally *came through with* an offer to negotiate rather than strike.

come to—to regain consciousness; add up to:

> After Dorothy *came to,* she saw that she was in her own bed in Kansas.

> That dress and those shoes will *come to* about $100 dollars.

come to terms with—to understand or absorb mentally:

> She had trouble *coming to terms with* her dog's death—it seemed so sudden.

do without—to get along without:

> During the drought, residents had to *do without* long, luxurious showers.

drop in/drop by—to visit casually and sometimes unexpectedly:

> After the movie, we'll *drop in* and see if Margie is home.

> On your way to the dorm, *drop by* the library to see if the book is on reserve.

fall back on—to turn to for help:

> Fortunately for John, after he lost all his spending money, he had some savings to *fall back on.*

fall behind—to fail to keep up with:

> Mark had *fallen behind* so badly in his studies, it seemed he'd never be able to finish all his work and pass his courses.

fall for—to be taken in by; duped:

> I can't believe that John *fell for* that trick—it was so obvious.

fill in—to substitute for:

> Mary Jones will *fill in* for Patty Smith during the race, as Patty is too ill to come today.

fit in—to make time for; to conform:

> The doctor will *fit* you *in* at about 3 o'clock for an appointment with her.

> Teenagers often try to *fit in* with their friends by wearing the same style clothes and listening to the same music.

give away—to make a gift of:

> The store was *giving away* a new scarf with every purchase in order to bring in more customers.

give in—to surrender:

> In Hesse's *Siddhartha*, the main character's father finally *gives in* and allows his son to leave home.

give up—to stop; to yield to; to part with:

> I finally *gave up* smoking after years of hearing all the health warnings.

> Nellie wouldn't sign the legal papers yet—she wasn't sure if she wanted to *give up* her right to a trial.

go along with—to agree to:

> The president would *go along with* the decision to hire more people if the department could bring in more revenue.

go down—when referring to food this means it can be swallowed and digested:

> Ice cream was the only food that would *go down* easily after her operation.

go far—to succeed:

> Laura would *go far* with her hard work and intelligence.

go on—to proceed with; to happen;

> "I don't want to *go on* a diet again in my lifetime!" exclaimed Bob.

> The speaker *went on* for almost three hours before stopping.

go through with—to do:

> Few people thought that the mayor would *go through with* his plans to close all the city's homeless shelters.

go under—to fail:

> Due to the poor economy, ten businesses have *gone under* in our town in the last year.

go up—to be erected:

> The building *went up* in a few months and soon there were tenants in the apartments.

hang on—to hold on to; to wait or persevere:

> Indiana Jones managed to grab onto the cliff and *hang on* for dear life.

> The receptionist told me to *hang on* while she consulted her appointment book.

hang around—to loiter:

> On a hot summer day, the kids like to just *hang around* at the beach.

hang up—to end a telephone conversation by putting the receiver down:

> Police tell you to just *hang up* if you get an obscene phone call.

heat up—to increase in pressure:

> The debate *heated up* significantly when Congressman Smithers mentioned plans for rezoning in the area.

Idiom Drill — Section 1

Directions: Choose the answer choice that best answers each question. Then check your answers on page 53.

1. (Woman) I heard that the award ceremony was wonderful.

   (Man) Yes, John broke down when he won the humanitarian award.

   What does the man mean?

   (A) John's award was broken.
   (B) John got emotional when he won.
   (C) John only received one award.
   (D) The award was humanitarian.

2. (Man) Will you help me clean the kitchen?

   (Woman) Sure. You clear away the dishes and I'll wash the pots.

   What does the woman want the man to do?

   (A) Wipe off the dishes.
   (B) Take the dishes off the table.
   (C) Take the pots away.
   (D) Put the dishes away.

3. (Man) It's so sad that Harvey isn't feeling well.

   (Woman) What a bad time for him to come down with chicken pox!

   What does the woman mean?

   (A) Harvey was coming over with chicken.
   (B) Harvey has chicken pox.
   (C) Harvey fell down.
   (D) Harvey is having a bad time.

4. (Woman) When did that new movie house open?

   (Man) I don't know—it seems like it went up in a week!

   What does the man suggest?

   (A) The movie house was built quickly.
   (B) The movie house is very tall.
   (C) He doesn't understand the woman's question.
   (D) It opened a week ago.

5. (Woman) Have you heard about the principal's new plan to make the school day longer?

   (Man) She'll never go through with it!

   What does the man mean?

   (A) He likes the principal's plan.
   (B) The principal went through the school.
   (C) Her plan is possible.
   (D) The principal will not carry out her plan.

6. (Man) How long have you been working on that paper?
   (Woman) Three hours—I give up!

   What does the woman want to do?

   (A) Give the man the paper.
   (B) Stop working on the paper.
   (C) Throw the paper up in the air.
   (D) Work longer.

7. (Man) Did you see John's new haircut?

   (Woman) I don't know if that crazy style will fit in with his conservative friends.

   What does the woman suggest?

   (A) John's haircut is not like any of his friends' haircuts.
   (B) John's hair won't fit his head.
   (C) John's friends are too conservative.
   (D) She hasn't seen John's haircut.

8. (Woman) What time do you want to wake up?

(Man) Well, I'll set the alarm to go off at eight in the morning.

What does the man want to do?

(A) Put off the alarm.
(B) Eat in the morning.
(C) Wake up at eight in the morning.
(D) Get a new alarm.

9. (Man) Did you hear about that new vaccine?

(Woman) What a breakthrough for people with that sickness!

What does the woman mean?

(A) It's good news for people with that sickness.
(B) People with that sickness will get sicker.
(C) The vaccine is broken.
(D) Scientists are not through with their study.

10. (Man) What do you want to do today?

(Woman) It's hot outside, let's just hang around.

What does the woman suggest?

(A) That they do nothing.
(B) That they go home.
(C) That they walk around.
(D) That they hang pictures.

Section 2

keep in touch with—to stay in communication with:

> Please *keep in touch with* us after you move to France.

kill off—to put to death:

> The use of that pesticide will *kill off* ants as well as fleas.

lay aside—to give up or set aside:

> The mayor warned the students to *lay aside* their angry feelings toward the rival school on the day of the big soccer game.

> Jan *laid aside* some money for just such an emergency.

lay off—to terminate someone's employment:

> The Brindley Corporation had to *lay off* ten percent of its employees due to decreased sales.

laid up—sick in bed or out of the action:

> Mr. Rodriquez was *laid up* for several weeks with a terrible flu.

leave out—to omit:

> "Don't *leave out* Aunt Mary from the wedding invitations!"

leave up to—to allow to decide:

> "I'll *leave* your punishment *up to* you to decide," Principal Skinner told the kids.

live up to—to fulfill:

> We expect that Jim will *live up to* our plans to become the first member of the family to attend college.

live down—to bear the embarrassment:

> He'll never *live down* the shame of forgetting all his lines in the class play.

move on—to go in another direction:

> "It's time for you to *move on*," Susan told her friend, who wanted to quit her job as an editor.

off limits—restricted:

> That area is *off limits* to cars, due to efforts in our community to cut down on pollution.

on the mark—exactly right:

> "Boy, were you *on the mark* about Irene—you were the only one who thought that she'd play so well in that concert."

overkill—excess:

> You really didn't need to prepare fifteen pages for that report—it really was *overkill*.

over with—finished:

> I was so relieved to be *over with* the TOEFL after six months of study.

pass by—to overlook:

> Marie was upset that the committee *passed* her *by* and chose a different finalist.

pass through—to go through:

> To get to New England by car from that town, it is necessary to *pass through* New York.

pass up—to refuse:

> We couldn't believe that Jose would *pass up* an opportunity to travel all around the country for free.

pour in—to arrive in a large amount:

> Cards and letters came *pouring in* to offer help and money after the news report about that young girl's need for an operation.

pull out—to take out:

> The United States *pulled* its last troops *out* of Vietnam in 1973, although soldiers had been leaving for years.

pull off—to do something in spite of problems:

> Jake could hardly believe that Amanda could *pull off* that deal after she'd made such a big mistake.

pushover—someone who is easily taken advantage of:

> That Mrs. Jones is a real *pushover*—she always lets you hand in papers late if you ask.

put down—to insult; to suppress:

> I can't believe the way John *puts down* his mother when she's standing right there.

> The leaders *put down* a rebellion in their country by appeasing the different groups.

put up—to allow or go along with:

> Mr. Smith doesn't *put up* with any troublemakers in his class—they are immediately punished.

run by—to tell someone about:

> Maria asked her accountant to *run* those figures *by* her one more time before she signed the contract.

send back—to return:

> President Clinton vetoed the bill and *sent* it *back* to Congress for changes.

Idiom Drill—Section 2

Directions: Match the idiom with its definition. Then check your answers on page 54.

1. pushover

2. pull off

3. pass up

4. pass by

5. over with

6. off limits

7. live down

8. laid up

9. lay off

10. keep in touch with

a) to refuse

b) to overlook

c) to bear an embarrassment

d) to do in spite of problems

e) to terminate someone's employment

f) to stay in communication with

g) restricted

h) someone easily taken advantage of

i) sick in bed

j) finished

Section 3

sign in—to sign your name to enter a place:

> Visitors must *sign in* at the front desk before going into the main auditorium.

speak out—to state publicly:

> Jones was afraid to *speak out* when he saw his boss stealing supplies—he didn't want to get in trouble.

speak up—to speak more loudly; to state publicly:

> "Please *speak up*—the rest of the group cannot hear you," Ms. Montgomery told Peter.

> Activists argue that we all have the responsibility to *speak up* wherever we see injustice, or no change will ever take place.

speed up—to increase one's speed:

> I have been practicing my reading comprehension with the hope that I will *speed up* and finish more passages in the time allotted.

step in—to intervene:

> The Town Board was forced to *step in* and put a stop to the development in the area when it was judged to be unsafe.

stick to—to persist:

> "*Stick to* your morals and you'll do a good job," my grandfather always advised.

stick around—to stay:

> I think I'll *stick around*—there's no reason to head home yet.

stop by—to make a brief visit:

> Could you *stop by* the grocery store on your way home from work and pick up a loaf of bread?

stop up—to clog or prevent from moving:

> The grease and hair *stopped up* the sink and Jan had to call a plumber to fix it.

> Traffic was *stopped up* for miles due to that horrible five-car accident.

think better of—to change your mind:

> Mark had considered dropping out of school to work, but a discussion with his parents made him *think better of* it, and he decided to stay in school.

think nothing of—to do without care:

> Some people in that town *think nothing of* throwing all their garbage into the river—don't they know the long-term effects?

think over—to consider:

Every time Steven writes a paper he has to *think over* his topic for a few days before he even begins to write.

think through—to consider all the effects:

"You obviously did not *think through* what would happen to you if you pulled that fire alarm," Principal Skinner told Marie.

tied up—busy; unavailable for use:

Mr. Jones cannot come to the meeting this afternoon—he'll be *tied up* downtown until 7:00 p.m.

Since most of their money was *tied up* in long-term investments, Jan and Mark couldn't spend any of it.

turn down—to refuse; to lower:

The Smiths were *turned down* for a loan because of their poor credit history.

The volume on the speakers was *turned down* because it was so late at night.

turnoff—something that disgusts a person:

"Guys who only talk about themselves are such a *turnoff!*" the magazine article proclaimed.

turn over—transfer:

By law, attorneys must *turn over* evidence to the court so that both sides may have a chance to review it.

turn to—to go to for guidance or inspiration:

Many teenagers *turn to* their friends and family to help them decide where to attend college.

turn up—to find or uncover:

It's always a good idea to browse the shelves in a library when you are doing a research paper—you never know what you may *turn up*.

up against—confronted with:

In spite of being *up against* strong opposition from the larger British forces, the United States won the Revolutionary War.

up to date—current:

Her clothes are always so stylish and *up to date*—she must read all the fashion magazines.

wake up—to rouse from sleep or inactivity:

The young Americans of the 1960s sent a *wake up* call to the country to get involved and work for change.

Young children may *wake up* at any time in the middle of the night.

Idiom Drill—Section 3

Directions: Choose the answer choice that best completes the sentence. Then check your answers on page 54.

1. "Pick one topic and _____ it throughout your term paper."

   (A) stick around
   (B) step on one's toes in
   (C) stick to
   (D) pull out of

2. "I'm in a real rush now, but _____ later and I'll have more time to talk."

   (A) stop by
   (B) drop out
   (C) turn over
   (D) turn off

3. Jane was _____ with work and couldn't be here.

   (A) up to date
   (B) tied up
   (C) filled up
   (D) touched up

4. Smitty felt that people who were rude were a real _____.

   (A) turnoff
   (B) turn down
   (C) turn over
   (D) stop up

5. Patty always sets her alarm so that she can _____ at 8:00 a.m.

   (A) think over
   (B) write down
   (C) think through
   (D) wake up

6. The beginning of the second book brings the reader _____ with what happened in the first book.

    (A)   up over
    (B)   up to date
    (C)   up against
    (D)   think over

7. At our school no one would even think to _____ against the administration for fear of getting in trouble.

    (A)   step in
    (B)   sign in
    (C)   speak out
    (D)   step up

8. Always a quiet boy, John was too shy to _____ in class.

    (A)   speed up
    (B)   step down
    (C)   speak up
    (D)   step in

9. "Why don't you _____; I'm sure that Mr. Smith will be here any second."

    (A)   step up
    (B)   sign in
    (C)   stick around
    (D)   think better of

10. Americans _____ being able to buy anything they want in a large convenience store; in other countries, it is not always so easy.

    (A)   think over
    (B)   think through
    (C)   think better of
    (D)   think nothing of

ANSWER KEY

Voice Emphasis Drill

1. *Louis*—The other person thought that someone else recycles his or her newspapers.

2. *always*—The other person implied that Louis hadn't recycled them at some time in the recent past; the speaker is surprised.

3. *recycles*—The other person thought that Louis did something else with his newspapers.

4. *his*—The other person thought that Louis recycled someone else's newspapers.

5. *newspapers*—The other person thought that Louis recycled something else.

6. *Diane*—The other person thought that someone else was coming.

7. *will*—The other person thought or implied that Diane wasn't coming.

8. *arrive*—The other person thought that Diane would be doing something else at three o'clock—leaving, for example.

9. *three o'clock*—The other person thought that Diane would arrive at a different time.

10. *Tuesday*—The other person thought that Diane would arrive on a different day.

11. *What*—The other person asked for something unusual or something which the speaker didn't understand.

12. *you*—The other person was talking about what someone else wanted, which is not what the speaker is interested in.

13. *want*—The other person was talking about what they have to do, or what they don't want, or something else entirely.

14. *This*—The speaker wants to make it clear that while this test may be easy, she finds other tests difficult.

15. *is*—The speaker anticipated a difficult test and therefore is surprised that it turned out to be so easy.

16. *pretty*—The speaker doesn't believe that the test is as easy as the other person implied.

17. *easy*—The speaker is disagreeing with the other person who found the test more difficult than the speaker did.

Idiom Drill — Section 1

1. B

2. B

3. B

4. A

5. D

6. B

7. A

8. C

9. A

10. A

Idiom Drill — Section 2

1. h

2. d

3. a

4. b

5. j

6. g

7. c

8. i

9. e

10. f

Idiom Drill — Section 3

1. C

2. A

3. B

4. A

5. D

6. B

7. C

8. C

9. C

10. D

SUMMARY

Voice Emphasis

- What's Important—focus on the words that are stressed or emphasized to understand the speaker's intention.

- What's Understood—short incomplete sentences often use the context supplied by the other speaker.

- What's Implied—emphasized words sometimes indicate sarcasm or exaggeration to make a point.

- Emphasized Expressions—some expressions have special meanings only when they are emphasized.

Cliches

- Overly familiar or commonplace phrases or expressions.

- Often used on the TOEFL CBT to express simple ideas.

- Have a friend or study partner quiz you using the examples on pages 29–32.

Homonyms

- Words that are spelled differently but sound alike.

- Often given on the TOEFL CBT to fool you.

- The key to handling homonyms is context. What did the other words in the sentence tell you about the word in question?

Idioms

- Words or phrases that do not translate literally.

- Generally the hardest part of any language to master.

- Fairly common on the TOEFL CBT; good to know for conversational English.

- Learn each of the three lists of idioms, quiz yourself (or work with a partner), and then complete the exercise at the end of each list.

Part A–Short Conversations

THE BASICS

In Part A of the TOEFL CBT Listening section, your task is to listen to short conversations and answer a question based on what is either stated or implied. The conversations will not be repeated. In other words, you have only chance to listen and remember.

Unfortunately, because ETS may include experimental questions, it is impossible to know in advance exactly how many short conversations you will hear. There are approximately 9 to 17 questions in Part A. Once you have listened to each short conversation, you will be able to read the question asked about it. But don't worry, the amount of time you are given to answer the questions will be proportional to the number of the questions you will see. Also, both the total number of questions in the section and the total time given for Listening are given in the directions. The questions each will appear at the top of the computer screen, just above the answer choices. You may take as much time as you wish to answer each question, but don't take too much time, the clock is running.

TUTORIAL

Volume

Prior to beginning the Listening section, ETS will provide a tutorial introducing the TOEFL CBT. Put on the headset supplied by the testing center to learn how to adjust the volume. Normally, the volume will be preset to an audible level. However, if you need to raise or lower the volume, do it right away. You do not want to waste valuable time adjusting the volume during the test.

Time

The time remaining is shown in the upper left-hand corner of the screen. You have the option of turning off the time by clicking on the Clock icon in the lower left corner of the screen. However, we strongly recommend that you leave the clock on. If you do turn off the clock, you will not be able to see how much time you have remaining and, consequently, you will have difficulty pacing yourself. *Fortunately, the clock does not run while any of the conversations are being spoken*. The time displayed in the upper left-hand corner is the time remaining for you to answer the questions. The time *does* run if you click on the Help icon. However, once you finish this book, the Help icon will not be necessary.

Directions

After the tutorial, the Listening section begins and the clock starts running. The first item to appear on the screen is the directions screen. You should learn the directions prior to the test so you don't waste valuable time reading them. When you click on the "Dismiss Directions" icon located on the right side of the screen, the directions will disappear and you will immediately be given the first question. The directions will look something like this:

You will not see the four answer choices until after the short conversation is finished.

Remember, the clock runs whenever you adjust the volume during the Listening section. So save time and adjust it properly before the clock starts.

The time shown in the upper left-hand corner is the time remaining for you to answer the questions.

Listening

Listening
49 questions

This section measures your ability to understand spoken English.

There are 50 questions in this section.

The listening material and questions about it will be presented only one time.

After you have confirmed an answer, you cannot return to previous questions. You may not take notes.

Click on the Volume icon below to make the sound softer or louder.

When you are ready to continue, click on the Dismiss Directions icon.

When finished reading directions click on the icon below

Dismiss Directions

Time · Volume · Help · Answer Confirm · Next

Look to see how many questions you will have to answer!

After you see the general Listening section directions, the specific directions for the short conversations will appear. They look very similar to the general Listening section directions. Click on the "Dismiss Directions" icon to immediately begin the test. Do not waste your time reading the directions. The clock is running.

Listening

Listening
49 questions

Question Directions – Part A

In the first part, you will hear short conversations between two people. Each conversation is followed by a question about it.

Each question in this part has four answer choices. Click on the best answer to each question. Answer the questions on the basis of what is stated or implied by the speakers.

During the questions, you can refer to these directions again by clicking on the Help icon. To change the volume, click on the Volume icon.

You cannot click on any icons during a conversation.

When you are ready to continue, click on the Dismiss Directions icon.

When finished reading directions click on the icon below

Dismiss Directions

Time · Volume · Help · Answer Confirm · Next

Question Types

In Part A of the TOEFL CBT, you will hear short conversations between two people: The first speaker usually introduces the topic of the conversation, but the question almost always asks about what the last speaker said. Most of the questions will be as follows:

What does the man mean?

What is inferred by the woman?

What will the man probably do next?

What does the woman say about . . . ?

What does the man suggest the woman do?

How to Answer

You can't skip a question.

Remember, because the Listening section is computer adaptive, the difficulty of any given question you receive depends upon your performance on all of the questions that came before it in the section. Therefore, you must answer the question on the screen before the next one will appear. Unfortunately, you cannot skip the hard questions and come back to them later (like you will in the Reading section). Every Listening question must be answered in the order in which it is served.

The questions will appear on your screen one at a time. After selecting the best answer from the four answer choices presented, click on the icon at the bottom right hand corner of the screen labeled "Next." At this point you may still change your answer. To move on, you must confirm your selection by clicking on "Answer Confirm." This action logs your answer, takes away the question on the screen forever, and brings up the next question.

Pictures

During the short conversations, you will see a picture of two people in some type of university setting on the computer screen. The two students will be holding books, walking across campus, or sitting at a table in a cafeteria. Their short conversations will *always* be about academic situations, (for example, home-work, a professor, living conditions, class rules, and so forth). On the next page is an example of the type of picture you might see during a short conversation in Part A of the Listening section.

Keep in mind, however, that the pictures ETS shows you in Part A of the Listening section serve only as "distractors." In some cases ETS will even use the same picture for different conversations. You do *not* need to look at the picture on the computer screen. Where the students are located, how they are dressed, what they are holding in their hands, and the color of their hair has absolutely *no* relevance to the question. The picture does not provide any visual information such as facial expressions, gestures, or emotional state that pertains to the upcoming question. Looking at the picture will not make answering the question any easier. In fact, it will make the question more difficult. Humans are much more visual than auditory; we are less inclined to listen if we can see. In other words, do *not* look at the picture. It will only divert your attention away from the conversation. So do your best to avoid looking at the pictures.

In the Listening section, the pictures are "distractors." Do not waste time looking at them.

After the short conversation is heard, the picture will disappear, and the question will appear along with four answer choices. Look at the example below:

```
┌─────────────────────────────────────────────────────────────┐
│                          Listening                          │
├─────────────────────────────────────────────────────────────┤
│                                                             │
│  ┌───────────────────────────────────────────────────────┐  │
│  │                                                       │  │
│  │                                                       │  │
│  │       What does the man mean?                         │  │
│  │                                                       │  │
│  │       ○    It follows a very strict schedule.         │  │
│  │       ○    It begins on Monday.                       │  │
│  │       ○    Attendance at orientation is mandatory     │  │
│  │            for all freshmen.                          │  │
│  │       ○    Its sole purpose is to help the freshmen   │  │
│  │            find jobs.                                 │  │
│  │                                                       │  │
│  │                                                       │  │
│  └───────────────────────────────────────────────────────┘  │
│  ┌────┐                      ┌────┐ ┌───┐ ┌───────┐ ┌─────┐ │
│  │ ◷  │                      │ ◁◁ │ │ ? │ │Answer │ │ ➡  │ │
│  │Time│                      │Volume│ │Help│ │Confirm│ │Next │ │
│  └────┘                      └────┘ └───┘ └───────┘ └─────┘ │
└─────────────────────────────────────────────────────────────┘
```

WHAT MAKES PART A SO DIFFICULT?

One of the biggest disadvantages you will face in the Listening section is that you are unable to read the questions before you actually hear the conversation. Also, on most tests (including the Reading section of the TOEFL CBT), if you come across a difficult question, you can skip it and come back to answer it later. That's usually a very good strategy. You've spent most of your life approaching questions this way, particularly in school, so it seems perfectly natural. What's not natural is the situation you'll find yourself in during the Listening section. First, you are shown an illogical picture of two strangers to represent the speakers of the short conversation you will hear, and then you'll hear (and read) the question. Be sure to listen to the conversation carefully; once it is finished, you'll never hear it again.

Say What?

Somewhere in the early part of the Listening section, you hear a statement that sounds something like this:

"Question number six. Hey, that's the blah over blah blah bee blah!"

In other words, you have no idea what the speaker said. Now, while you're trying to remember when in your English studies you ever heard "*blah blah bee*" (or was it "*bee blah blah*"?), you hear "*. . . blah blah*, don't you think?"

You panic. You only heard part of what the speakers said and now you have just a few words to base your answer choice on. What do you do?

No Context

The short conversations that ETS gives you in Part A do not accurately depict real conversations. As we've already pointed out, in real, face-to-face conversations you rely on many visual factors, such as facial expressions and hand gestures, to help you understand what the other person is saying. Also, knowing something about the person or the topic gives additional meaning to the words used. Furthermore, if he or she uses some words or expressions that you're not familiar with, you can use the context of the rest of the conversation to help figure out what they mean.

All of these cues are absent in Part A of the Listening section. The largest hurdle to get over in order to do well on this section is the lack of context. For the questions in Part A, the information presented is completely isolated. The questions can be about anything. However, there is some good news. The questions you will be asked are almost always about what the *second* speaker means, what he will do, or what he infers. Luckily for you, you can rely on what the first speaker says to help orient yourself as to what the main idea of the conversation will be about. Then listen closely to what the second speaker says to help you answer the upcoming question.

As you move through Part A, you may encounter conversations in which one or both of the people speak more than once. Don't panic, just keep listening. The same rules apply when one or both of the people speak twice: The statements at the beginning of the conversation generally just set up the more important statements at the end of the conversation. So remember to keep listening after the second person speaks because there may be more dialogue to come. Also, keep in mind that longer conversations usually give you a little more time to think about what is being said. This is a good thing.

> Part A questions are almost always about what the second speaker means, what he will do, or what he infers.

The Good News

Although there are some problems with the TOEFL CBT, one of the test's weaknesses can make your job much easier. To help you understand how this works, we're going to explain some of the reasons why the TOEFL CBT is constructed the way it is.

Most tests you take in school are not multiple choice. The primary reason for this is that teachers don't like them. Teachers don't like multiple-choice tests because they don't do what tests are supposed to do: Provide some meaningful indication of how much a student has learned. Here's why. Complete the following sentence:

> When I haven't had time to prepare for an exam, I would have the best luck if my teacher asked me to
>
> ○ write an essay
> ○ answer questions orally
> ○ write short answers to pointed questions
> ○ choose the best answer from among four options

Most people would pick "Choose the best from among four options." Why? Because on a multiple-choice test you don't necessarily have to *know* the right answer; you can eliminate some answer choices, and then guess! Remember that the correct answer is *always* in front of you on the computer screen.

> On multiple-choice tests, the answer is always in front of you!

ETS's Dilemma

Let's say that two people are taking the TOEFL CBT. One of them speaks English almost fluently. The other hardly speaks English at all. The one who hardly speaks English has a lot of trouble understanding the words on the recording and hears something like this:

Question number 12.

(Woman) Will Mary blah bee blah blah Sunday?

(Man) Sunday blah bee blah Mary's blah blah.

(Narrator) What does the man mean?

Now look at the answer choices. Remember, the only words this person understood were *Sunday* and *Mary*.

- ○ School is in session nine months out of the year.
- ○ Hats are not usually worn during dinner.
- ○ Mary rarely works on Sunday.
- ○ The operation was very expensive.

So which answer would he choose? "Mary rarely works on Sunday" of course, because it contains the words he recognized from the question. "Mary rarely works on Sunday" is also the right answer, so this person who hardly understands English just answered the question correctly.

This presents ETS with a problem. Of course the person whose English is very good is also going to answer the question correctly. He will understand the question word for word. According to this particular question, both test takers now have the same level of English proficiency. If this happens on too many questions, it is a disaster for ETS. It means the test is a failure.

ETS had to come up with a way to keep people from guessing correctly on too many of its questions. Now look at the same question with different answer choices:

Question number 12.

(Woman) Will Mary blah bee blah blah Sunday?

(Man) Sunday blah bee blah Mary's blah blah.

(Narrator) What does the man mean?

- ○ Sunday is a day Mary often works.
- ○ Mary rarely works on Sunday.
- ○ Some days Mary's work is awful.
- ○ Mary has had a terrible cough since Sunday.

Would you be able to tell which is the right answer? Probably not. Now, most of the answer choices contain those same two words that you could hear in the statement, so it would be hard to choose among them. Although the statement remained the same, this question just became much harder. Nothing has changed but the answer choices.

The first example was much too easy to have ever appeared on an actual TOEFL CBT. Too many people would correctly guess the answer. To fix this, ETS had to change the answer choices so that the wrong answers don't seem so wrong. In fact, ETS tries to make the wrong answers sometimes look *better* than the right answers. In other words, ETS creates "distractors" to divert your attention from the correct answer. Let's look at how they do it.

A Brief Lesson In Question Writing

First ETS comes up with the short conversation:

> (Woman) Will Mary be in on Sunday?
>
> (Man) Sunday is usually Mary's day off.
>
> (Narrator) What does the man mean?

and the right answer:

> ◯ Mary rarely works on Sunday.

Now comes the hard part for ETS. It has to come up with three wrong "distractors" that don't *seem* wrong. On many questions, ETS will phrase an answer choice so that it's very close to the right answer but means just the opposite:

> ◯ Sunday is a day Mary often works.

This wrong answer will attract thousands of test takers who *almost* understood the stem. If you ever see two answer choices that are opposites, chances are, one of them is the correct. Make your best guess and click on it!

ETS will also include answer choices that contain some of the same sounds and words as the stem:

> ◯ Some days Mary's work is awful.
> ◯ Mary has had a terrible cough since Sunday.

Some days sounds like *Sunday*; and *awful* and *cough* sound like *off*. These answers will attract those who were able to pick out the sounds of the statement, but didn't understand the sense of it. If answer choices contain these types of "sound-alikes" you can bet they are wrong.

Eliminate the opposite answer choice.

Eliminate the "sound-alikes."

Finally, take a look at what has happened to the answer choices.

○ Sunday is a day Mary often works.
○ Mary rarely works on Sunday.
○ Some days Mary's work is awful.
○ Mary has had a terrible cough since Sunday.

Three out of four of them mention Sunday, three out of four of them mention work, and they all include Mary. In order to make it harder for you to guess, ETS regularly includes words from the conversation in both correct and incorrect answer choices. So don't be fooled into thinking you can select the correct answer just by looking for words from the conversation.

QUESTION TYPES

In Part A of the TOEFL CBT, questions can be put into one of four main categories. The question types below are listed in order of frequency:

- Meaning questions
- Infer/imply questions
- Action questions
- Detail questions

1. Meaning Questions

There is basically one type of meaning question:

What does the man/woman mean?

Meaning questions contain the word mean.

These questions are easy to identify because they contain the word *mean*. Meaning questions always refer to what the *second* speaker has said. The first speaker sets up the conversation with a direct/indirect question or a general statement to which the second speaker responds. The second speaker most likely will use an idiomatic expression, or just simply respond to what the first speaker has asked or stated. In any event, the second speaker holds the answer to the question ETS presents. For example:

(Woman) Have you heard about the new periodical wing that the administration wants to add on to the south side of the library?

(Man) Yeah, I can barely wait until it is finished.

(Narrator) What does the man mean?

○ The library has just opened a new section.
○ He is eager to take advantage of the new library wing.
○ The new library will be extra crowded.
○ The administration wants to close the library.

For meaning questions on the TOEFL CBT, repeat as much of the conversation in your head as possible. Ask yourself the question, "What did the second speaker say?" If there are any words or phrases you don't understand, you can bet ETS is asking about them. But don't worry, however, if you can't understand everything. Concentrate on what the second speaker says. In this example, even if you didn't hear the first speaker, you can tell from the answer choices that she must have said something about a library! The second speaker says "I can barely wait . . .," an idiom which means he is "eager." Eliminate all the answer choices that don't say this and the answer is "He is eager to take advantage of the new library wing." Focus on the answer choices and use POE. Later in this chapter, you will see more helpful hints to strengthen your POE strategy.

2. Infer/Imply Questions

Some typical infer/imply questions are:

> What can be inferred about the woman?
>
> What does the woman imply?
>
> What can be inferred about the conversation?
>
> What does the man imply about . . . ?

To *imply* means to express a thought indirectly.
To *infer* means to draw a conclusion.

These questions are easy to recognize because you will read the word "imply" or "infer" in the question. Basically, to imply something is to express it indirectly, and to infer something is to draw a conclusion from given facts. What makes these questions difficult is that you must click on the answer choice that paraphrases the conversation. Again, the strategy for answering infer/imply questions is to listen to how the first speaker sets up the conversation, and how the second speaker responds. Try to form a picture in your mind as to what they are talking about. For example, you might hear:

> (Man) I have to stop at the bank before dinner. I'm down to my last few dollars.
>
> (Woman) Why bother? I thought we'd use the gift certificates I got for my graduation present.
>
> (Narrator) What does the woman imply?
>
> ○ Dinner has been canceled.
> ○ The man will not be able to afford dinner.
> ○ Dinner will be free of charge.
> ○ The bank is too far away.

Again, the first speaker's words are not nearly as important as the second speaker's words. The best answer, "Dinner will be free of charge," correctly paraphrases "Why bother? I'd thought we'd use the gift certificates I got for my graduation present." Later in this chapter, you will see more helpful hints to strengthen your POE strategy.

3. Action Questions

Some typical sample action questions are:

> What does the man/woman suggest the man/woman do?
>
> What will the man/woman probably do?
>
> What will the man/woman probably do next?

These are questions that center on the verb in the conversation. Again, listen closely to the second speaker for clues as to what will happen next. For example:

> (Man) I'm just about sick of all this chemistry homework. I don't even have a spare minute to cook.
>
> (Woman) Well, if it would help at all, I could run to the cafeteria and pick something up for you.
>
> (Narrator) What will the woman probably do?
>
> ○   Help the man with his homework.
> ○   Get some food for the man.
> ○   Find out where the man can exercise.
> ○   Buy some medicine for the man.

The answer choice "Get some food for the man" best paraphrases the woman's statement, "I could run to the cafeteria and pick something up for you." Notice how the first speaker introduces the situation, and how the second speaker responds. Action questions are either about what the *second* speaker will do, or what the *second* speaker recommends the first speaker do. Therefore, try to think of synonyms for the verb the second speaker uses. Use POE to avoid the traps and distractors that ETS presents and click on the answer that best represents what the second speaker will do next. Later in this chapter, you will learn more helpful hints to strengthen your POE strategy.

Answer choices for action questions always begin with verbs.

4. Detail Questions

Recently, ETS has begun to ask more specific questions about the details of the short conversation. Luckily, this is the least-asked type of question. Detail questions may appear in several forms, yet you will be able to recognize them because they refer to specific items mentioned in the conversation. Some typical detail questions are:

> What does the man want to know?
>
> What do the speakers say about . . . ?
>
> What happened to the . . . ?
>
> What does the woman say about . . . ?
>
> What is the man/woman's problem?

Detail questions are those that center on the nouns of the short conversation. For example:

> (Woman) John, have you stopped by the registrar to drop off your reservation voucher for a seat at next week's graduation?
>
> (Man) You know what my schedule has been like recently, so I just got Jennifer to do it yesterday.
>
> (Narrator) What happened to the reservation voucher?
>
> ○ The woman forgot to give it to Jennifer.
> ○ Jennifer took it to the registrar.
> ○ It was lost at graduation.
> ○ John traded it for a seat.

Detail questions refer to specific items mentioned in the conversations.

The question asks about a detail—the reservation voucher—mentioned by the first speaker. Pay attention to the second speaker: " . . . I just got Jennifer to do it yesterday." The correct answer choice will say that Jennifer did something with the voucher. Only one answer fits. The answer choice "Jennifer took it to the registrar" best answers the detail question, "What happened to the reservation voucher?"

In Part A of the TOEFL CBT, time is on your side. Remember to be extra careful on the first eight questions. They have the most influence on the question types to come that will help improve your score.

Be extra careful on the first eight questions.

FOUR POE TECHNIQUES

The following four POE techniques will help you narrow down your choices whether or not you have actually understood what is spoken on the recording.

1. Opposites

When composing the wrong answer choices for a given question, ETS often tries to trap test-takers who *almost* understood the conversation. One wrong answer choice will look pretty similar to the correct answer, but will mean the opposite. For example:

> ○ Sunday is a day Mary often works.
> ○ Mary rarely works on Sunday.
> ○ Some days Mary's work is awful.
> ○ Mary has had a terrible cough since Sunday.

In the example above, "Sunday is a day Mary often works" and "Mary rarely works on Sunday" are what we call opposites; that is, it is impossible for *both* statements to be true. In a typical Listening section, one-fourth of the questions contain opposites. This is good news for you because if there is a pair of opposites in the answer choices, one of them is likely to be the right answer!

Even if you don't understand the question, you still have a 50 percent chance of answering this question correctly. For example, you hear:

> (Man) I thought Josh had a huge mid-term final tomorrow. Why is he outside playing frisbee?
>
> (Woman) If there's one thing Josh hates, it's cramming for an exam.
>
> (Narrator) What does the man mean?

Next, your four answer choices appear. You read:

- ⬭ Josh does not enjoy studying.
- ⬭ Josh ate while he studied.
- ⬭ Studying is a pleasure for Josh.
- ⬭ Josh doesn't have enough time to study.

In this example, the opposites are "Josh does not enjoy studying" and "Studying is a pleasure for Josh." Now, think of what the woman just said. The answer choice "Josh does not enjoy studying" best represents "If there's one thing Josh hates, it's cramming for an exam."

Now try another one. You hear:

> (Man) I can't seem to find my biology notes. I had them just a minute ago and suddenly they are gone.
>
> (Woman) Well, maybe you should try tidying up your desk a bit!
>
> (Narrator) What does the woman imply?

Next, your four answer choices appear. You read:

- ⬭ She thinks his desk is too tiny.
- ⬭ His desk is too messy.
- ⬭ He needs to buy a new desk.
- ⬭ His desk is far too organized.

The opposites are "His desk is too messy" and "His desk is far too organized." If you didn't recognize the opposites, you need to broaden your understanding of the term *opposites*. "His desk is too messy" simply states that the desk is messy, and "His desk is far too organized" implies that the desk is clean. That's enough for them to be considered opposites. So now all you need to do is remember what you just heard. The answer choice "His desk is too messy" best paraphrases the woman's statement, "Well, maybe you should try tidying up your desk a bit!" Use POE to eliminate the other answer choices and click on the best answer.

2. Extremes

The people who write the TOEFL CBT have very conservative tastes. None of their statements or short conversations will contain anything controversial, violent, passionate, or silly.

Use POE to eliminate extreme answer choices.

Use common sense and POE to eliminate any answer choices that are too extreme.

Remember Mary?

- ◯ Sunday is a day Mary often works.
- ◯ Mary rarely works on Sunday.
- ◯ Some days Mary's work is awful.
- ◯ Mary has had a terrible cough since Sunday.

The answer choice "Some days Mary's work is awful" is too extreme. ETS would probably say someone's work was "unsatisfactory" or even "bad," but not "awful." Just remember, ETS can't afford to offend anyone: Any answers that might be controversial are automatically wrong.

3. Literal Meanings of Idioms

Idiomatic expressions in English mean something different from their apparent meaning. They are a group of words known individually, but together, the words make no sense. For example, "to egg someone on" doesn't mean to put an egg on someone, but to encourage someone to do something bad.

Use POE to eliminate direct translations of idiomatic expressions.

In the TOEFL CBT, the second speaker will frequently use an idiomatic expression. In this case you can eliminate any answer choice that gives a literal translation. Look at an example.

(Woman) How did Rob perform in the fall production of Romeo and Juliet last night?

(Man) You wouldn't have believed it! He was head and shoulders above the rest of the cast.

(Narrator) What does the man mean?

- ◯ Rob is too tall to be an actor.
- ◯ Rob's performance was excellent.
- ◯ Rob was suspended above the stage.
- ◯ No one believed how terrible his performance was.

The answers "Rob is too tall to be an actor" and "Rob was suspended above the stage" directly translate the idiomatic expression "He was head and shoulders above the rest of the cast." Therefore, you may use POE to eliminate these answer choices. The answer choice "No one believed how terrible his performance was" is an opposite of "Rob's performance was excellent." Based on what you just heard the man say, click on one of these two answer choices. The statement "Rob's performance was excellent" correctly answers the question, "What does the man mean?"

Use POE to eliminate answer choices that sound like the short conversation.

4. Sound-Alikes

Another of ETS's favorite trap answers is what we call a sound-alike. Sound-alikes take some of the words and sounds from the statement or dialogue and rearrange them so that they have a totally different meaning. Remember this example?

○ Sunday is a day Mary often works.
○ Mary rarely works on Sunday.
○ Some days Mary's work is awful.
○ Mary has had a terrible cough since Sunday.

The conversation was:

(Woman) Will Mary be in on Sunday?

(Man) Sunday is usually Mary's day off.

(Narrator) What does the man mean?

We already found the opposites in these answers, and one extreme answer. So now look at how ETS might trap you with sounds. Notice how many things in the answer choices echo the word *off* in the statement—*often*, *awful*, and *cough*. In the answer choice "Some days Mary's work is awful," the phrase *Some days* is meant to confuse the test-taker with the sound of *Sunday*. The right answer "Mary rarely works on Sunday," is one of the opposites, is not extreme, and contains the fewest sound-alikes.

You'll notice that many sound-alikes can be eliminated using common sense and rigorous POE.

Summary of Listening Part A Strategy

Step 1: Avoid looking at the picture.

Step 2: Listen to how the first speaker sets up the random topic of conversation.

Step 3: Listen *extra* closely to how the second speaker responds. Remember, the question will almost always be about the second speaker.

Step 4: Don't stop listening after the second person speaks. On up to half of the conversations you will hear, one or both of the people will speak twice. Listen extra closely to the information at the end of the conversation.

Step 5: While reading the answer choices, look for those that contain:

- Extremes

- Opposite pairs in the answer choices

- Answer choices that directly translate idiomatic expressions

- Sound-alikes

Step 6: Use POE on as many answer choices as possible and then click on your answer. If you are still undecided, choose the answer choice containing the fewest sounds from the statement or dialogue.

LISTENING PART A

Drill 1 - CD Track 2

Directions: In this drill, you will hear short conversations between two people. Place the disk that came with this book into your CD player, advance to track 2, and press play. Listen to the following short conversations while looking at the pictures in the book. Do not turn the pages to preview the answer choices. Listen to the short conversations only one time. After you hear the short conversation between the two people and listen to the question, press pause. Then, turn the page and fill in the oval that best answers the question based on what is stated or implied. After you have filled in the oval, press play, and listen to the next conversation. Continue this pattern until the end of the drill. On the TOEFL CBT, you are not allowed to see the answer choices until after you hear the conversation. Therefore, do not turn the page and read the four choices until you have heard the conversation and the question. Remember, on the TOEFL CBT, the next question will appear only after you click on the "Next" icon and the "Answer Confirm" icon. Then check your answers on page 105.

Transcriptions for these drills can be found in the Appendix. You should only refer to them after you complete the exercises. Remember, on the real test you will only hear the passage once and you will not see anything in writing.

Listening

Time   Volume   Help   Answer Confirm   Next

What does the woman imply?

○ She isn't quite ready to go.
○ She'll meet them after the movie.
○ She can't finish the chapter.
○ She wants the man to wait for her.

Time
Volume   Help   Answer Confirm   Next

What does the woman say about Jim?

○ He isn't able to study for his mid-term exam.
○ He's preparing for a mid-term exam.
○ His mid-term exam is tomorrow.
○ He has been excused from the meeting.

Time   Volume   Help   Answer Confirm   Next

Listening

Time

Volume

? Help

Answer Confirm

→ Next

What does the man suggest the woman do?

○ Go out of town the week before the concert.
○ Reschedule her flight for a later date.
○ Find a new travel agent.
○ Lengthen her vacation by a week.

Time

Volume Help Answer Confirm Next

Listening

Time Volume Help Answer Confirm Next

What does the woman say about the scholarship?

○ It doesn't provide much money.
○ She's applying for another one soon.
○ It was easy to win.
○ She regrets applying for it.

Time

Volume Help Answer Confirm Next

What happened to the videotapes?

- ○ Bob lost the tapes in the library.
- ○ Ellen returned the tapes for Bob.
- ○ Bob left the tapes in the library.
- ○ Ellen never borrowed the tapes.

Time

Volume   Help   Answer Confirm   Next

What does the man imply about Lara?

○ She doesn't know how to use a calculator.
○ She finished her algebra exam first.
○ She was cheating during the exam.
○ She is an excellent math student.

Time

Volume

? Help

Answer Confirm

Next

Listening

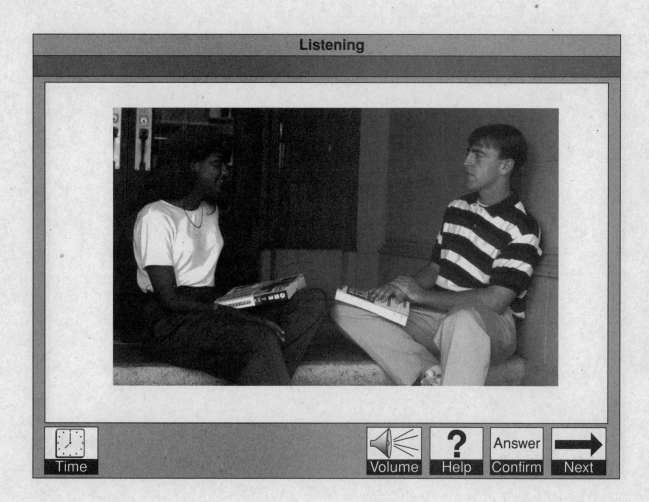

Time

Volume Help Answer Confirm Next

What had the woman assumed about the man?

○ He wouldn't be able to attend the party.
○ He didn't know the way to the party.
○ He thought he had to wear formal clothes.
○ He needed a ride home from the party.

Time

Volume

? Help

Answer Confirm

→ Next

What can be inferred about the man?

○ He usually does well on his biology tests.
○ He likes to watch television shows on biology.
○ He was watching television while studying for his biology test.
○ He needs to spend less time watching television.

Time

Volume   Help   Answer Confirm   Next

What does the woman mean?

○ John probably did well on his final.
○ She's not sure if John has taken the final yet.
○ She is happy to see John.
○ She is also trying to pass the final.

Time   Volume   Help   Answer Confirm   Next

What does the woman mean?

○ He will have no problem waking up.
○ She will wake him up tomorrow.
○ He should ask his roommate to wake him up.
○ Nobody can help him wake up.

Time

Volume

Help

Answer
Confirm

Next

Time Volume Help Answer Confirm Next

What does the man suggest the woman do?

- ◯ Take a break from writing.
- ◯ Choose a different essay topic.
- ◯ Continue working on her essay.
- ◯ Extend the length of her essay.

Time   Volume   Help   Answer Confirm   Next

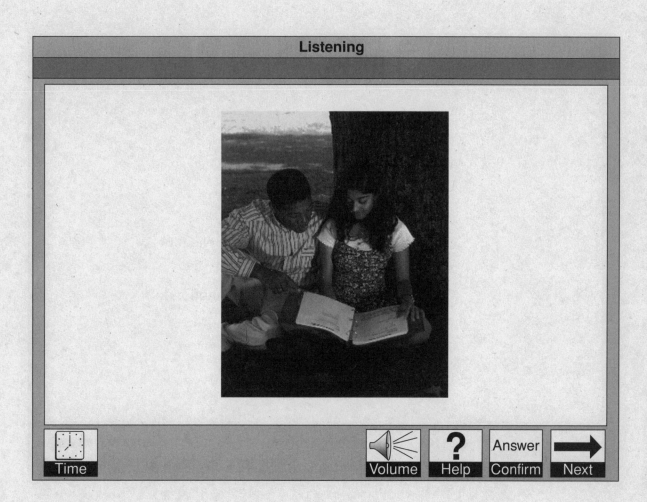

What does the woman mean?

○ Jeff was late sending in his application.
○ Things are going well for Jeff.
○ Jeff will earn a lot of money.
○ The graduation ceremony will honor Jeff.

Time

Volume Help Answer Confirm Next

Listening

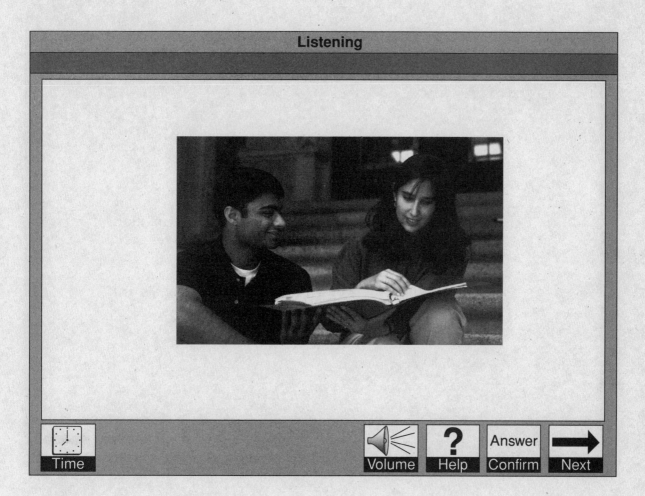

Time · Volume · Help · Answer Confirm · Next

What does the man mean?

○ He told the woman to get a job at the recreation center.
○ He forgets what he told the woman.
○ He thought the woman wouldn't believe him.
○ He knew the woman would be helped by his suggestion.

Time

Volume Help Answer Confirm Next

ANSWER KEY

1. Concentrate on finishing their paper.

2. She isn't quite ready to go.

3. He's preparing for a mid-term exam.

4. Reschedule her flight for a later date.

5. It doesn't provide much money.

6. Ellen returned the tapes for Bob.

7. She is an excellent math student.

8. He wouldn't be able to attend the party.

9. He was watching television while studying for his biology test.

10. It will not be completed on time.

11. John probably did well on his final.

12. He should ask his roommate to wake him up.

13. Continue working on her essay.

14. Things are going well for Jeff.

15. He knew the woman would be helped by his suggestion.

Part B—Long Conversations and Lectures

THE BASICS

In Part B of the TOEFL CBT Listening section, your task is to listen to long conversations and lectures, after which you'll be asked questions about the information you just heard. Just as in Part A, you are *not* allowed to look at the questions during the long conversations or lectures. Also, neither the long conversations nor the lectures will be repeated. In other words, you have one chance to listen and remember.

Unfortunately, ETS may include experimental questions in this section, so it is impossible to say exactly how many long conversations and lectures you will hear. There can be anywhere from 5 to 7 long conversations and lectures, with 2 to 6 questions each. Once you have listened to the long conversation or lecture, you will be able to read the questions that are asked. They will appear at the top of the computer screen, just above the answer choices. You may also take as much time as you wish to answer each question, but remember, the clock is running.

Computer-adaptive tests use your performance on previous questions to determine which question you'll be asked next.

THE TUTORIAL

VOLUME

You are allowed to adjust the volume for the Listening section at the beginning of Part B. Normally, the volume will be preset to an audible level; however, if you need to raise or lower the volume, do so now. Once you have decided on the volume level, you won't have to think about it during the remainder of the Listening section. Furthermore, if you adjust it after the section begins, the clock will run.

TIME

The time remaining is shown in the upper left-hand corner of the screen. You have the option of turning off the time by clicking on the Clock icon in the lower left corner of the screen. However, we strongly recommend that you leave the clock on. If you do turn off the clock, you will not be able to see how much time you have remaining and, consequently, will have difficulty pacing yourself. Fortunately, the clock does not run while any of the conversations are being spoken. The time displayed in the upper left-hand corner is the time remaining for you to answer the questions. The time *does* run if you click on the Help icon. However, once you finish this book, the Help icon will not be necessary.

The clock stops running while the long conversations or lectures are being spoken.

Directions

Take a look at the directions for Part B:

HOW TO ANSWER

During the long conversations, a picture will appear on the computer screen of a professor, and four to six students either sitting around a table or in some other type of university setting. The professor will lead a discussion on an undetermined academic subject. Although the professor will do the majority of the speaking, two or three students *at most* will also participate in the discussion. After the conversation, you will be asked 2 to 4 questions about what was discussed.

During the lectures, a professor will give a talk about various academic subjects such as biology, geography, music, and so forth. The lecture may last anywhere from 2 to 3 minutes. After the lecture you will be asked 4 to 6 questions about what you heard.

After clicking on the best answer, you *must* then click on the two icons in the bottom right-hand corner of the computer screen. The first is the "Next" icon on the far right. After you click on "Next," you must click on "Answer Confirm." You may change you answer at any time *before* you click on "Answer Confirm." However, once you click on "Answer Confirm," you will never see that question again. As was the case in part A, you must answer the question on the screen before the next one will appear.

Pictures

In Part A of the TOEFL CBT Listening section, you do not need to study the pictures shown. However, in Part B, you have to pay a little more attention. Before you hear a long conversation or lecture, you will see the topic of the conversation or lecture you are about to hear. The screen will look similar to the following:

Pay close attention to how the narrator introduces the long conversation or lecture. It might hold valuable information to what the main idea is.

Next, you will see a picture of a professor standing and the lecture or conversation will begin. Do *not* be distracted by the professor. What the professor is wearing, holding, or doing will not be tested. You only have to be concerned with what the professor is saying. Here is a typical lecture picture:

PICTURE FLIPS

Pay close attention to the picture flips.

Due to the new question types ETS has introduced on the TOEFL CBT, occasionally the picture of the lecturing professor disappears, and a word, diagram, graph, or picture appears on the computer screen. These "picture flips" occur during the lectures of the TOEFL CBT. You *must* pay close attention to what is being said about the word, diagram, graph, or picture that appears on the screen. ETS *will* ask you a question about that word, diagram, graph, or picture in the questions following the lecture. Look at the following example:

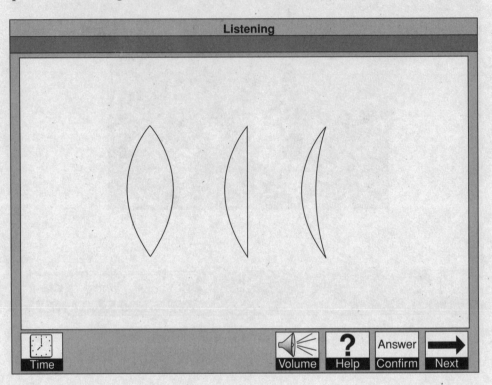

WHAT MAKES PART B SO HARD?

What many test-takers find most difficult is simply remembering what was said long enough to answer the questions. Each long conversation or lecture lasts between two to three minutes and contains a lot of information. Even many native English speakers cannot remember every word.

WHY CAN'T YOU TAKE NOTES?

You may not take notes during the TOEFL CBT.

This part of the test is probably the best proof that the TOEFL CBT is not a very good predictor of how well you could function in an American university setting. Can you imagine a professor at a college or university who forbids you to take notes in class? Of course not! But that's what this section of the TOEFL CBT does.

This restriction exists on no other test administered by ETS, and according to ETS it exists "for security reasons." Does that sound logical to you? It doesn't make much sense to us either.

We believe that it is primarily Part B of the TOEFL CBT Listening section that prompted ETS to decide that you should not be allowed to take notes. Since most of the language in this section is so simple, ETS knows you're not going to have much difficulty *understanding* what was said. What is difficult, however, is trying to *remember* what was said. Perhaps ETS should rename Part B the "memory" section, instead of the "listening" section. The truth is, if ETS allowed note taking in Part B, most people would have no problem answering the questions. In other words, test-takers could easily score too many points on this part of the test.

Pacing

In Part B of the TOEFL CBT Listening section, you may take as much time as you wish to answer. Always read each answer choice carefully before choosing. However, just because you have all the time in the world doesn't mean you can let your mind wander and spend two minutes on each question. You need to work efficiently. The time remaining is displayed in the upper left-hand corner of the computer screen. Refer to it to see exactly how much time remains. In the upper right-hand corner of the computer screen, the number of questions remaining is displayed. Keep an eye on the both of them to make sure you don't run out of time. You should try to answer each question in 45 seconds or less.

Pace yourself. Don't spend too much time on any one question.

General Strategy

ETS will only ask 4 to 6 questions about each long conversation or lecture; therefore, you only need to remember 4 to 6 pieces of information. Your short-term memory will be most helpful here. Once you answer the questions, you will never have to use any of the information again. The trick is to figure out which pieces of information you need to remember. Although there is no surefire way to know exactly what ETS will ask, there are some recognizable patterns that you can look for.

Introductions

Before the conversations and lectures begin, you will be able to read the introductory academic subject heading. The topics could be about biology, art history, geography, chemistry, history, or any other academic subjects. As you read the topic, the narrator will say several introductory sentences. Listen for any key words that give you clues as to the main topic. For example, you might hear:

> (Narrator) Listen to a professor discuss the side effects of an experimental drug being tested on cancer patients.

Now you have some idea as to what the lecture is about. As you hear the phrases "side effects," "experimental drugs," and "cancer patients," you can safely assume the lecture is something about the various side effects different cancer patients have experienced as a result of taking a new type of drug. This eliminates any new surprises about the topic.

Questions/Definitions

A rhetorical question is one usually asked for the purpose of making a point, with no answer expected.

If at any time during the conversations or lectures the speakers pose rhetorical questions or ask the students questions, listen closely for the answers. More than likely, ETS will ask you similar questions after the conversations or lectures are finished. Also, if the speakers at any time define vocabulary words, or if vocabulary words appear on the screen, listen closely and remember the definitions. ETS loves to ask questions about the words they define.

Lists and Examples

The speakers will frequently give lists of items to illustrate or clearly provide details about what they are discussing. They also give examples to support their claims. If you hear lists of words or examples, listen for and remember any specific or unusual details that surround them. ETS might ask questions concerning these lists and examples.

Comparisons

From time to time, the speakers will compare two or more objects. Listen closely for the similarities and differences among the objects being compared. ETS might use these comparisons for matching questions.

Processes/Chronological Order

During the long conversations and lectures, be aware of any series of events that are presented or explained in a particular or specific order. ETS might ask you to place the events in chronological order.

QUESTION TYPES

Besides teaching you about volume, time, and how to answer, ETS will also introduce the question types you will encounter on Part B of the TOEFL CBT Listening section. Although they may sound confusing at first, you will become quite familiar with them after finishing our practice questions. There are 4 basic question types.

1. Single Answer Questions

Single answer questions are just like those on the old paper-and-pencil version, except now you are able to read the questions along with the four answer choices. Basically, you are asked to click on one of four choices that best answers the question you are asked. There are two types of single answer questions: main idea questions and detail questions.

Main Idea Questions

The first question you'll encounter in the Part B Listening section will most likely be a main idea question. Main idea questions test how well you understand and interpret the general content of the talk. The answer is *not* directly mentioned; rather, it has to be inferred from other information you hear. These question types do *not* involve pictures. Main idea questions are usually asked in the following forms:

What is the purpose of the talk?

What is the main purpose of the talk?

What is the purpose of the instructor's talk?

What is the main topic of the talk?

What is the professor mainly discussing?

To answer main idea questions, try to remember how the lecture or conversation was introduced. Think about what the general topic of the talk was. Ask yourself which words or phrases were constantly repeated. Then look at your four answer choices, and use POE to eliminate any that introduce any new material *not* mentioned during the conversations or lectures. You will have to rely on your paraphrasing skills. Once you have clicked on your answer choice, you must click on the "Next" and the "Answer/Confirm" icons.

Detail Questions

Detail questions ask for specific facts mentioned in the conversations or lectures. Unlike the short conversations in the Listening section Part A, there are no tricks or traps, such as sound-alikes and idiom interpretations. Three of the four answer choices simply were *not* mentioned in the passage, or were mentioned in association with a topic other than the one asked about. These question types do *not* involve pictures. Detail questions will appear on the test as follows:

What does the professor say about the way steamer ships sail?

According to the speaker, why do ants live in colonies?

How does the student manage to take so many courses?

The question types are endless. However, as you read the question at the top of the computer screen, try to remember as much as possible about the topic being asked. Then read the answer choices and eliminate any new information, or any information that was spoken about in regards to another topic. Once you have clicked on your answer choice, you must click on the "Next" and the "Answer/Confirm" icons.

2. Other Single Answer Questions

Other single answer questions may come in two different forms: clicking on one of four letters (A, B, C, or D) in a picture, or clicking on one of four pictures. In any case, you need to click on just *one* answer choice in the picture before clicking on the "Next" and the "Answer/Confirm" icons.

Clicking on One of Four Letters

There is a good chance that you will encounter at least one of these question types on Part B. Like detail questions, they ask for specific information that you heard during the long conversation or lecture. These question types always refer to a picture, map, or diagram. Look at the following example. At the top of the computer screen you read:

Click on the letter that indicates the location where cork farmers obtain their product.

Using your mouse, point and click on the letter that best answers the question. When answering these question types, try to remember the picture you were shown during the lecture. ETS is fairly predictable. If they show you a word, diagram, graph, or picture during the talk, pay *close* attention to what is being said. They will definitely ask you a question about it.

However, be sure to answer the question you are being asked. Many students answer hastily and misread the question. Once you have clicked on your answer choice, you must click on the "Next" and the "Answer/Confirm" icons.

Clicking on One of Four Pictures

The only difference between "clicking on one of four pictures" and "clicking on one of four letters" is you have four individual pictures rather than just one picture with four letters. There is a good chance that you will encounter at least one of these question types on Part B. Like detail questions, they ask for specific information that you heard during the long conversation or lecture. These question types always refer to a picture, map, or diagram.

Approach these questions like you would for clicking on one of four letters. Using your mouse, point and click on the picture that best answers the question. When answering these question types, try to remember the pictures you were shown during the lecture. Again, ETS is fairly predictable. If they show you a word, diagram, graph, or picture during the talk, pay *close* attention to what is being said. They will definitely ask you a question about it.

3. Multiple Answer Questions

Multiple answer questions ask for specific facts mentioned in the conversations or lectures. However, they ask you to click on **TWO** choices that best answer the question instead of just one. Interestingly enough, ETS places squares next to the four answer choices rather than ovals. These question types do *not* involve pictures. Unlike the Listening section Part A, there are no tricks or traps, such as sound-alikes and idiom interpretations. Simply, two of the four answer choices simply were *not* mentioned in the passage or were mentioned in association with another topic other than the one being asked about. Multiple answer questions will appear on the test as shown on the next page.

Read the question carefully before clicking on the best answer.

Some question types ask you to pick two correct answers.

According to the speaker, what were
two ways that early Colonial Americans
traveled?

Click on 2 answers.

☐ Covered wagon.
☐ Carriage.
☐ Sleigh.
☐ Wagon.

Time | Volume | ? Help | Answer Confirm | → Next

One simple strategy to
remember when answering
multiple answer questions is
to not click on opposite
answer choices. If two
statements contradict each
other, it is impossible for
them both to be correct.

Multiple-answer questions are basically detail questions and should be approached as such. As you read the question at the top of the computer screen, try to remember as much as possible about the topic being asked. Then read the answer choices and use POE to get rid of any new information or any information that was spoken about in regards to another topic. One simple strategy to remember when answering these question types is to *not* click on opposite answer choices. If two statements contradict each other, it is impossible for them both to be correct. Once you have clicked on your *two* answer choices, you must click on the "Next" and the "Answer/Confirm" icons. If you just click on *one* answer choice, you will *not* be allowed to proceed with the test until you click on *two* answer choices.

4. Matching/Order Questions

Matching/Order questions are the most time consuming of all the Part B Listening questions. They require extensive mouse clicking and moving. Unfortunately, you do *not* get half-credit for getting the question partially correct... It's all or nothing. These questions are also the most difficult because rather than having to remember just one piece of information, you are required to remember many.

MATCHING QUESTIONS

Matching questions ask that you match three items in one category with three items in another category. This question type does *not* refer to a picture that you may have seen; rather, it is based on what is spoken in the conversations or lectures. As referred to in the General Strategy section above, you want to pay close attention to any similarities and differences among objects being compared during the conversations or lectures. ETS might use these comparisons for matching questions. On the TOEFL CBT test, matching questions will be similar to the following:

```
┌──────────────────────────────────────────────────────────────┐
│                          Listening                            │
├──────────────────────────────────────────────────────────────┤
│                                                                │
│  ┌────────────────────────────────────────────────────────┐   │
│  │                                                         │   │
│  │   Based on the description in the passage, classify     │   │
│  │   the following types of animals.                       │   │
│  │                                                         │   │
│  │   ┌──────────────────────────────────────────────┐      │   │
│  │   │ Click on a word. Then click on the space where │     │   │
│  │   │        it belongs. Use each word only once.    │     │   │
│  │   └──────────────────────────────────────────────┘      │   │
│  │                                                         │   │
│  │                       Whale                             │   │
│  │                        Ant                              │   │
│  │                      Piranha                            │   │
│  │                                                         │   │
│  │   ┌──────────┐    ┌──────────┐    ┌──────────┐          │   │
│  │   │  Mammal  │    │   Fish   │    │  Insect  │          │   │
│  │   ├──────────┤    ├──────────┤    ├──────────┤          │   │
│  │   └──────────┘    └──────────┘    └──────────┘          │   │
│  │                                                         │   │
│  └────────────────────────────────────────────────────────┘   │
│                                                                │
│  ┌────┐              ┌────┐ ┌────┐ ┌────────┐ ┌────────┐       │
│  │Time│              │Vol │ │ ?  │ │ Answer │ │  Next  │       │
│  └────┘              └────┘ └Help┘ └Confirm ┘ └───────→┘       │
└──────────────────────────────────────────────────────────────┘
```

Using the three words in the first category as memory stimulators, try to remember what was stated or implied about each. Most likely they were compared to each other. Click on the first word in the list to highlight it. Then click on the space in which you would like to insert it.

ORDER QUESTIONS

This question type is all about chronological order. ETS gives you approximately four sentences and asks you to put them in correct chronological order. Order questions do *not* refer to any picture that you have seen; rather, they are based on what is spoken in the conversations or lectures. As referred to in the General Strategy section above, you want to pay close attention to a series of events that are presented or explained in a particular or specific order. On the TOEFL CBT, order questions will be similar to the following:

Listening

The professor briefly explains a process. Summarize the process by putting the events in order.

Click on a sentence. Then click on the space where it belongs.
Use each sentence only once.

The top of the mountain spews molten magma.

Trees, shrubs, and all other plants begin to grow.

Cities and towns are evacuated.

The dormant volcano sides begin to expand.

1 [＿＿＿＿＿＿]   3 [＿＿＿＿＿＿]

2 [＿＿＿＿＿＿]   4 [＿＿＿＿＿＿]

Time | Volume | Help | Answer Confirm | Next

For order questions, you should read all the sentences and determine which of the statements begins the chronological order. Next, determine which of the remaining sentences comes last.

For order questions, you should first read the four or five sentences and determine which of the statements *begins* the chronological order. Try to remember the series of events the professor described in the passage (and use your common sense) to select the best answer. Next, determine which of the remaining sentences come **last**. Your next step is to simply fill in the middle answer choices. After you have made your selections, re-read them to make sure they flow in chronological order. You may rearrange them at any time before you click on the "Next" and the "Answer/Confirm" icons.

Listening Part B

Drill 1 - CD Track 3

Now that you have been introduced to strategies and different question types, use what you have learned and practice the techniques. Listen to the following conversation or lecture. Do *not* turn the pages back to review any words, diagrams, graphs, or pictures that might be presented in the lecture. Listen to the lecture only *one* time. After the conversations and lectures are finished, press pause. Then, turn the page and fill in the oval that best answers the question based on what is stated or implied. After you have filled in the oval, press play and listen to the next conversation. Continue this pattern until the end of the drill. On the TOEFL CBT, you are *not* allowed to see the answer choices until after you hear the conversation. Therefore, *do not* turn the page and read the four choices until you have heard the conversation and the question. Remember, on the TOEFL CBT, the next question will appear only after you click on the "Next" icon and the "Answer Confirm" icon. Now get ready to listen to the first conversation.

Answers to these drills can be found at the end of this chapter. Transcriptions for these drills can be found in the Appendix. You should only refer to them after you complete the exercises. Remember, on the real test you will only hear the passage once and you will not see anything in writing.

Listening

Time

Volume

? Help

Answer Confirm

Next

Why did the woman go to see the chemistry professor?

- ⬭ To apply for a job as a research assistant.
- ⬭ To discuss a problem concerning a letter.
- ⬭ To make an appointment with the registrar.
- ⬭ To register for advanced chemistry class.

Time

Volume

?
Help

Answer
Confirm

Next

What can be inferred about the research grant for the project?

- ○ The electrochemistry project isn't possible without it.
- ○ It was more generous than originally anticipated.
- ○ It isn't enough to pay for the woman's salary.
- ○ It was approved sooner than was expected.

Time

Volume　Help　Answer Confirm　Next

What does the professor say about academic probation?

- ○ There are many reasons for someone to be on academic probation.
- ○ Academic probation is common for senior students.
- ○ Students with high grade point averages seldom have academic probation.
- ○ Academic probation interferes with graduation.

Time   Volume   Help   Answer Confirm   Next

What does the professor suggest the woman do?

- ⬭ Return the book to the library.
- ⬭ Contact the campus police.
- ⬭ Pay for the missing book.
- ⬭ Contest the academic probation.

Time

Volume Help Answer Confirm Next

Listening Part B

Drill 2 - CD Track 4

Now that you have been introduced to strategies and different question types, use what you have learned and practice the techniques. Listen to the following conversation or lecture. Do *not* turn the pages back to review any words, diagrams, graphs, or pictures that might be presented in the lecture. Listen to the lecture only *one* time. After the conversations and lectures are finished, press pause. Then turn the page and fill in the oval that best answers the question based on what is stated or implied. After you have filled in the oval, press play and listen to the next conversation. Continue this pattern until the end of the drill. On the TOEFL CBT, you are *not* allowed to see the answer choices until after you hear the conversation. Therefore, *do not* turn the page and read the four choices until you have heard the conversation and the question. Remember, on the TOEFL CBT, the next question will appear only after you click on the "Next" icon and the "Answer Confirm" icon. Now get ready to listen to the next conversation.

Transcriptions for these drills can be found in the Appendix. You should only refer to them after you complete the exercises. Remember, on the real test you will only hear the passage once and you will not see anything in writing.

Listening

Time

Volume　Help　Answer
Confirm　Next

According to the professor, when were peace pipes smoked?

Click on 2 answers.

☐ Treaties
☐ Pacts
☐ Weddings
☐ Banquets

Time Volume Help Answer Confirm Next

According to the professor, why were the peace pipes regarded as valuable objects?

- ⭕ The pipes were rarely used by the tribesmen.
- ⭕ The materials needed to make the pipes were scarce.
- ⭕ The same pipes were smoked generation after generation.
- ⭕ The pipes signified communication with higher powers.

Time

Volume | Help | Answer Confirm | Next

Listening

The professor briefly explains a process. Summarize the process by putting the events in order.

Click on a sentence. Then click on a space where it belongs. Use each sentence only once.

Verbal agreements were decided.

Native Americans leaders gathered in living quarters.

The women of the tribes harvested tobacco.

The peace pipe was smoked.

1 _____

2 _____

3 _____

4 _____

Time | Volume | ? Help | Answer Confirm | Next

According to the discussion, why were the locations of the tobacco fields kept confidential?

◯ To ensure an abundant harvest.
◯ To protect them from neighboring tribes.
◯ To please the higher powers.
◯ To keep the children from smoking.

Time

Volume Help Answer Confirm Next

LISTENING PART B

Drill 3 - CD Track 5

Now that you have been introduced to strategies and different question types, use what you have learned and practice the techniques. Listen to the following conversation or lecture. Do *not* turn the pages back to review any words, diagrams, graphs, or pictures that might be presented in the lecture. Listen to the lecture only *one* time. After the conversations and lectures are finished, press pause. Then, turn the page and fill in the oval that best answers the question based on what is stated or implied. After you have filled in the oval, press play, and listen to the next conversation. Continue this pattern until the end of the drill. On the TOEFL CBT, you are *not* allowed to see the answer choices until after you hear the conversation. Therefore, *do not* turn the page and read the four choices until you have heard the conversation and the question. Remember, on the TOEFL CBT, the next question will appear only after you click on the "Next" icon and the "Answer Confirm" icon. Now get ready to listen to the next conversation.

Transcriptions for these drills can be found in the Appendix. You should only refer to them after you complete the exercises. Remember, on the real test you will only hear the passage once and you will not see anything in writing.

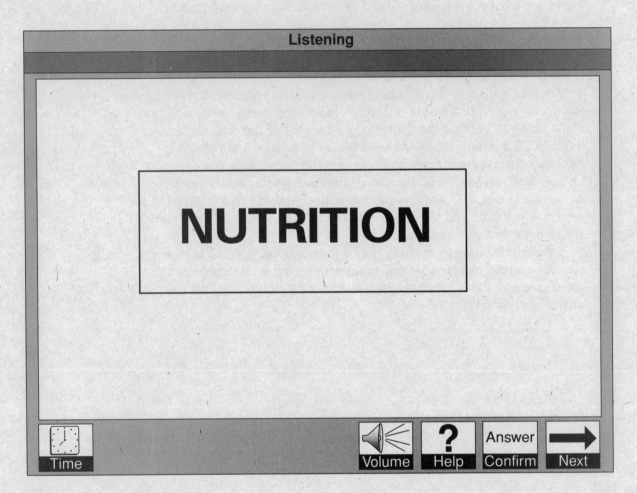

What is the main purpose of the lecture?

- ⬭ To review material for an upcoming nutrition examination.
- ⬭ To convince students to carefully watch their weight.
- ⬭ To inform the students of recent controversial diets.
- ⬭ To associate weight with personal and physical characteristics.

Time | Volume | Help | Answer Confirm | Next

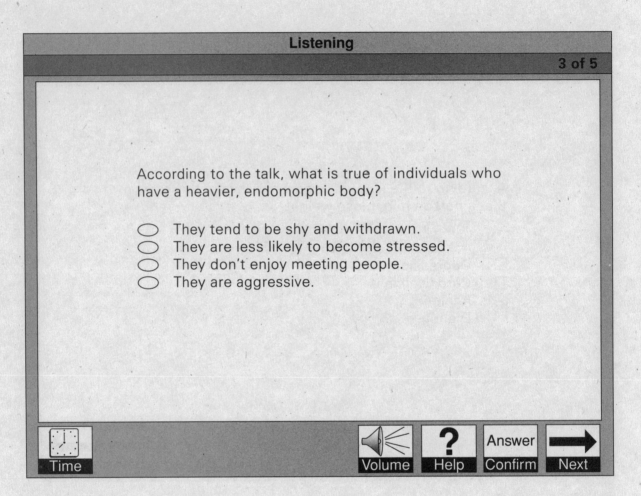

Based on the professor's lecture, what can be concluded about the recent controversial research linking personality traits to physical appearance?

○ Children are likely to develop personalities based on their physical appearance.

○ Physical appearance can drastically change without any personality change.

○ Individuals suffering from multiple personalities could gain and lose weight rapidly.

○ Personality traits are often linked with cultural upbringing.

Time   Volume   Help   Answer Confirm   Next

What does the speaker advise to do if rapid weight gain or loss is experienced?

○   Consult a physician.
○   Purchase new clothing.
○   Try to return to normal weight.
○   Confide in a psychologist.

Time   Volume   **?** Help   Answer Confirm   Next

LISTENING PART B

Drill 4 - CD Track 6

Now that you have been introduced to strategies and different question types, use what you have learned and practice the techniques. Listen to the following conversation or lecture. Do *not* turn the pages back to review any words, diagrams, graphs, or pictures that might be presented in the lecture. Listen to the lecture only *one* time. After the conversations and lectures are finished, press pause. Then, turn the page and fill in the oval that best answers the question based on what is stated or implied. After you have filled in the oval, press play, and listen to the next conversation. Continue this pattern until the end of the drill. On the TOEFL CBT, you are *not* allowed to see the answer choices until after you hear the conversation. Therefore, *do not* turn the page and read the four choices until you have heard the conversation and the question. Remember, on the TOEFL CBT, the next question will appear only after you click on the "Next" icon and the "Answer Confirm" icon. Now get ready to listen to the next conversation.

Transcriptions for these drills can be found in the Appendix. You should only refer to them after you complete the exercises. Remember, on the real test you will only hear the passage once and you will not see anything in writing.

What does the professor mainly discuss?

○ The complex social order of ants.
○ A procedure for exterminating ants.
○ The creation of ant colonies.
○ The cultivation practices of ant species.

Time   Volume   Help   Answer Confirm   Next

According to the passage, ants build their colonies in which of the following?

Click on two answers.

☐ Soil
☐ Ships
☐ Logs
☐ Rocks

Time

Volume

? Help

Answer Confirm

Next

Based on the professor's lecture, match the responsibility to the correct caste of ants.

Click on a word. Then click on the space where if belongs. Use each word only once.

Protection

Construction

Reproduction

Queens	Workers	Males

Time

Volume

? Help

Answer Confirm

Next

What does the lecturer say about the three classes of ants in the caste system?

- ◯ They compete with one another for food.
- ◯ The queen caste is considered the most essential.
- ◯ They are dependent upon each other for survival.
- ◯ They live in separate colonies.

Time Volume Help Answer Confirm Next

The professor briefly explains a process of reproduction. Summarize the process by putting the events in correct chronological order.

Click on a sentence. Then click on the space where it belongs. Use each sentence only once.

The males die.

The mature generation of ants leaves on a mating flight.

The female lays eggs.

The females excavate an egg chamber.

1 [   ]   3 [   ]

2 [   ]   4 [   ]

Time   Volume   Help   Answer Confirm   Next

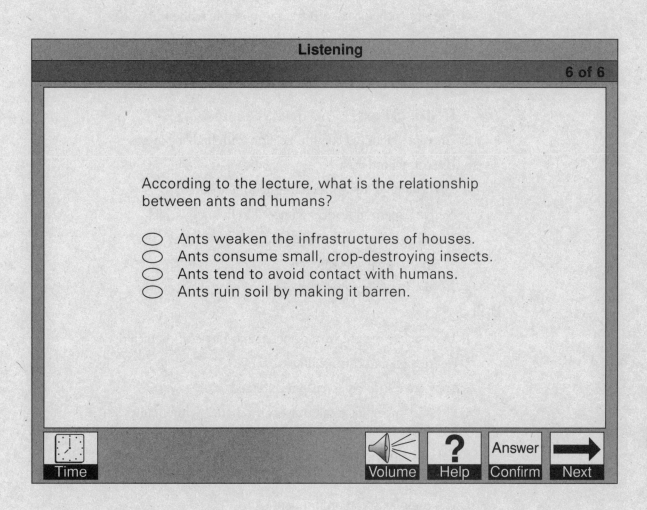

According to the lecture, what is the relationship between ants and humans?

- ⬭ Ants weaken the infrastructures of houses.
- ⬭ Ants consume small, crop-destroying insects.
- ⬭ Ants tend to avoid contact with humans.
- ⬭ Ants ruin soil by making it barren.

Time

Volume Help Answer Confirm Next

Answer Key

Drill 1

1. To discuss a problem concerning a letter

2. The electrochemistry project isn't possible without it.

3. There are many reasons for someone to be on academic probation.

4. Pay for the missing book.

Drill 2

1. Treaties and pacts

2. The pipes signified communication with higher powers.

3. The correct order is:

   The women of the tribes harvested the tobacco.

   Native American leaders gathered in living quarters.

   Verbal agreements were decided.

   The peace pipe was smoked.

4. To ensure an abundant harvest

Drill 3

1. To associate weight with personal and physical characteristics

2. Depression and chronic illness

3. They are less likely to become stressed.

4. Physical appearance can drastically change without any personality change.

5. Consult a physician.

Drill 4

1. The complex social order of ants

2. Soil and logs

3. Protection = Workers

   Construction = Males

   Reproduction = Queens

4. They are dependent upon each other for survival.

5. The correct order is:

   The mature generation of ants leaves on a mating flight.

   The males die.

   The females excavate an egg chamber.

   The female lays eggs.

6. Ants consume small, crop-destroying insects.

PART III

Structure

THE BASICS

The second section of the TOEFL CBT is the Structure section. It tests your basic knowledge of English grammar. The Structure section is computer adaptive, meaning the difficulty of any given one question depends on your performance on all previous questions in the section. Also, you must answer each question before the next one will appear. You will be expected to answer anywhere from 20 to 25 questions in approximately 15 to 20 minutes.

There are two types of questions in the TOEFL CBT Structure section: Sentence Completion and Error Identification. ETS presents them one by one in random order. It is impossible to determine how many of each you will see.

DIRECTIONS

The first computer screen you will see in the Structure section of the TOEFL CBT contains the directions. You should learn the directions prior to the test so you don't waste valuable time reading them. By clicking on the "Dismiss Directions" icon located in the upper right side of the screen, the directions will disappear and the first question will appear. The directions will look something like this:

Structure

20 Question

This section is designed to measure your ability to recognize language that is appropriate for standard written English. There are two types of questions in this section.

In the first type of question, there are incomplete sentences. Beneath each sentence there are four words or phrases. You will click on the one word or phrase that best completes the sentence.

> Example: Geysers have often been compared to volcanoes____they both emit hot liquids below the Earth's surface.
> ○ due to
> ○ because
> ○ in spite of
> ○ regardless

The second type of question has four underlined words or phrases. You will click on the one underlined word or phrase that must be changed for the sentence to be correct.

> Example: Guppies <u>are</u> sometimes <u>call</u> rainbow fish <u>because</u> of the males' bright <u>colors</u>.

Now begin working on the Structure questions. When you are ready to continue, click on the Dismiss Directions icon.

When finished reading directions click on the icon below

Dismiss Directions

Time   **?** Help   Answer Confirm   ➡ Next

SENTENCE COMPLETION

For sentence completion questions, a sentence will appear in the middle of the computer screen. You must then click on one of the four answer choices that is grammatically correct and best completes the sentence. Look at an example:

Structure

Directions: Click on the one word or phrase that best completes the sentence.

With time, the thickness of human eyelashes decreases, _____ them less likely to protect the eyes from dust and disease.

○ making
○ which they make
○ and is making
○ make

Time | **?** Help | Answer Confirm | ➡ Next

Three of the above four answer choices are incorrect, meaning if they were inserted into the blank, the sentence would *not* make sense in accordance with the standard rules of English grammar. (By the way, the correct answer is "making.")

ERROR IDENTIFICATION

For Error Identification questions, you only have to identify the error, *not* correct it.

The second type of Structure question you will encounter is Error Identification. You will see sentences in which four words or phrases are underlined. One of these words or phrases is incorrect and makes the entire sentence grammatically incorrect. The good news in this section is that you are not asked to correct or name the error; you only have to *identify* it. This means that it doesn't really matter if you are not completely sure *why* a particular word or phrase is wrong. Recognizing that it is incorrect is all you need to do. You will not have to supply the correct word or phrase to get the questions corrrect.

One of the most obvious things to keep in mind regarding Error Identification questions on the TOEFL CBT is that the parts of the sentence that are *not* underlined are *correct* as written. Many times, you can look to the non-underlined parts, the parts you know are correct, and use them to guide you. Articles and adjectives can tell you whether nouns are plural or singular. Pronouns replace nouns. **So don't ignore the non-underlined parts of the sentence when you are looking at Error Identification questions**. Look at a typical TOEFL CBT Error Identification question:

Use non-underlined words to help you determine the error.

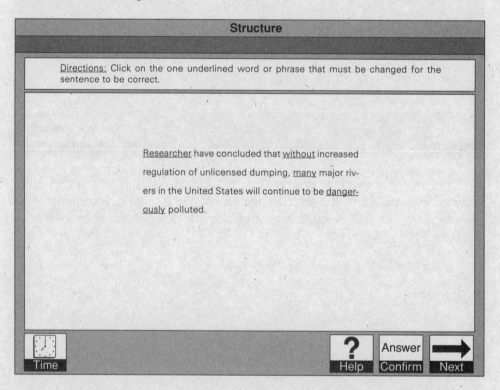

Three of the above four answer choices are correct, meaning they are *grammatically* correct. You want to "click on" the answer choice that is *grammatically incorrect* in accordance with the standard rules of English grammar. (By the way, the correct answer is "Researchers.")

What Does It Test?

ETS says that the Structure section "measures your ability to recognize language that is appropriate for standard written English." The key word here is "recognize." You never have to come up with the answer yourself, you simply have to "recognize" the best answer. Think about it this way. Every day, you go to the same grocery store where you see the same manager. Although you don't know the name of the manager, his face is familiar. If you see that same manager in the subway, at the library, or in the park, you still don't know his name or anything else about him, but you will be able to "recognize" him and know that he works at the grocery store. The Structure section of the TOEFL CBT works the same way. It tests the same grammar rules over and over again.

ETS is not that creative with its questions. Once you "recognize" the limited grammar rules that ETS tests, "recognizing" the best answer is simple. Since ETS uses multiple choice testing, you must simply "click on" one of four possible choices that you "recognize." Once you memorize and practice the different question types, your score will improve significantly. So, the Structure section of the TOEFL CBT simply tests how well you can "recognize" grammar mistakes.

Process of Elimination (POE)

As you learned in the Listening section, sometimes you aren't quite sure which answer you should "click on." By eliminating the answer choices you know are wrong, you can greatly increase your chances of clicking on the best answer—even if you guess. Guessing and clicking on an answer from one of two choices makes your odds of getting the best answer much greater than guessing from four choices.

Use Process of Elimination to rule out wrong answer choices, and as a last resort, *guess*.

How Much Will My Scores Improve?

Improvement is directly related to practice. But keep this in mind: If grammar is your strong point, and you are already scoring fairly high, room for improvement is significantly *less* than if grammar is your weak point and you are scoring fairly low. There are a lot of drills in this book. If you use the techniques we teach and practice, practice, practice, your scores will improve.

Scoring

Half of your score for the Structure and Writing section is determined by how well you do on the grammar questions—that is, the 20 to 25 Sentence completion and Error Identification questions. The other half of your score is determined by how well you write your essay in the Writing section, formerly known as the Test of Written English (TWE). The Writing section is covered in chapter 7 of this book.

On test day, the computer will immediately determine your score for the Structure part of the Structure and Writing section. As we mentioned in the Introduction section, what happens next at the end of the test is little more complicated. Because your essay will not yet have been graded, the first Structure and Writing score you receive will be presented as a range. The high number indicates the maximum score you could receive (if your essay is rated highly), while the low number indicates the minimum score you could receive (if your essay is very poor). The overall score you receive on test day will also represent a range for the same reason. Again, we'll talk more about the essay and how it's scored, in chapter 7.

5

Grammar and Usage

APPROACHING THE SECTION

Fortunately for you, ETS is not very creative with its question types. They tend to test the same incorrect grammar points over and over. The following is a list of the most common types of errors found in Error Identification questions on the TOEFL CBT Structure section. Each one is described in detail and followed by practice questions like those frequently found on the TOEFL CBT.

Once you have reviewed and learned how to recognize the most common errors, you simply have to "click on" the underlined answer choice that makes the sentence grammatically incorrect.

The Sixteen Most Common Errors
Subjects
Verbs
Nouns
Singular and Plural
Articles
Pronouns
Appositives
Adjectives
Adverbs
Subordination
Noun Cases
Passive and Active Modifiers
Gerunds and Infinitives
Prepositions
Conjunctions
Comparisons and Superlatives

SUBJECTS

A sentence is a group of words that expresses a grammatically complete thought. The main subject and the main verb are at the heart of every written sentence in English. The basic parts of a sentence are:

main subject	the noun that does the main action
main verb	the word that expresses the main action

The subject is the part of the sentence that tells you who or what is doing the main verb. On the TOEFL CBT, you should always try to find and isolate the main subject and the main verb. This will greatly increase your chances of using POE to eliminate the incorrect answer choices and selecting the best answer.

> Every sentence *must* have a main subject and a main verb.

The subject of every sentence must be a noun. A noun is a word that represents a person, place, or thing. However, nouns that function as subjects of sentences are not always a single word. Nouns that act as subjects can take on many forms.

Nouns:	*Astrologers* divide the hemisphere into twelve parts.
Pronouns:	*There* are fewer than 100 panda bears alive in the wild.
	It was Robert Goddard who successfully fired the world's first liquid-fuel rocket.
Gerunds:	*Exercising* is recommended by all health care professionals.
Infinitives:	*To learn* how to read music requires diligence.
Noun Clauses:	*That the dog had bitten her* gave her a reason to fear it.

In the TOEFL CBT Structure section, ETS will test your basic knowledge of subjects. The majority of the subject questions are found among the sentence completions. Rarely will you find a question testing subjects in the Error Identification questions.

The first and most common way ETS tests your basic knowledge of subjects on the TOEFL CBT is by having you identify the noun functioning as the subject. Sometimes the subject is a gerund—a form of a verb, ending in *–ing*, which acts as a noun—but usually the subject is just a regular noun. ETS sometimes tries to confuse you by hiding the subject behind a modifying phrase or by including the main verb in the answer choice. However, always determine whether a main subject and main verb exist. If they are not present, ETS wants you to find them. Look at a typical *subject* question that frequently appears on the TOEFL CBT.

The seventeenth child of slaves, _____ President Roosevelt's policies on minority affairs.

- ○ Mary Bethune developed
- ○ and Mary Bethune was developing
- ○ because Mary Bethune developed
- ○ Mary Bethune, to develop

Since modifying phrases must either precede or follow what they modify, you can use POE to get rid of the second and third answer choices. The fourth answer choice does not provide a main verb. The first (and correct) answer choice fulfills main subject and main verb requirements. Look at another typical *subject* question.

_____ among constituents is just one of the many ways that politicians attempt to increase their popularity in opinion polls.

- ○ If similarities are found
- ○ Similarities are found
- ○ Finding similarities
- ○ When finding similarities

In this *subject* question, the main subject is missing but the main verb is "is." The first answer choice uses the conditional "if," and ETS never tests conditionals. The second answer choice provides another main verb. Remember, every sentence needs only one main verb. The third (and correct) answer choice provides the gerund *finding* and the noun *similarities* that completes the noun clause.

Another way ETS tests your knowledge of subjects is by using the pronoun *there*. If the subject sentence begins with the word *there*, you must determine what noun the pronoun *there* is referring to. Look at a typical "there" question that frequently appears on the TOEFL CBT:

_____ many viruses that attack the immune system and leave the victim vulnerable to infections, malignancies, and other neurological disorders.

- ○ They are
- ○ Of the
- ○ There are
- ○ The

This question needs a main subject and a main verb. The answer choices "Of the" and "The" lack a main verb. The pronoun in the first answer choice, "They are," cannot refer to "viruses" in a statement of fact. The third (and correct) answer choice supplies the pronoun *there*, which refers to "viruses," and the plural verb *are*, which agrees with "viruses."

ETS may also test your knowledge of subjects by using the pronoun subject *it*, which is used to identify a person who accomplishes something. Look at a typical "it" question that frequently appears on the TOEFL CBT:

_____ who was the first African American writer to win the Nobel Prize for Literature.

- ○ Toni Morrison
- ○ When Toni Morrison
- ○ Toni Morrison was
- ○ It was Toni Morrison

This type of question frequently appears on the TOEFL CBT and is easy to recognize. The first two answer choices create dependent clauses and lack main verbs. The third answer choice incorrectly places the verb in front of the relative pronoun *who*. The last answer choice provides a subject, a verb, and a noun for the relative pronoun "who" to modify.

A final way ETS may test your knowledge of subjects is by using the negatives "not only" and "not until." Whenever a sentence begins with this negative, the auxiliary of the verb *must* come immediately before the subject. Look at an example.

> Not only are dogs some of the most
> Negative aux   sub
> loyal animals, but they also provide
> safe protection.

Notice how the auxiliary "are" precedes the subject "dogs." This type of negative question would appear as follows on the TOEFL CBT:

> Not only _____ some of the most loyal
> animals, but they also provide safe
> protection.
>
> ◯   are dogs
> ◯   dogs
> ◯   they are dogs
> ◯   dogs are

The first answer choice, "are dogs," is the correct answer. It correctly places the auxiliary before the subject. The second answer choice, "dogs," lacks a main verb. The third answer choice, "they are dogs," repeats the subject. The last answer choice, "dogs are," incorrectly places the subject before the verb.

The subject questions that sometimes appear in Error Identification questions simply insert a "double subject" in the form of a pronoun. Look at a typical subject question that frequently appears on the TOEFL CBT in the Error Identification section.

> Many bookstores in <u>most</u> large
> American cities <u>they offer</u> gourmet
> coffee and food, in addition to
> <u>shelves full</u> of <u>popular books</u>.

In this type of question, the pronoun *they* incorrectly repeats the subject, "bookstores."

PRACTICE SUBJECT QUESTIONS

The following exercises contain **subject** questions most frequently found on the TOEFL CBT Structure section. Click on (in this case circle) the one word or phrase that best completes the sentence, or the one underlined word or phrase that must be changed for the sentence to be correct. Answers to these questions can be found at the end of this chapter.

Click on the one word or phrase that best completes the sentence.

_____ more than 60 types of grains, and although they are all edible, only a few types are digestible by humans.

○ There are
○ Of the
○ The
○ They are

Time   Help   Answer Confirm   Next

Click on the one word or phrase that best completes the sentence.

_____ adopted by President Franklin D. Roosevelt was the New Deal, which helped alleviate the effects of the Great Depression

○ A most significant program
○ The more significant program
○ The most significant program
○ More significant program

Time   Help   Answer Confirm   Next

Click on the one word or phrase that best completes the sentence.

_____ of animal life is known as zoology.

○ The scientific study
○ To study scientifically
○ That the scientific study
○ Studying scientific

Time   ? Help   Answer Confirm → Next

Click on the one word or phrase that best completes the sentence.

While studying at Magdalene College, Oxford, _____ himself for his wit and eccentricity in dress, taste, and manners.

○ that the playwright Oscar Wilde distinguished
○ playwright Oscar Wilde distinguished
○ distinguished Oscar Wilde, a playwright
○ there playwright Oscar Wilde distinguished

Time   ? Help   Answer Confirm → Next

Click on the one word or phrase that best completes the sentence.

Not until a modern physician employs laboratory tests in addition to physical examinations _____.

○ when the disease is diagnosed
○ the diagnosis of the disease
○ are diseases diagnosed
○ that the disease can be diagnosed

Time   ? Help   Answer Confirm   → Next

Click on the one word or phrase that best completes the sentence.

The first European _____ the Mississippi River was Hernando De Soto, a Spanish explorer who traversed North America in search of gold, silver, and jewels.

○ discover
○ discovering
○ that he discovered
○ to discover

Time   ? Help   Answer Confirm   → Next

Click on the one word or phrase that best completes the sentence.

_____ fame and fortune before reaching their twenties.

- ○ Many professional athletes gain
- ○ Since many professional athletes gain
- ○ For many professional athletes who gained
- ○ That many professional athletes gain

Time   Help   Answer Confirm   Next

Click on the one word or phrase that best completes the sentence.

Working much like a drill, _____ through soil by twisting its long and muscular body in a clockwise direction.

- ○ which bores an earthworm
- ○ and boring an earthworm
- ○ an earthworm bores
- ○ an earthworm which bores

Time   Help   Answer Confirm   Next

Click on the one word or phrase that best completes the sentence.

_____ to raise tropical salt-water fish in a controlled environment, despite the vast amount of information available on the subject.

○ Not only is it easy
○ It is not easy
○ That it is much easier
○ Why it is not easy

Time   Help   Answer Confirm   Next

Click on the one word or phrase that best completes the sentence.

_____ the habitual use of any chemical substance to alter states of body or mind.

○ If drug addiction is
○ With drug addiction
○ While drug addiction is
○ Drug addiction is

Time   Help   Answer Confirm   Next

Click on the one underlined word or phrase that must be changed for the sentence to be correct.

Biological warfare, the <u>employment</u> of <u>destructive</u> chemical weapons <u>to destroy</u> human beings, animals, or crops, <u>it was</u> prohibited by the Geneva Convention in 1925.

Time   **Help**   Answer Confirm   Next

Click on the one word or phrase that best completes the sentence.

Soon after the Iron Age, _____ method ancient tribes had to obtain food.

◯ to hunt quickly was probably
◯ hunting was probably the quickest
◯ the quickest hunt
◯ to hunt quickly was probably

Time   **Help**   Answer Confirm   Next

Click on the one word or phrase that best completes the sentence.

_____ to make honey is just one of the many responsibilities a drone bee has to ensure the survival of its colony.

- ◯ Collection nectar
- ◯ Collect nectar
- ◯ Nectar that collects
- ◯ Collecting nectar

Time

? Help | Answer Confirm | → Next

Click on the one word or phrase that best completes the sentence.

Although fairly new in their application, _____ relax muscles, adjust blood flow, and alleviate anxiety.

- ◯ biofeedback programs help patients
- ◯ and help biofeedback programs' patients
- ◯ is helping patients in biofeedback programs
- ◯ are biofeedback programs to help

Time

? Help | Answer Confirm | → Next

Click on the one underlined word or phrase that must be changed for the sentence to be correct.

Fish <u>living</u> in complete darkness at the bottom of deep-sea trenches <u>they have</u> evolved <u>incredibly</u> sensitive eyes <u>and</u> phosphorescent organs.

Time

Help

Answer Confirm

Next

VERBS

A verb is a word that expresses a mental or physical action, a state of being, or a condition. Even though there may be more than one verb in a sentence, try to identify the *main* verb. This is the word that identifies the main action of the main subject. The main verb must always be conjugated. This means that it will *not* be in the "to _____" form, or with an -ing (by itself) at the end. For example:

to speak	can *not* be a main verb
speaking	can *not* be a main verb by itself
speak, speaks, spoke	can be a main verb

Usually, in the Structure section of the TOEFL CBT, ETS will use an incorrect verb tense. Look at a common TOEFL CBT verb tense test question:

> When he <u>lands</u> on the moon in 1969,
> <u>astronaut</u> Neil Armstrong was considered a
> <u>national hero</u> by <u>every</u> American.

In these types of sentences, ETS will most likely give you a time clause. In this example, the action took place in the past, 1969. Therefore, the verb should be in the past tense, *landed*.

In an English sentence, the subject and the verb must always agree. Singular subjects must take singular verbs, and plural subjects must take plural verbs. ETS will also try to confuse you by inserting long modifying clauses between the subject and the verb to make it difficult for you to know the correct verb conjugation. Look at a common TOEFL CBT subject/verb test question:

> Russia's <u>immense</u> areas of <u>barren</u> tundra
> <u>draws</u> many species of wildlife that depend
> on the foliage for <u>survival</u>.

In these types of sentences, ETS will hide the verb behind a prepositional phrase. What is the main subject in this sentence? Remember, the main verb and the main subject must agree. The subject, "areas," is plural. The main verb, "draws," must also be in the plural form, *draw*. You will also encounter verb questions in the Sentence Completion type of question in the Structure section of the TOEFL CBT. For example:

> During the brief prohibition era, the local
> police force _____ thousands of gallons
> of illegally distilled alcohol.
>
> ○ destroyed
> ○ who destroyed
> ○ destroying that which
> ○ to destroy

This type of sentence needs a main verb. The second and third answer choices create a dependent clause. The infinitive form "to destroy" cannot act as a main verb. The first answer choice "destroyed" completes main verb requirements.

Occasionally, ETS will try to confuse you with the passive form of the verb. The passive construction switches the object and the subject, and the "be" verb is added to the past participial verb. Look at a common TOEFL CBT passive test question:

> One of the first grains <u>cultivated</u> in the New World, corn <u>was growing</u> by the settlers <u>who</u> landed on the <u>eastern shores</u> of Massachusetts.

The active sentence would read, "settlers grew corn." When the object and subject are switched the sentence should read, "corn was *grown* by the settlers." The verb *must* be in the past participial form.

PRACTICE VERB QUESTIONS

The following exercises contain the sort of **verb** questions most frequently found in the Structure section of the TOEFL CBT. Click on (in this case circle) the one word or phrase that best completes the sentence, or the one underlined word or phrase that must be changed for the sentence to be correct. Answers to these questions can be found at the end of this chapter.

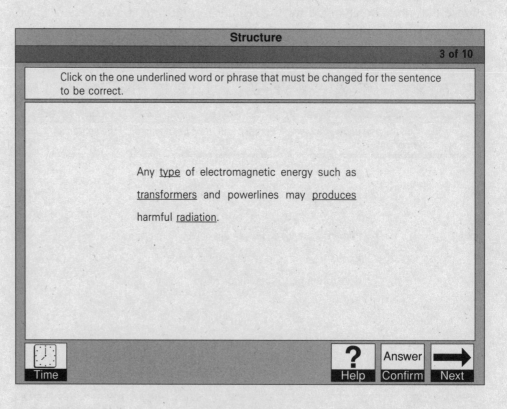

Click on the one word or phrase that best completes the sentence.

Most mammals give birth to live offspring, but a few rare species _____ eggs in the soil until they hatch.

- ○ to incubate
- ○ they incubate
- ○ incubate
- ○ to have incubated

Time   Help   Answer Confirm   Next

Click on the one underlined word or phrase that must be changed for the sentence to be correct.

Any <u>type</u> of electromagnetic energy such as <u>transformers</u> and powerlines may <u>produces</u> harmful <u>radiation</u>.

Time   Help   Answer Confirm   Next

Click on the one underlined word or phrase that must be changed for the sentence to be correct.

Seven out of ten <u>practicing</u> health care <u>professionals</u> in Alaska <u>prescribes</u> anti-depressants to <u>their</u> patients.

Time

? Help

Answer Confirm

→ Next

Click on the one word or phrase that best completes the sentence.

One of the most historically significant cities of the Eastern United States, Philadelphia, the original capital, ——— the City of Brotherly Love.

○ to name it
○ it names
○ is naming it
○ is named

Time

? Help

Answer Confirm

→ Next

Click on the one underlined word or phrase that must be changed for the sentence to be correct.

<u>Although</u> synthetic nylon is mainly <u>synthesize</u> for fabric, it is also manufactured <u>to make</u> ropes, insulation, fiberglass, and other common household <u>utensils</u>.

Time   Help   Answer Confirm   Next

Click on the one word or phrase that best completes the sentence.

Many recently built suburban communities, including the hundreds that surround New York City, _____ city councils or chambers of commerce.

○ not having
○ have no
○ they do not have
○ that have no

Time   Help   Answer Confirm   Next

Click on the one underlined word or phrase that must be changed for the sentence to be correct.

One small tablespoon of parmesan cheese container approximately two grams of saturated fat, more than the daily recommended allowance.

Click on the one word or phrase that best completes the sentence.

Although most drama critics believe his work to be insignificant, Neil Simon's plays _____ more performances than those of any other contemporary playwright.

- ◯ receive
- ◯ they have received
- ◯ receiving
- ◯ which receive

Click on the one word or phrase that best completes the sentence.

All metal <u>containers</u> used for <u>food storage</u> must first be thoroughly washed and then <u>disinfection</u> to protect against <u>harmful</u> bacteria.

Time

? Help

Answer Confirm

→ Next

NOUNS

In the subject section above, you briefly encountered nouns that function as subjects. However, ETS also tests your ability to recognize nouns, noun clauses, and gerunds; whether nouns are singular or plural; and the articles that come before nouns. ETS does *not* test capitalization of proper nouns.

Simply, a noun is a word that names a person, place, thing, or idea. On the TOEFL CBT, ETS will test your ability to recognize nouns by incorrectly substituting them with either an adjective or verb. Look at a typical noun question that appears in the Structure section of the TOEFL CBT.

> The <u>current</u> definition of <u>dead</u> is the irreversible cessation of <u>all</u> functions of the <u>entire</u> brain, including the brain stem.

In this example, ETS has incorrectly substituted the adjective "dead" for the noun "death." If you have trouble distinguishing the adjective form from the noun form, rely on your POE techniques to eliminate the other three answer choices. In this example, the adjectives "current", "all," and "entire" correctly modify the nouns they precede.

PRACTICE NOUN QUESTIONS

The following exercises contain **noun** questions most frequently found on the TOEFL CBT Structure section. Click on (in this case circle) the one word or phrase that best completes the sentence, or the one underlined word or phrase that must be changed for the sentence to be correct. Answers to these questions can be found at the end of this chapter.

A noun is a word that names a person, place, thing, or idea.

Click on the one underlined word or phrase that must be changed for the sentence to be correct.

Although difficult to master, the guitar is embraced by many beginning music students because of <u>its</u> musical <u>versatile</u>, relative low <u>cost</u>, and <u>extreme</u> popularity.

Time · Help · Answer Confirm · Next

Click on the one underlined word or phrase that must be changed for the sentence to be correct.

<u>The discover</u> of prehistoric mammoth remains have validated the <u>accuracy</u> of the creature's picture <u>depicted</u> by cave dwellers <u>who</u> once resided in the south of France.

Time · Help · Answer Confirm · Next

Click on the one word or phrase that best completes the sentence.

The texture, temperature, and general appearance of a dog's nose tell _____ about its physical condition.

○ as much
○ much more
○ much
○ that much as

Time   Help   Answer Confirm   Next

Click on the one underlined word or phrase that must be changed for the sentence to be correct.

Much like the fangs of venomous snakes, the

duck-billed platypus protects their young with a

pair of poisonous fangs.

Time   Help   Answer Confirm   Next

Click on the one word or phrase that best completes the sentence.

Harry S Truman _____ as chairman of a committee investigating government spending during World War II.

○ first gained national prominence
○ national gained first prominence
○ gained first prominence national
○ gained nation prominence first

Time   Help   Answer Confirm   Next

Click on the one underlined word or phrase that must be changed for the sentence to be correct.

Tooth decay could be the result of poor hygiene

or from bacteria decaying food particles.

Time   Help   Answer Confirm   Next

Click on the one underlined word or phrase that must be changed for the sentence to be correct.

Left untreated, even a small wound could lead

to a dangerous infectious.

Time   Help   Answer Confirm   Next

Click on the one word or phrase that best completes the sentence.

While hi-fidelity vinyl records can record _____ of sound than compacts discs can, they tend to scratch easily.

○ where a great range
○ and great ranges
○ great ranges
○ a greater range

Time   Help   Answer Confirm   Next

Click on the one word or phrase that best completes the sentence.

<u>Astronomers</u> estimate that one planet <u>in</u> eleven billion has an environment suitable <u>to sustain</u> biological <u>live</u>.

Time Help Answer Confirm Next

Click on the one underlined word or phrase that must be changed for the sentence to be correct.

Cartilage, a firm yet <u>flexible</u> tissue <u>that</u> is vital to the skeletal <u>structural</u>, <u>is categorized</u> as a fibrous collagen.

Time Help Answer Confirm Next

SINGULAR AND PLURAL NOUNS

ETS will also test your basic knowledge of whether a noun should be singular or plural. The singular and plural noun questions always appear in Error Identification questions on the TOEFL CBT exam. Ninety-nine percent of the time, ETS will either drop the "s" on words that should be plural, or add the "s" on words that should be singular. Only rarely does ETS confuse irregular plural nouns and irregular singular nouns (feet for foot, people for person, and so forth).

Ninety-nine percent of the time, ETS will either drop the "s" on words that should be plural, or add the "s" on words that should be singular.

How do you know if a noun is singular or plural? It's simple. If the underlined noun is talking about several objects, or referring to an object in general, the noun should be plural. In this case, the underlined noun is often preceded by a quantitative adjective such as "several", a "few", "many", "other", "various", and so forth. If the underlined noun is referring to just one specific or special object, the noun should be singular. Look at a typical singular and plural question frequently found on the TOEFL CBT.

> <u>Earthquakes</u> occur in several geographical
>
> <u>location</u>, <u>many of which</u> are in conjunction
>
> with <u>faults</u>, the areas where opposing
>
> plates pass one another.

The quantitative (meaning "how many") adjective "several" indicates that the noun "location" should be plural. The other underlined nouns in the sentence, "earthquakes" and "faults," are *not* referring to one in particular, and therefore must be plural. Remember that singular nouns must be preceded by the indefinite articles "a" and "an."

COUNTABLE AND NON-COUNTABLE NOUNS

Some nouns that appear on the TOEFL, such as "children," "tables," or "fish," can be counted and are therefore called **countable** nouns. Others cannot be counted. These are called **non-countable** nouns:

air	water
wheat	equipment
money	gold
petroleum	literature
chemistry	weather
editing	grass

Many nouns refer to abstract ideas instead of concrete things or people. These abstract nouns are examples of rarely countable nouns:

beauty	courage
fear	wealth
determination	blindness
charity	grace
equality	hate

PRACTICE SINGULAR AND PLURAL QUESTIONS

The following exercises contain **singular** and **plural** questions most frequently found on the TOEFL CBT Structure section. Click on (in this case circle) the one underlined word or phrase that must be changed for the sentence to be correct. Answers to these questions can be found at the end of this chapter.

Click on the one underlined word or phrase that must be changed for the sentence to be correct.

Known more <u>for</u> his novels than his poetry, William Faulkner <u>actually</u> published several <u>collection</u> of poems before writing his most famous <u>piece</u> *As I Lay Dying* in 1930.

Time

?
Help

Answer
Confirm

Next

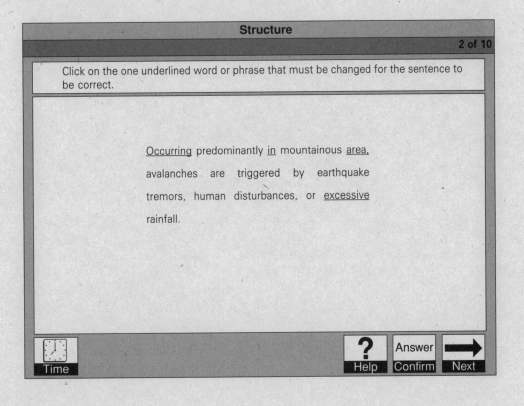

Click on the one underlined word or phrase that must be changed for the sentence to be correct.

<u>Occurring</u> predominantly <u>in</u> mountainous <u>area,</u> avalanches are triggered by earthquake tremors, human disturbances, or <u>excessive</u> rainfall.

Time

?
Help

Answer
Confirm

Next

Click on the one underlined word or phrase that must be changed for the sentence to be correct.

<u>Pain</u> and other <u>symptom</u> affecting the head, jaw,
and face are <u>the</u> result of <u>muscles and ligaments</u>
not correctly working together.

Time   ? Answer   →
       Help Confirm Next

Click on the one underlined word or phrase that must be changed for the sentence to be correct.

The Chinese province of Liaoning is believed
<u>to have</u> one of the most extensive <u>site</u> of
dinosaur fossils known <u>to</u> <u>archeologists</u>.

Time   ? Answer   →
       Help Confirm Next

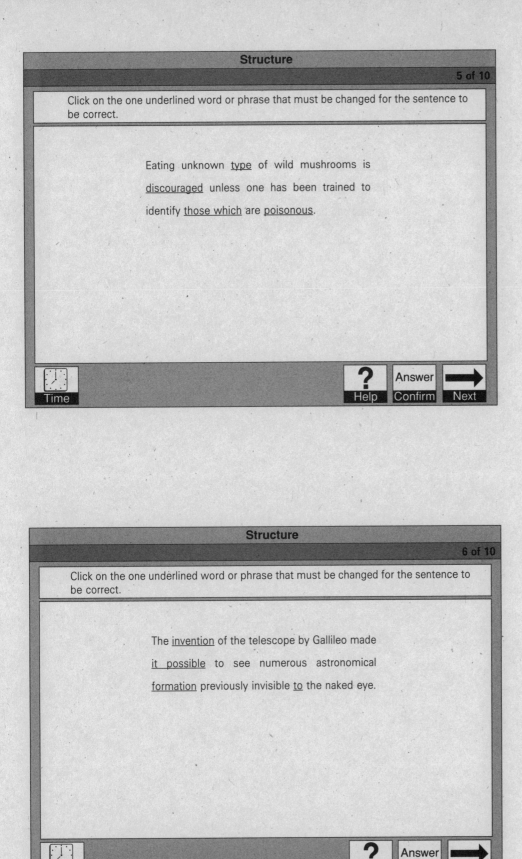

Structure

Click on the one underlined word or phrase that must be changed for the sentence to be correct.

Eating unknown <u>type</u> of wild mushrooms is <u>discouraged</u> unless one has been trained to identify <u>those which</u> are <u>poisonous</u>.

Time

? Help

Answer Confirm

→ Next

Structure

Click on the one underlined word or phrase that must be changed for the sentence to be correct.

The <u>invention</u> of the telescope by Gallileo made <u>it possible</u> to see numerous astronomical <u>formation</u> previously invisible <u>to</u> the naked eye.

Time

? Help

Answer Confirm

→ Next

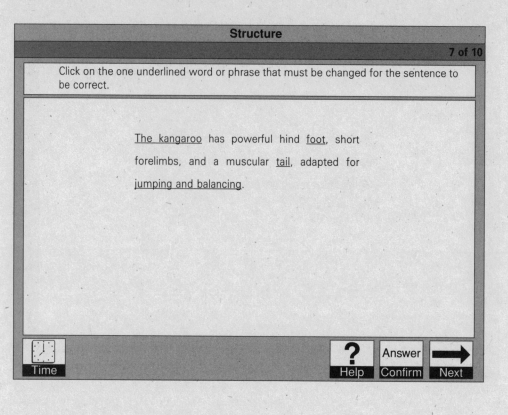

Click on the one underlined word or phrase that must be changed for the sentence to be correct.

The <u>kangaroo</u> has powerful hind <u>foot</u>, short forelimbs, and a muscular <u>tail</u>, adapted for <u>jumping and balancing</u>.

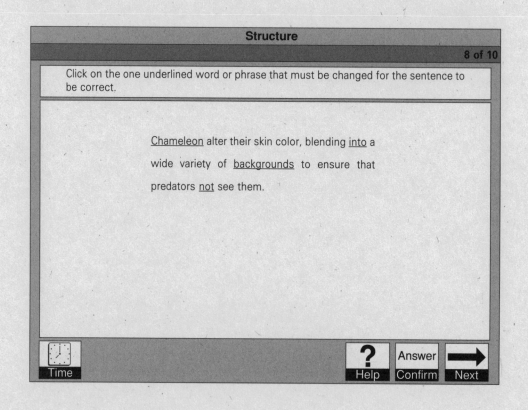

Click on the one underlined word or phrase that must be changed for the sentence to be correct.

<u>Chameleon</u> alter their skin color, blending <u>into</u> a wide variety of <u>backgrounds</u> to ensure that predators <u>not</u> see them.

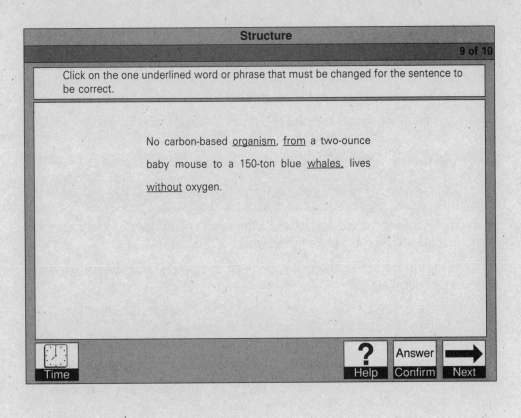

Click on the one underlined word or phrase that must be changed for the sentence to be correct.

No carbon-based <u>organism</u>, <u>from</u> a two-ounce baby mouse to a 150-ton blue <u>whales</u>, lives <u>without</u> oxygen.

Time

Help

Answer
Confirm

Next

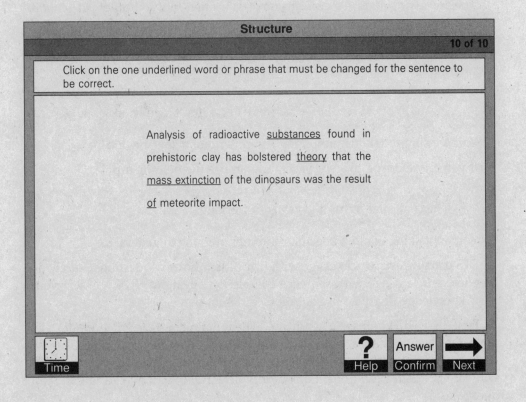

Click on the one underlined word or phrase that must be changed for the sentence to be correct.

Analysis of radioactive <u>substances</u> found in prehistoric clay has bolstered <u>theory</u> that the <u>mass extinction</u> of the dinosaurs was the result <u>of</u> meteorite impact.

Time

Help

Answer
Confirm

Next

ARTICLES

In the Structure section of the TOEFL CBT, ETS tests your knowledge of correct article usage. There are many rules and exceptions to article usage; however, ETS tests your basic knowledge and makes most of the test questions fairly simple.

Articles modify nouns. There are two types of articles, definite and indefinite.

Definite:	There is only one definite article: **the**.
Indefinite:	There are two types of indefinite articles: **a** or **an**.

To study the use of articles, let's use the noun "computers" as an example. First, imagine all the computers in the world.

If you are referring to the *entire group* of computers, you do *not* need an article. For example:

Computers cost less than they did ten years ago.

You are talking about computers *in general*, not a specific computer.

If you are talking about a specific group of computers, not computers in general, use the definite article with the plural noun.

The computers on the third floor were damaged in the fire.

You are talking about a *specific* group of computers, not computers in general.

If you are referring to any *single* computer from this entire group, but not any one in particular, use the indefinite article. Indefinite articles must precede a singular noun!

I want to buy **a** computer for my sister. I don't care what kind.

You are simply talking about any computer, not a specific one.

If you are referring to a *specific* computer, use the definite article.

The computer in front of me isn't working.

You are talking about a specific computer, not one in general.

ETS usually tests article usage with Error Identification questions. Rarely do they test article usage with sentence completion questions. ETS will test your basic knowledge of article usage in four different ways.

First, they will confuse "a" and "an." The indefinite article "a" precedes any noun that begins with a consonant. The indefinite article "an" precedes any noun that begins with a vowel. There are some exceptions to this rule, but ETS will *not* test these exceptions. Look at a typical TOEFL CBT "a" and "an" test question.

> The spider monkey, native to Madagascar,
> emits <u>an</u> yell so loud that <u>it</u> acts <u>to frighten</u>
> away <u>potential</u> predators.

Clearly, the indefinite article "an" is incorrectly substituted for the indefinite article "a." Remember, ETS will also test the opposite situation, substituting "a" for "an."

Second, ETS will insert the indefinite article "a" for the definite article "the." Remember your rules. Use the indefinite article when referring to a general noun, and a definite article when referring to a specific noun. Remember, it is *impossible* for the indefinite articles "a" and "an" to come *before* a *plural noun!* Look at a typical TOEFL CBT "a" for "the" test question:

Indefinite articles precede singular nouns!

> Usually handed down <u>from</u> one generation
> to the next, hymns <u>were perhaps</u> one of <u>a</u>
> earliest types of music <u>performed</u> by
> humans.

Clearly, the indefinite article "a" is incorrectly substituted for the definite article "the." Not only is the sentence speaking about a specific type of music, but the noun is also plural. Remember, indefinite articles can't precede plural nouns.

Third, in the Error Identification questions, ETS will also omit the definite ("a" or "an") or indefinite ("the") article. In this case, the two words on either side of the omitted article will be underlined. This gives you a clue that something might need to be inserted. Look at a typical TOEFL CBT article omission test question:

> <u>Rather</u> than <u>purchasing</u> real estate,
> Americans <u>have</u> been investing in mutual
> funds ever <u>since beginning</u> of the 1980s.

The definite article ("the") has been omitted between the preposition "since" and the specific noun "beginning." ETS will also omit the indefinite article "a" as well.

Fourth, ETS will insert an extra definite article ("the") in front of a noun that is speaking in general terms about an entire group, or in front of academic subjects such as mathematics, astronomy, or art. Look at a typical TOEFL CBT definite article addition test question:

> <u>Whether</u> documented or <u>orally</u> transmitted,
> <u>the history</u> is perhaps one of the oldest
> fields of study <u>known to</u> scholars.

In this case, the general noun "history" is *not* specifically referring to anything in particular.

PRACTICE ARTICLE QUESTIONS

The following exercises contain **article** questions most frequently found in the Structure section of the TOEFL CBT. Click on (in this case circle) the one underlined word or phrase that must be changed for the sentence to be correct. Answers to these questions can be found at the end of this chapter.

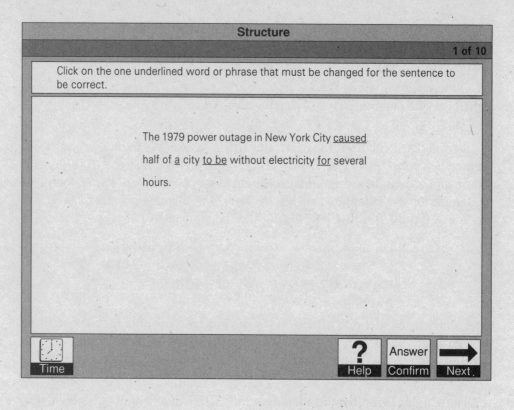

Click on the one underlined word or phrase that must be changed for the sentence to be correct.

The 1979 power outage in New York City <u>caused</u> half of <u>a</u> city <u>to be</u> without electricity <u>for</u> several hours.

Click on the one underlined word or phrase that must be changed for the sentence to be correct.

<u>Glamorized</u> in the United States by <u>recent</u> films, <u>an</u> 1960s will always be remembered <u>for</u> the Vietnam war, hippies, and the assassination of John F. Kennedy.

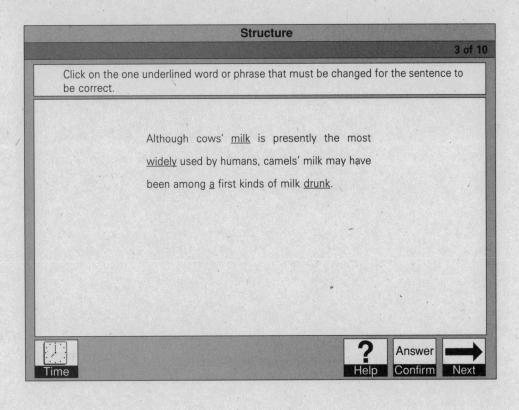

Click on the one underlined word or phrase that must be changed for the sentence to be correct.

Although cows' <u>milk</u> is presently the most <u>widely</u> used by humans, camels' milk may have been among <u>a</u> first kinds of milk <u>drunk</u>.

Time   ?   Answer   Next
        Help Confirm

Click on the one underlined word or phrase that must be changed for the sentence to be correct.

Encephalitis is <u>a</u> inflammation of the brain that can be caused <u>by</u> rabies; it may also follow <u>serious cases</u> of influenza <u>or</u> scarlet fever.

Time   ?   Answer   Next
        Help Confirm

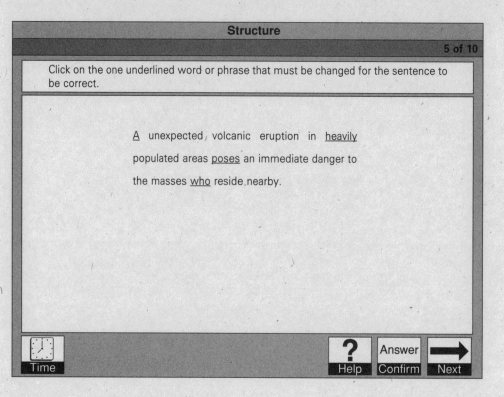

Click on the one underlined word or phrase that must be changed for the sentence to be correct.

<u>A</u> unexpected, volcanic eruption in <u>heavily</u> populated areas <u>poses</u> an immediate danger to the masses <u>who</u> reside nearby.

Time   Help   Answer Confirm   Next

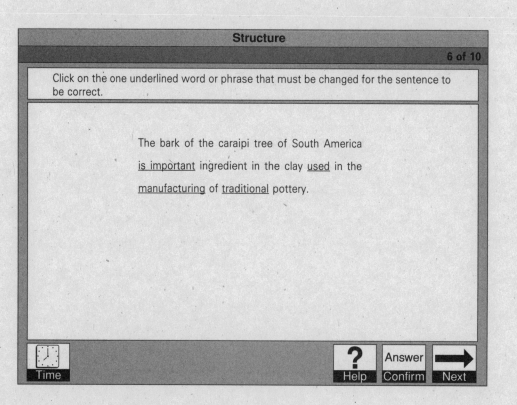

Click on the one underlined word or phrase that must be changed for the sentence to be correct.

The bark of the caraipi tree of South America <u>is important</u> ingredient in the clay <u>used</u> in the <u>manufacturing</u> of <u>traditional</u> pottery.

Time   Help   Answer Confirm   Next

Click on the one underlined word or phrase that must be changed for the sentence to be correct.

The <u>archaeology</u> began in Athens with the excavation of ancient Greek sculptures in the <u>fifteenth century</u> and is now <u>an</u> exceptional technique for enhancing <u>historical</u> knowledge.

Click on the one underlined word or phrase that must be changed for the sentence to be correct.

<u>After beginning</u> of any industrial revolution, the rural population <u>steadily</u> shifts <u>toward</u> <u>urban centers</u>.

Click on the one underlined word or phrase that must be changed for the sentence to be correct.

According to <u>his</u> journals, Charles Darwin was

amazed <u>for</u> <u>the</u> rich <u>diversity</u> of animal species

he discovered in the Galapagos Islands.

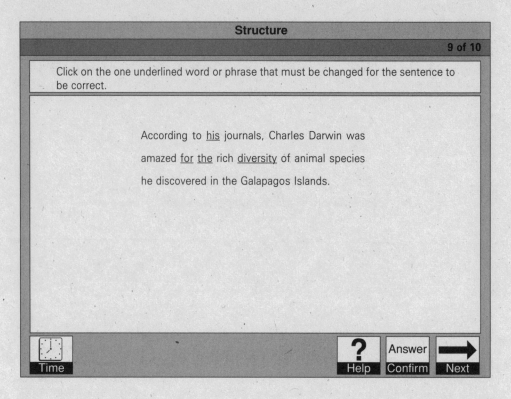

Time

? Help

Answer Confirm

→ Next

Click on the one underlined word or phrase that must be changed for the sentence to be correct.

The <u>mating calls</u> of <u>some</u> tree frogs can be

<u>heard</u> for <u>many á miles</u>.

Time

? Help

Answer Confirm

→ Next

PRONOUNS

A pronoun is a word that takes the place of a noun. It stands for a person, place, thing, or idea *already* mentioned in a sentence. ETS only tests pronouns in the third person. Fortunately, ETS does *not* test pronouns in the first or second person, or any reflexive pronouns. The list of pronouns ETS tests is as follows:

ETS does not test reflexive pronouns.

Subject	Object	Possessive
he	him	his
she	her	hers
it	it	its
they	them	their
that		
those		

Pronoun questions appear only in the Error Identification questions in the Structure section of the TOEFL CBT. ETS often switches the object pronoun for the possessive pronoun, substitutes a singular pronoun for a plural one (or vice versa), confuses singular and plural possessives, or eliminates the pronoun completely. Look at a typical example that appears on the TOEFL CBT.

> Balancing the ecosystems of Australia's wetlands is an <u>extremely</u> delicate process: even the <u>introduction of</u> an alien insect species could cause <u>serious</u> damage to <u>it</u>.

The singular object pronoun "it" has been incorrectly substituted for the plural object pronoun "them." A pronoun must agree with the noun to which it refers. In this sentence, the pronoun refers to the plural noun "ecosystems." Remember, a pronoun represents another noun already present in the sentence. You have just two simple tasks: Find out if the pronoun agrees with the noun it is referring to, and determine if a possessive is necessary.

Pronouns represent another noun already present in the sentence.

PRACTICE PRONOUN QUESTIONS

The following exercises contain the sort of **pronoun** questions most frequently found on the TOEFL CBT Structure section. Click on (in this case circle) the one underlined word or phrase that must be changed for the sentence to be correct. Answers to these questions can be found at the end of this chapter.

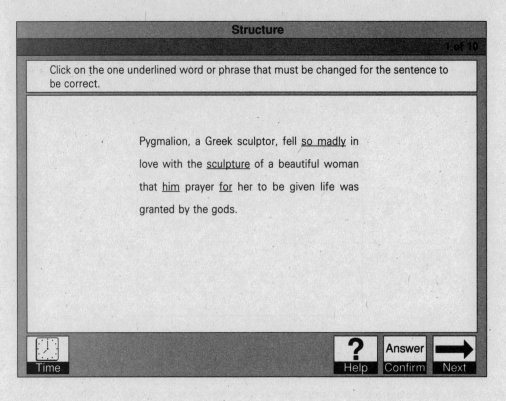

Click on the one underlined word or phrase that must be changed for the sentence to be correct.

Pygmalion, a Greek sculptor, fell <u>so madly</u> in love with the <u>sculpture</u> of a beautiful woman that <u>him</u> prayer <u>for</u> her to be given life was granted by the gods.

Time

Help Answer Confirm Next

Click on the one underlined word or phrase that must be changed for the sentence to be correct.

Stuart Davis had <u>little</u> patience with hesitation, and he was one of the few modern <u>artist</u> to paint <u>his</u> subjects in <u>under</u> 10 minutes.

Time

Help Answer Confirm Next

Click on the one underlined word or phrase that must be changed for the sentence to be correct.

The trademark of Frank Lloyd Wright's style was <u>his</u> ability <u>to blend</u> the essence of modernity with <u>those</u> of nature in <u>his</u> architecture.

Time Help Answer Confirm Next

Click on the one underlined word or phrase that must be changed for the sentence to be correct.

Research in Germany on the <u>physical build</u> of the individual has attempted to link <u>them</u> with specific <u>personality</u> traits and <u>mental illness</u>.

Time Help Answer Confirm Next

Click on the one underlined word or phrase that must be changed for the sentence to be correct.

The study of the group dynamic <u>has</u> gained <u>popularity</u> as business managers attempt <u>to find</u> the optimal work environments for <u>its</u> employees.

Time   Help   Answer Confirm   Next

Click on the one underlined word or phrase that must be changed for the sentence to be correct.

The Van Allen belts are the <u>magnetic</u> fields <u>that</u> surround the Earth and help <u>shield surface</u> <u>from</u> cosmic rays.

Time   Help   Answer Confirm   Next

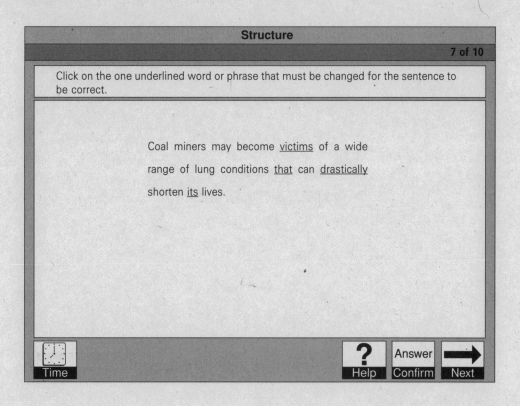

Click on the one underlined word or phrase that must be changed for the sentence to be correct.

Coal miners may become <u>victims</u> of a wide range of lung conditions <u>that</u> can <u>drastically</u> shorten <u>its</u> lives.

Time

Help

Answer
Confirm

Next

Click on the one underlined word or phrase that must be changed for the sentence to be correct.

Male rodents are often chased away <u>from</u> nests by females because <u>they</u> have a tendency to attack the <u>young</u> <u>of own</u> species.

Time

Help

Answer
Confirm

Next

Click on the one underlined word or phrase that must be changed for the sentence to be correct.

All <u>rays</u> of light <u>passing</u> through a lens are refracted except <u>them</u> that pass directly through a point <u>called</u> the optical center.

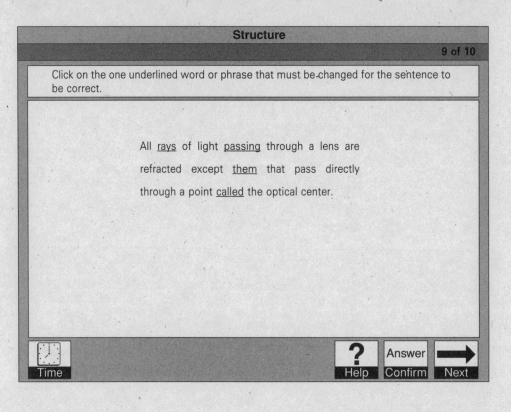

Time   Help   Answer   Next
                Confirm

Click on the one underlined word or phrase that must be changed for the sentence to be correct.

Alvin Ailey was an American choreographer <u>who</u> dance works combined the movements of ballet <u>with</u> <u>those</u> of <u>modern methods</u>.

Time   Help   Answer   Next
                Confirm

APPOSITIVES

Some of the Sentence Completion questions in the Structure section of the TOEFL CBT will test all or a part of the appositive construction. An appositive is simply a noun phrase that defines the subject. It must be identical to the subject and must provide additional information. A comma must immediately precede and follow the appositive. For example:

Smallpox, _____, causes a high fever and severe skin eruptions.

○ which infecting diseases
○ diseases are highly infectious
○ a highly infectious disease
○ infects disease

To click on the correct appositive answer, use POE to get rid of any answer choice that contains a verb or a relative pronoun (who, that, which, etc). In this case, the first, second, and fourth answer choices contain either relative pronouns or verbs. Only the third answer choice, "a highly infectious disease," correctly restates the subject and follows appositive requirements. It is preceded by a comma and gives you more information about the subject, smallpox.

Practice Appositive Questions

The following exercises contain **appositive** questions most frequently found in the Structure section of the TOEFL CBT. Click on (in this case circle) the one word or phrase that best completes the sentence. Answers to these questions can be found at the end of this chapter.

Click on the one word or phrase that best completes the sentence.

Claude Monet, _____, is considered to be the founder of Impressionism .

- ⬭ paints French landscapes
- ⬭ is a landscape painter of France
- ⬭ a French landscape painter
- ⬭ French landscapes are painted

🕐 Time   ? Help   Answer Confirm   ➡ Next

Click on the one word or phrase that best completes the sentence.

The Mississippi, _____ longest river in North America, flows along the border of 10 states.

- ⬭ is the
- ⬭ the
- ⬭ it is by
- ⬭ is an

🕐 Time   ? Help   Answer Confirm   ➡ Next

Click on the one word or phrase that best completes the sentence.

The jaguar, _____, is similar to the shorter-limbed and stockier leopard.

○ a more adaptable animal
○ adapts more animal
○ is an adaptable animal
○ which adapting animal

Time   Help   Answer Confirm   Next

Click on the one word or phrase that best completes the sentence.

The concept of the greenhouse, _____ plants inside glass houses, is just one of the results of an industrial revolution.

○ for cultivation
○ cultivates to
○ the cultivation of
○ the cultivating

Time   Help   Answer Confirm   Next

Click on the one word or phrase that best completes the sentence.

Viruses, _____, do not carry out the functions of living cells, such as respiration and growth.

- ⬭ microscopic parasites
- ⬭ are microscopic parasites
- ⬭ parasites are microscopic
- ⬭ to parasite a microscope

Time

? Help

Answer Confirm

→ Next

MODIFIERS

On the TOEFL CBT, ETS will test your basic knowledge of modifiers. In an English sentence, all other words except the subject and verb are called modifiers. Modifiers describe or give more information about the subject, verb, or other modifiers.

Modifiers describe or give more information about the subject, verb, or other modifiers.

> <u>Canada</u>, <u>which has a small population</u>, <u>covers</u>
> subject   modifier   verb
>
> <u>slightly more</u> <u>territory</u> <u>than</u> <u>the United States</u> <u>does</u>.
>   modifier   object   than   subject   verb
>
> <u>Wolfgang Amadeus Mozart</u> <u>wrote</u>
>   subject   verb
>
> <u>his first</u> <u>symphony</u> while <u>he</u> <u>was</u> <u>still</u> a very young child.
> modifier   object   subject verb modifier

As shown in the diagramed sentences above, a modifier is a word or a group of words that describes another word in the sentence. Adjectives and adverbs are just two types of modifiers.

ADJECTIVES

Simply, adjectives modify nouns. They report the *quality*, *quantity*, or *condition* of nouns. In a typical TOEFL CBT sentence, the adjectives will usually precede the noun, follow an adverb, or exist alone after the "be" verb. Adjectives can not modify adverbs. Look at the following typical TOEFL CBT sentence with all the modifiers and nouns labeled.

> <u>All</u> <u>flightless</u> <u>waterfowl</u> are <u>still</u> <u>equipped</u> with <u>hollow</u>
> adj.   adj.   noun   adv.   verb   adj.
> <u>wingbones</u>, giving them an <u>incredibly</u> <u>acute</u> <u>sense</u> of balance.
>   noun   adverb   adj. noun

Paying attention to the word order will drastically increase your chances of clicking on the best possible answer. Always make sure the parts of speech come in the right order. Look at the following chart:

Word #1	Word #2	Word #3	Word #1	Word #2	Word #3
Adjective			fresh		
Adjective	Noun		fresh	bread	
Adjective	Adjective	Noun	tasty	fresh	bread
Adverb	Adjective		surprisingly	fresh	
Adverb	Adjective	Noun	surprisingly	fresh	bread

Here are the types of adjectives that frequently appear on the exam:

Qualitative	Comparative	Superlative	Distributive	Quantitative
colorful	faster than	the fastest	both	less admired
rapid	smaller than	the smallest	each	many
severe	greater than	the greatest	every	fifteenth
slender	longer than	the longest	another	some
evident	lower than	the lowest	other	few
complex	larger than	the largest		
capable	more abundant	the most abundant		

You will encounter "adjectival" questions as both sentence completion and Error Identification questions in the Structure section of the TOEFL CBT. For sentence completion questions, you must be able to click on the adjective that best completes the sentence.

Choose on the correct answer in this typical adjectival question found in the Structure section of the TOEFL CBT.

_____ the root and the foliage of the red beet are safe for consumption.

- ○ While
- ○ Both
- ○ Either
- ○ Though

ETS tries to make adjectival questions confusing by adding in a few conjunctions and other parts of speech. In this case, "while" and "though" create dependent clauses that lack main verbs. The conjunction "either" must be paired with "or," not "and."

For Error Identification questions, ETS will replace the adjective with either an adverb or a noun.

Find the error in this typical adjectival question found in the Structure section of the TOEFL CBT.

John Quincy Adams, <u>like</u> his father President John Adams, was intelligent, strong-willed, <u>energetically</u>, and totally <u>dedicated to</u> serving <u>his</u> country.

Remember, many of the Error Identification questions contain lists of adjectives separated by commas. If one of the words in this list is underlined, make sure it parallels the other listed words. In this case, "intelligent," "strong-willed," and "dedicated" are all adjectives. However, "energetically" is an adverb. It should also be an adjective: "energetic."

Circle the error in this typical adjectival question found in the Structure section of the TOEFL CBT.

> <u>Much</u> like movies, <u>radio</u> could not have
> been developed <u>without</u> the remarkable
> and <u>technology</u> advances of the times.

Remember, adjectives modify nouns. Nouns *cannot* modify nouns. In this sentence, the noun "technology" is modifying the noun "advances." It should be the adjective "technological."

On the TOEFL CBT, ETS will also test your basic knowledge of adjectives by placing a noun *in front of* an adjective, or an adverb *after* an adjective. Take a look at this type of question commonly found in the Structure section of the TOEFL CBT.

> Under <u>current</u> tax laws, couples who
> have more than one child <u>receive</u> a
> <u>reduction significant</u> in <u>their</u> income tax.

Remember, adjectives used alone must precede the nouns that they modify. In this sentence, the adjective "significant" must come before the noun "reduction."

PRACTICE ADJECTIVE QUESTIONS

The following exercises contain the sort of **adjective** questions most frequently found in the Structure section of the TOEFL CBT. Click on (in this case circle) the one word or phrase that best completes the sentence, or the one underlined word or phrase that must be changed for the sentence to be correct. Answers to these questions can be found at the end of this chapter.

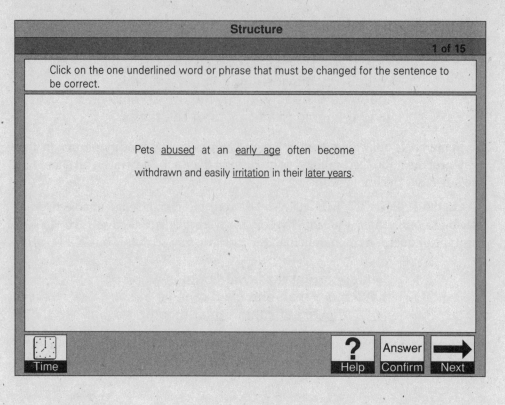

Click on the one underlined word or phrase that must be changed for the sentence to be correct.

Pets <u>abused</u> at an <u>early age</u> often become withdrawn and easily <u>irritation</u> in their <u>later years</u>.

Time | Help | Answer Confirm | Next

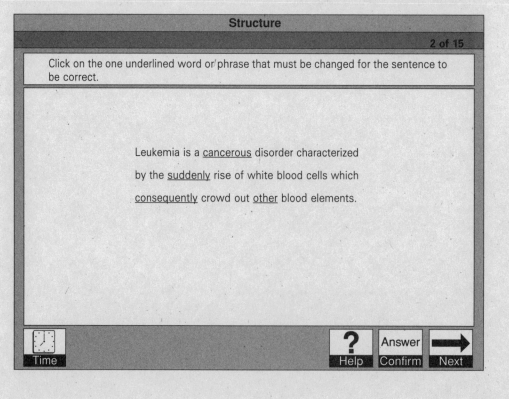

Click on the one underlined word or phrase that must be changed for the sentence to be correct.

Leukemia is a <u>cancerous</u> disorder characterized by the <u>suddenly</u> rise of white blood cells which <u>consequently</u> crowd out <u>other</u> blood elements.

Time | Help | Answer Confirm | Next

Click on the one word or phrase that best completes the sentence.

The exact representation of surface features with reference to area, scale, and direction, can only _____ a globe.

○ be accomplished with
○ accomplish with
○ with accomplishment
○ accomplish

Time ? Help Answer Confirm Next

Click on the one underlined word or phrase that must be changed for the sentence to be correct.

It is <u>possibly</u> <u>to determine</u> the <u>chemical</u> composition of a sample by using <u>a</u> spectroscope.

Time ? Help Answer Confirm Next

Click on the one underlined word or phrase that must be changed for the sentence to be correct.

The hemlock, one of many coniferous trees, <u>is</u> frequently confused <u>with</u> the <u>poison</u> herb having the <u>same name</u>.

Time   Help   Answer Confirm   Next

Click on the one word or phrase that best completes the sentence.

The summer of 1967, sometimes called the Summer of Love, was ironically a period of profound civil and _____.

- ○ an ethnic unrest
- ○ it was of ethnic unrest
- ○ ethnically unrestful
- ○ ethnic unrest

Time   Help   Answer Confirm   Next

Click on the one underlined word or phrase that must be changed for the sentence to be correct.

The <u>recently</u> epidemic of church fires in southern communities <u>is</u> a <u>painful reminder</u> of the <u>violent</u> civil rights battles of the 60s.

Time   ?   Answer   Next
        Help   Confirm

Click on the one word or phrase that best completes the sentence.

During the 1950s, Chinese and North American ginseng became so popular among herbalists that _____ species were almost exterminated.

○ both
○ the both
○ and both
○ both of

Time   ?   Answer   Next
        Help   Confirm

Click on the one word or phrase that best completes the sentence.

The periodic table contains all the elements, _____ has a particular atomic weight and number.

○ which of each
○ which each
○ each of which
○ each

Click on the one underlined word or phrase that must be changed for the sentence to be correct.

Of the <u>much</u> nervous systems in mammals, the peripheral nervous system is responsible <u>for</u> <u>controlling</u> cranial, spinal, and autonomic <u>nerves</u>.

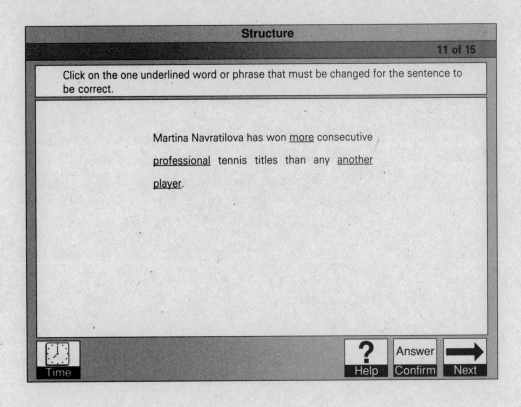

Click on the one underlined word or phrase that must be changed for the sentence to be correct.

Martina Navratilova has won <u>more</u> consecutive <u>professional</u> tennis titles than any <u>another</u> <u>player</u>.

Help Answer Confirm Next

Time

Click on the one word or phrase that best completes the sentence.

Airplanes that used to take more than half a day to cross the Atlantic are now _____ to make the crossing in several hours.

- ⬭ faster than
- ⬭ fast enough
- ⬭ so fast
- ⬭ faster

Help Answer Confirm Next

Time

Click on the one underlined word or phrase that must be changed for the sentence to be correct.

Often seen <u>close to</u> the entrances of <u>their</u> burrows, fiddler crabs possess a <u>four-inched</u> claws used for <u>both</u> courtship rituals and defense.

Click on the one word or phrase that best completes the sentence.

Club mosses, considered to be advanced because they are vascular, _____ in tropical and subtropical forests.

- ⬭ inhabit often moist places
- ⬭ moist places often inhabit
- ⬭ often inhabit moist places
- ⬭ places inhabit moist often

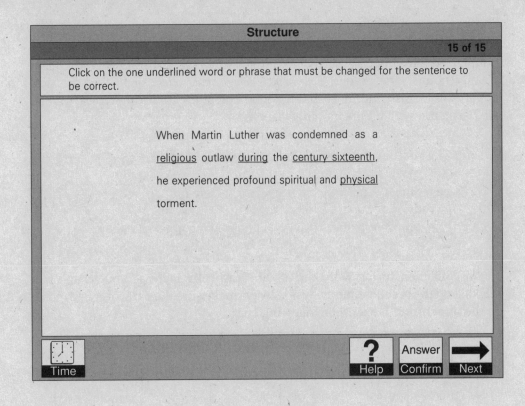

Click on the one underlined word or phrase that must be changed for the sentence to be correct.

When Martin Luther was condemned as a religious outlaw during the century sixteenth, he experienced profound spiritual and physical torment.

Time   ? Help   Answer Confirm   → Next

ADVERBS

Simply, adverbs modify verbs, adjectives, or other adverbs. Adverbs *never* modify nouns. They report *how, when, where, how often,* or *how much*. Most adverbs in English end in -ly, but not all. Look at the following typical TOEFL CBT sentence with all the modifiers labeled.

Most of the <u>hastily</u> <u>built</u> platforms of the subway are <u>so</u>
           adv.   adj.   adv.
<u>incredibly</u> <u>decrepit</u> that warning signs were <u>finally</u>
  adv.   adj.   adv.
<u>hung</u> to protect riders from <u>potentially</u> <u>dangerous</u> situations.
 verb   adv.   adj.

Paying attention to the word order will drastically increase your chances of clicking on the best possible answer. Always make sure the parts of speech come in the right order. Look at the following chart:

Word #1	Word #2	Word #3	Word #1	Word #2	Word #3
Adverb	Verb		quickly	ran	
Adverb	Adverb	Verb	very	quickly	ran
Adverb	Adjective		very	pretty	
Adverb	Adverb	Adjective	still	very	pretty

Here are the types of adverbs that frequently appear on the TOEFL CBT exam:

Manner	Time	Frequency	Degree
dramatically	still	rarely	so
typically	today	seldom	very
thoroughly	soon	occasionally	hardly
intentionally	now	frequently	rather
originally	yet	never	instead

You will encounter a few adverbial questions in the sentence completion questions, but mainly they will be tested in Error Identification questions. Look at a typical adverbial question found in the Structure section of the TOEFL CBT.

_____ a national catastrophe such as an earthquake, tornado, or flood destroys property, insurance companies require that all policyholders complete the necessary forms.

- ◯ Being
- ◯ Whenever
- ◯ Are
- ◯ When can

ETS tries to make adverbial questions confusing by adding in gerunds, verbs, and other parts of speech. In this sentence, "whenever" answers the question, "*When* do insurance companies require that all policy holders complete the necessary forms?" The other answer choices fail to do so.

For Error Identification questions, ETS will replace the adverb with either an adjective or a noun. Look at some typical adverbial questions found in the Structure section of the TOEFL CBT.

> The claim that humans only use ten
> percent of their intellectual capacity has
> never been scientific confirmed.

Remember, adverbs usually precede the verbs they modify. In this sentence, the adjective "scientific" has been incorrectly substituted for the adverb "scientifically." Look at another typical adverbial question found in the Structure section.

> Emile Zola's surprise accusation of the
> French military following the scandalous
> Dreyfus Affair ultimate resulted in the
> pardon of the unfairly accused Dreyfus.

Remember, adverbs must modify verbs or adjectives. Adjectives can **NOT** modify verbs. In this sentence the main verb "resulted" is being modified by an adjective. It should be the adverb "ultimately."

On the TOEFL CBT, ETS will also test your basic knowledge of adverbs by replacing an adverb for another adverb. Look at this type of question found on the TOEFL CBT.

> During the civil rights movement of the
> 1960s, Martin Luther King Jr. proved that
> one could accomplish more with pacifistic
> measures instead than violence.

The adverb "instead" has been incorrectly substituted for the adverb "rather." The fixed pattern is "rather than" and "instead of." Remember, you never have to correct the answer on the TOEFL CBT; you simply must recognize that it is incorrect.

PRACTICE ADVERBIAL QUESTIONS

The following exercises contain **adverbial** questions most frequently found in the Structure section of the TOEFL CBT. Click on (in this case circle) the one word or phrase that best completes the sentence, or the one underlined word or phrase that must be changed for the sentence to be correct. Answers to these questions can be found at the end of this chapter.

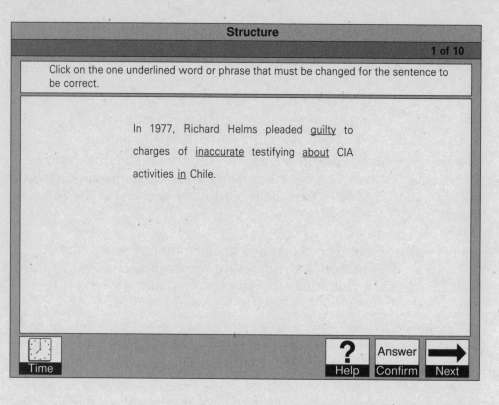

Click on the one underlined word or phrase that must be changed for the sentence to be correct.

In 1977, Richard Helms pleaded <u>guilty</u> to charges of <u>inaccurate</u> testifying <u>about</u> CIA activities <u>in</u> Chile.

Time   Help   Answer Confirm   Next

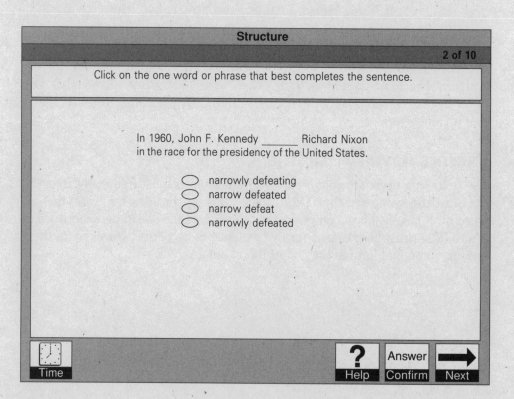

Click on the one word or phrase that best completes the sentence.

In 1960, John F. Kennedy _____ Richard Nixon in the race for the presidency of the United States.

- ○ narrowly defeating
- ○ narrow defeated
- ○ narrow defeat
- ○ narrowly defeated

Time   Help   Answer Confirm   Next

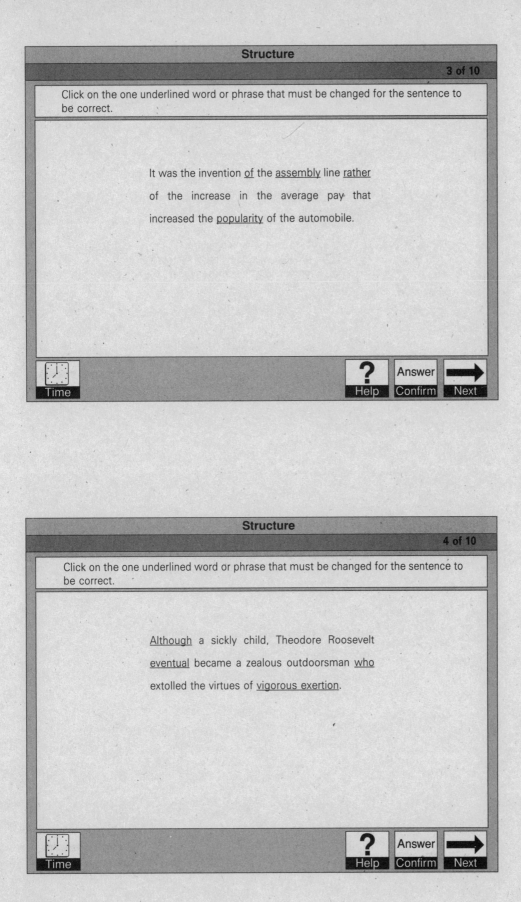

Click on the one underlined word or phrase that must be changed for the sentence to be correct.

It was the invention <u>of</u> the <u>assembly</u> line <u>rather</u> of the increase in the average pay that increased the <u>popularity</u> of the automobile.

Time ? Help Answer Confirm Next

Click on the one underlined word or phrase that must be changed for the sentence to be correct.

<u>Although</u> a sickly child, Theodore Roosevelt <u>eventual</u> became a zealous outdoorsman <u>who</u> extolled the virtues of <u>vigorous exertion</u>.

Time ? Help Answer Confirm Next

Click on the one word or phrase that best completes the sentence.

Although the CIA was an established information source during the Cold War, it was taken _____ the Berlin Wall fell in 1989.

- ⬭ surprised
- ⬭ surprised when complete
- ⬭ when it was completely surprised
- ⬭ completely by surprise when

Time — Help — Answer Confirm — Next

Click on the one underlined word or phrase that must be changed for the sentence to be correct.

A <u>so</u> loud sound, <u>such as</u> a rocket launch, carries more than a billion times more <u>energy</u> than the sound of <u>a</u> mosquito buzzing.

Time — Help — Answer Confirm — Next

Click on the one underlined word or phrase that must be changed for the sentence to be correct.

The natterjack, _easy_ identified by the yellow line _running_ along _its_ back, is _considered_ the most common toad on the European continent.

Time | Help | Answer Confirm | Next

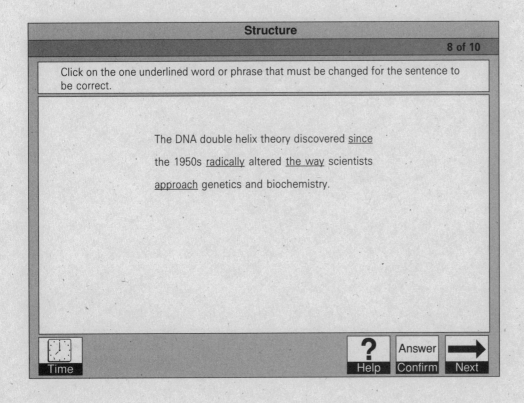

Click on the one underlined word or phrase that must be changed for the sentence to be correct.

The DNA double helix theory discovered _since_ the 1950s _radically_ altered _the way_ scientists _approach_ genetics and biochemistry.

Time | Help | Answer Confirm | Next

Click on the one word or phrase that best completes the sentence.

The Internet, with all its advanced technology, relies _____ on infrastructures built over a generation ago.

- ○ more heavy than
- ○ as heavily
- ○ heavily
- ○ that heavy

Time   Help   Answer Confirm   Next

Click on the one underlined word or phrase that must be changed for the sentence to be correct.

<u>Throughout</u> the Middle Ages, many <u>highly</u> educated scholars <u>thought</u> the Earth to be round <u>rather</u> of flat.

Time   Help   Answer Confirm   Next

SUBORDINATION

In the English language, subordination (also known as modifying clauses) is used to combine two or more sentences into one sentence. The subordinate clause usually contains a relative pronoun, and must appear immediately after the words it modifies. Look at the following three sentences:

> Some types of rice are grown for their large kernels.
>
> The kernels have a high protein content.
>
> The high protein content reduces malnutrition in many third-world countries.

Although these three sentences are grammatically correct, they are repetitive and a little awkward to read. By using subordination, the three sentences can become one.

> Some types of rice are grown for their large kernels, **which** have a high protein content **that** reduces malnutrition in many third world countries.

Notice how the relative pronouns connect the clauses to that which they are modifying. Look at the list of the relative pronouns ETS uses on the TOEFL CBT:

who	that	when
whose	where	which

On the TOEFL CBT, one way that ETS tests your basic knowledge of subordination is by substituting one relative pronoun for another. Look at a typical TOEFL CBT example:

> Some types of rice are grown for their large kernels, who have a high protein content that reduces malnutrition in many third world countries.

In this sentence, the subordination is providing more specific information about "kernels." Since the word "kernels" is not a person, the relative pronoun cannot be "who." The relative pronoun "who" has been incorrectly substituted for "which." Don't worry about the difference between "that" and "which." This point is *never* tested on the TOEFL CBT.

- **RULE #1**—The relative pronoun that you use in subordination depends on what you are modifying. If the relative pronoun is

    who, the subordination must modify a person.
    whose, the subordination must indicate possession.

ETS never tests the difference between "that" and "which."

that, the subordination must modify a thing by defining it, and answering the question, "which one?"
which, the subordination must modify a thing by providing more specific information.
where, the subordination must modify a place.
when, the subordination must refer to a time.

- **RULE #2**—Every subordinate clause *must* have a subject and verb. If the relative pronoun serves as the subject, no additional subject is needed. In the following example, the entire modifier is in bold:

The Statue of Liberty, **which** **was given** **to the United States by France,**
             Sub.   Verb   Preposition
still greets many new immigrants to the United States every year.

On the TOEFL CBT, ETS will insert another pronoun into the sentence, or omit part of the verb. Look at the example again:

The Statue of Liberty, <u>which it was</u> given to the United States <u>by</u> France, <u>still</u> greets <u>many</u> new immigrants to the United States every year.

OR

The Statue of Liberty, <u>which given</u> to the United States <u>by</u> France, <u>still</u> greets <u>many</u> new immigrants to the United States every year.

In the first sentence, the pronoun "it" unnecessarily repeats the relative pronoun "which." In the second example, the auxiliary verb "was" is omitted. Look for these subordination question patterns on the TOEFL CBT.

PRACTICE SUBORDINATION QUESTIONS

The following exercises contain the sort of **subordination** questions most frequently found in the Structure section of the TOEFL CBT. Click on (in this case circle) the one word or phrase that best completes the sentence, or the one underlined word or phrase that must be changed for the sentence to be correct. Answers to these questions can be found at the end of this chapter.

Click on the one word or phrase that best completes the sentence.

Now a mandatory practice in most urban areas, recycling recovers and reuses most waste products that otherwise _____.

- ⬭ not having a use
- ⬭ no use
- ⬭ have no use
- ⬭ they were not used

Time   ? Help   Answer Confirm   ➡ Next

Click on the one underlined word or phrase that must be changed for the sentence to be correct.

Sioux City, Iowa, was named <u>since</u> the Native

American Sioux, a tribe <u>that</u> practiced a <u>typical</u>

Plains area culture, <u>including</u> buffalo hunting

and sun dancing.

Time   ? Help   Answer Confirm   ➡ Next

Click on the one word or phrase that best completes the sentence.

Robert Duncan's paintings, _____ the Midwest as a serene and settled landscape, inspired many Easterners to relocate to the West.

- ◯ they portrayed
- ◯ portrays
- ◯ which portrayed
- ◯ the portrayal of

Time Help Answer Confirm Next

Click on the one underlined word or phrase that must be changed for the sentence to be correct.

Since the 1960s, population and <u>development</u>

have steadily increased <u>along</u> the Amazon River,

all of <u>which it</u> is <u>easily</u> accessible to ships.

Time Help Answer Confirm Next

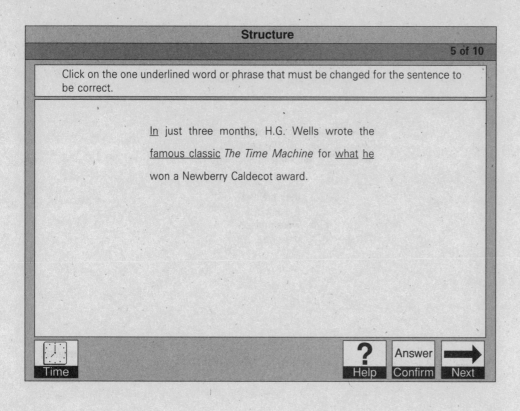

Click on the one underlined word or phrase that must be changed for the sentence to be correct.

<u>In</u> just three months, H.G. Wells wrote the <u>famous classic</u> *The Time Machine* for <u>what</u> <u>he</u> won a Newberry Caldecot award.

Time

? Help

Answer Confirm

Next

Click on the one word or phrase that best completes the sentence.

Cloud formations are categorized into four basic groups, based on their altitude, appearance, and the amount of water _____.

- ○ contain of
- ○ they contain
- ○ contain
- ○ they are contained

Time

? Help

Answer Confirm

Next

Click on the one word or phrase that best completes the sentence.

While living in the White House, Eleanor Roosevelt was harshly criticized by those who later _____ her humanitarian efforts.

- ○ they praised
- ○ praised
- ○ were praised
- ○ praising

Time | Help | Answer Confirm | Next

Click on the one underlined word or phrase that must be changed for the sentence to be correct.

There <u>was</u> great concern in the 1950s when <u>it</u>

was discovered <u>that</u> the paint used on <u>certainly</u>

dining sets contained radioactive uranium.

Time | Help | Answer Confirm | Next

Click on the one underlined word or phrase that must be changed for the sentence to be correct.

Some honeybees <u>are raised</u> for <u>their</u> ability to pollinate, <u>which</u> ensures plant fertilization <u>for</u> increases fruit yields.

Click on the one word or phrase that best completes the sentence.

The remora, _____ itself to turtles, is not considered a parasite since it does not take sustenance away from the host.

○ attaches
○ which it attaches
○ which attaches
○ of which attaches

Time   Help   Answer Confirm   Next

NOUN CLAUSES

A noun clause is a special type of subordinate clause that does not modify another noun, but rather acts as a subject or object. The following sentence has the noun clause in bold.

> During the Pleistocene epoch, glaciers covered **what is now named the Rocky Mountains.**

A noun clause always begins with a relative pronoun. If the relative pronoun serves as the subject of the noun clause, no additional subject is needed. Look at a list of relative pronouns that begin noun clauses on the TOEFL CBT.

what	where	when	whether
how	that	which	

ETS tests your basic knowledge of noun clauses by confusing the word order, and presenting incorrect relative pronouns or conjunctions in the answer choices. Noun clause questions are tested in the Sentence Completion section of the TOEFL CBT. Look at the following example of a typical TOEFL CBT noun clause question.

> According to some scientists, the goal of technology is to provide the masses with what _____ to comfortably live a self-sufficient life.
>
> ○ do they need
> ○ needs
> ○ they need
> ○ they are needed

In this question, the relative pronoun "what" does not function as the subject of the noun clause, so the subject "they" is needed. Therefore, you may use POE to eliminate the answer choice "needs" because it lacks a subject. In the answer choice "do they need," the auxiliary "do" incorrectly precedes the subject. The fourth answer choice, "they are needed," incorrectly uses the passive voice. Only the third answer choice, "they need," contains a subject and verb that correctly fulfills noun clause requirements.

PRACTICE NOUN CLAUSE QUESTIONS

The following exercises contain the sort of **noun clause** questions most frequently found in the Structure section of the TOEFL CBT. Click on (in this case circle) the one word or phrase that best completes the sentence. Answers to these questions can be found at the end of this chapter.

Click on the one word or phrase that best completes the sentence.

The five Great Lake basins in central North America were carved out of the earth and filled with water at a time _____.

○ when glaciers covered the area
○ covered the area were glaciers
○ the area in which glaciers covered
○ covered glaciers the area

Time

? Help

Answer Confirm

→ Next

Click on the one word or phrase that best completes the sentence.

Affirmative Action, an equal opportunity employment program in the United States, has long been the subject of disagreement over _____ the racial imbalance in the American workplace.

○ either the elimination
○ eliminating
○ how to eliminate
○ if elimination

Time

? Help

Answer Confirm

→ Next

Click on the one word or phrase that best completes the sentence.

People hoping to see unidentified flying objects are often fooled by unusual atmospheric conditions that appear _____.

- ○ on the horizon which clouds form
- ○ do clouds form on the horizon
- ○ clouds forming on the horizon
- ○ when clouds form on the horizon

Time Help Answer Confirm Next

Click on the one word or phrase that best completes the sentence.

Built in 1598 and destroyed by fire in 1644, The Globe Theater in London is _____ the playwright William Shakespeare wrote most of his plays.

- ○ it where
- ○ where
- ○ which is where
- ○ where is

Time Help Answer Confirm Next

Click on the one word or phrase that best completes the sentence.

Just inside the outer layer of the earth's atmosphere _____ needed to protect it from foreign substances.

○ are the elements
○ where the elements are
○ the elements are
○ which are the elements

Time | Help | Answer Confirm | Next

Click on the one word or phrase that best completes the sentence.

Essentially, a hologram is a three-dimensional, projected image of _____ to be a real object.

○ what is perceived
○ to perceive what
○ that perceiving
○ which perceiving

Time | Help | Answer Confirm | Next

Click on the one word or phrase that best completes the sentence.

One of the first Native American tribes to live in _____ was the Apache, who are known principally for their fierce fighting qualities and matriarchal organization.

○ this is Arizona now
○ Arizona is now
○ what is now Arizona
○ is now Arizona

Time   Help   Answer Confirm   Next

Click on the one word or phrase that best completes the sentence.

Phosphorus is nearly insoluble in water, but _____ it ignites spontaneously, burning to form white fumes.

○ the exposure to air
○ exposed when to air
○ when exposed to air
○ it is exposed to air

Time   Help   Answer Confirm   Next

Click on the one word or phrase that best completes the sentence.

Human survival rates in serious motor vehicle accidents depend mostly on _____ and passengers are wearing their seatbelts.

○ the driver
○ either the driver
○ whether the driver
○ that the driver

Time   Help   Answer Confirm   Next

Click on the one word or phrase that best completes the sentence.

According to developers, the purpose of virtual reality software is to provide the users with what _____ to explore otherwise unattainable environments.

○ they want
○ do they want
○ so they want
○ they are wanted

Time   Help   Answer Confirm   Next

PASSIVE AND ACTIVE MODIFIERS

In addition to functioning as verbs, verbs can also act as other parts of speech. Two parts of speech that use a verb form are passive and active modifiers (also called verbal modifiers). Passive modifiers take the past participial form of the verb, that is, the "third" verb form. For example, *given, taken, chosen, compared, known, provided, unparalleled*, and *located* are verbs in the participial form. Active modifiers are verbs that take the present participial form, the *-ing* ending. For example, *beginning, making, using, including,* and *maintaining* can all act as active modifiers.

In the subordination section, you learned that subordination is used to combine several sentences into one. Passive and active modifiers are used for the same reason. Look at the two following sentences:

> The National Institute of Technology was established in 1901.
>
> The National Institute of Technology dedicates its services to strengthening and advancing the application of science for national interest.

Although these two sentences are grammatically correct, they are repetitive and a little awkward to read. By using a passive modifier, the two sentences can become one. The passive modifier in the following sentence is in bold.

> **Established** in 1901, the National Institute of Technology dedicates its services to strengthening and advancing the application of science for national interest.

Passive modifiers are used to replace passive clauses and must immediately precede or follow the word they are modifying. Regardless of the main tense of the sentence, the passive modifier is always the past participle.

Active modifiers work the exact same way as passive modifiers, except they take the *-ing* form of the verb. They are also used to combine more than one sentence into one. Look at the two following sentences:

> After it hatches, the caterpillar experiences several stages of metamorphosis.
>
> The metamorphosis begins with a pupa.

Although these two sentences are grammatically correct, they are repetitive and a little awkward to read. By using an active modifier, the two sentences can become one. The active modifier in the following sentence is in bold.

> After it hatches, the caterpillar experiences several stages of metamorphosis, **beginning** with a pupa.

Active modifiers are used to replace active clauses and must immediately precede or follow the word or phrase they are modifying. Regardless of the main tense of the sentence, the active modifier always takes the *-ing* ending.

On the Error Identification questions of the TOEFL CBT, ETS will test your basic knowledge of passive and active modifiers by simply substituting one for the other. Look at a typical passive/active modifier question found on the Structure section of the TOEFL CBT.

> <u>Establishing</u> in 1901, the National Institute of Technology dedicates <u>its</u> services to <u>strengthening and advancing</u> the application of science <u>for</u> national interest.

To solve these types of questions, identify what the passive/active modifier is modifying and ask a question. For example, in this sentence, "The National Institute of Technology" is being modified. Simply ask the question, "Can the National Institute of Technology be establishing?" No. *An institute cannot establish anything*, but it *can* be established by someone.

Look at another typical passive/active modifier question found on the Structure section of the TOEFL CBT.

> After it hatches, the caterpillar experiences several stages of metamorphosis, _____ with a pupa.
>
>   ◯ began
>   ◯ is begun
>   ◯ beginning
>   ◯ begin

In this sentence, use POE on the answer choices that function as main verbs or change the tense of the sentence ("begin," "is begun," "began"). The "stages of metamorphosis" is active because it can begin with something. Therefore the best answer to select is "beginning."

PRACTICE PASSIVE/ACTIVE MODIFIER QUESTIONS

The following exercises contain **passive/active modifier** questions most frequently found in the Structure section of the TOEFL CBT. Click on (in this case circle) the one word or phrase that best completes the sentence, or the one underlined word or phrase that must be changed for the sentence to be correct. Answers to these questions can be found at the end of this chapter.

Click on the one word or phrase that best completes the sentence.

With time, the thickness of human eyelashes decreases, _____ them less likely to protect the eye from dust and disease.

- ○ make
- ○ which they make
- ○ and is making
- ○ making

Click on the one word or phrase that best completes the sentence.

The Native American group _____ as the Cherokee Nation established their own constitution and elected their own leaders.

- ○ known
- ○ were known
- ○ the unknown
- ○ are unknown

Click on the one underlined word or phrase that must be changed for the sentence to be correct.

<u>Was constructed</u> between 1959 and 1972, Lincoln Center in New York City is <u>dedicated to</u> the encouragement of new artists <u>and</u> to the presentation of <u>internationally</u> acclaimed performers.

Time Help Answer Confirm Next

Click on the one word or phrase that best completes the sentence.

Modern navigators make use of global satellites _____ in the outer atmosphere to determine their exact location on the sea.

- ○ to station
- ○ stationed
- ○ stationing
- ○ stations

Time Help Answer Confirm Next

Click on the one underlined word or phrase that must be changed for the sentence to be correct.

Many of the ancient Egyptian tombs <u>discovering</u> in the early <u>nineteenth</u> century offered <u>a</u> new store of knowledge on art, style <u>of</u> government, and way of life.

Time   Help   Answer Confirm   Next

Click on the one word or phrase that best completes the sentence.

In the United States every person _____ of a crime has the right to a trial by a jury of their peers.

○ accused
○ accusing
○ to accuse
○ be accused

Time   Help   Answer Confirm   Next

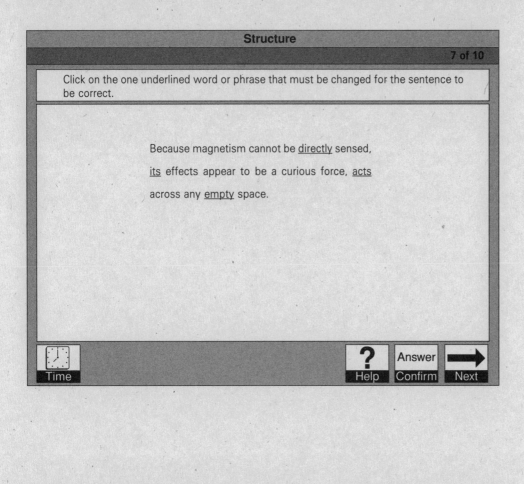

Click on the one underlined word or phrase that must be changed for the sentence to be correct.

Because magnetism cannot be <u>directly</u> sensed,

<u>its</u> effects appear to be a curious force, <u>acts</u>

across any <u>empty</u> space.

Time | ? Help | Answer Confirm | Next

Click on the one word or phrase that best completes the sentence.

The giant sea tortoises _____ extinction on the Galapagos Islands come ashore only to breed and lay eggs.

- ○ are facing
- ○ faced
- ○ facing
- ○ face

Time | ? Help | Answer Confirm | Next

Click on the one underlined word or phrase that must be changed for the sentence to be correct.

Every theatre is required by law <u>to install</u> a curtain <u>that</u> can drop across the stage, <u>protecting</u> the audience <u>for</u> backstage fires.

Time   ? Help   Answer Confirm   → Next

Click on the one underlined word or phrase that must be changed for the sentence to be correct.

The beefalo is an animal <u>engineering</u> by breeding <u>the</u> indigenous America buffalo <u>with</u> a strain of the <u>common cow</u>.

Time   ? Help   Answer Confirm   → Next

GERUNDS AND INFINITIVES

When the *-ing* ending is added to a verb, making it function as a *noun*, it is called a "gerund." A gerund represents the performance of the verb in noun form. To clarify what a gerund is, compare the *-ing* ending with the *-er* ending. If you add the *-er* ending to any verb—for example, *swimmer, runner, teacher,* and so forth— the verb expresses the performer of the verb. Likewise, adding the *-ing* form to any verb—for example, *swimming, running, teaching,* and so forth—the verb expresses the performance of the verb. Like a noun, a gerund can function as a subject, object, and complement. For example:

> Since its invention in 1834, refrigeration has greatly improved the **buying** and **selling** of food products.

On the TOEFL CBT, ETS tests your basic knowledge of gerunds that either follow verb/preposition combinations or adjective/preposition combinations. Identify the error in this typical TOEFL CBT question.

> <u>Some</u> politicians complain <u>about</u> border guards' <u>inability</u> to prevent people from illegally <u>cross</u> the Texan-Mexican border.

In this example, the gerund in the fixed phrase "to prevent someone from *doing* something" has been replaced with the infinitive. The sentence should read:

> <u>Some</u> politicians complain <u>about</u> border guards' <u>inability</u> to prevent people from illegally <u>crossing</u> the Texan-Mexican border.

The following is a common list of fixed adjectival and verbal phrases followed by a gerund that frequently appear on the TOEFL CBT. Try to memorize a few each day. Learning these fixed expressions will not only improve your TOEFL CBT Structure score, but they can also be used in the Writing section of the TOEFL CBT, and improve your level of conversational English.

Adjectival and Verbal Phrases Followed by a Gerund	
1. object to doing something	11. participate/take part in doing something
2. prevent/stop someone from doing something	12. admit/confess to doing something
3. responsible for doing something	13. accuse someone of doing something
4. punish someone for doing something	14. succeed in doing something
5. capable of doing something	15. excited about doing something
6. interested in doing something	16. keep/prohibit someone from doing something
7. known for doing something	17. accuse someone of doing something
8. believe in doing something	18. blame someone for doing something
9. committed to doing something	19. consist of doing something
10. forgive someone for something	20. guilty of doing something

On the TOEFL CBT, ETS will also test your ability to recognize if a gerund or an infinitive comes after another verb. Look at the following TOEFL CBT sentence.

> As minister of justice, Nicolas Avellaneda
> worked _____ the failing banks of
> Argentina reform into respectable financial
> institutions.
>
> ⬭ help
> ⬭ for helping
> ⬭ to help
> ⬭ the help that

In English, when one verb follows another, it must take *either* the gerund or the infinitive form. There is no rule as to why some verbs take a gerund and others take an infinitive. In the example above, the missing verb would take the infinitive form: to help.

The following is a reference list of verbs followed by either gerunds or infinitives that frequently appear on the TOEFL CBT. Try to memorize a few each day. Learning these verb patterns will not only improve your TOEFL CBT Structure score, but also help in the Writing section of the TOEFL CBT and improve your level of conversational English.

Verbs Followed by Infinitives	Verbs Followed by Gerunds
1. continue	1. mention
2. appear	2. postpone
3. consent	3. resist
4. pretend	4. tolerate
5. hesitate	5. consider
6. promise	6. delay
7. appear	7. keep
8. claim	8. enjoy
9. begin	9. mind
10. work	10. practice
11. threaten	11. risk
12. manage	12. finish
13. expect	13. recall
14. beg	14. avoid
15. refuse	15. anticipate

On the TOEFL CBT, ETS tests your basic knowledge of infinitives that follow verb/noun combinations. Identify the error in this typical TOEFL CBT question.

> <u>Composers</u> of the late twentieth century
> rely heavily <u>on</u> computers and specialized
> software <u>to helping</u> <u>write</u> their scores.

In this example the infinitive in the fixed phrase "to rely on something to do something" has been replaced with the gerund. The sentence should read:

> <u>Composers</u> of the late twentieth century
> rely heavily <u>on</u> computers and specialized
> software <u>to help</u> <u>write</u> their scores.

The following is a common list of fixed verb/noun phrases followed by an infinitive that frequently appear on the TOEFL CBT. Try to memorize a few each day. Learning these fixed expressions will not only improve your TOEFL CBT Structure score, but they can also be used in the Writing section of the TOEFL CBT, and improve your level of conversational English.

Verb/Noun Phrases Followed by Infinitives

1. persuade someone to do something
2. make it possible to do something
3. enable someone to do something
4. lead someone to do something
5. rely on something/someone to do something
6. equip someone to do something
7. permit someone to do something
8. cause someone to do something
9. encourage someone to do something
10. convince someone to do something
11. need someone to do something
12. remind someone to do something
13. challenge someone to do something
14. allow someone to do something
15. expect someone to do something

Practice Gerund/Infinitive Questions

The following exercises contain **gerund/infinitive** questions most frequently found in the Structure section of the TOEFL CBT. Click on (in this case circle) the one word or phrase that best completes the sentence, or the one underlined word or phrase that must be changed for the sentence to be correct. Answers to these questions can be found at the end of this chapter.

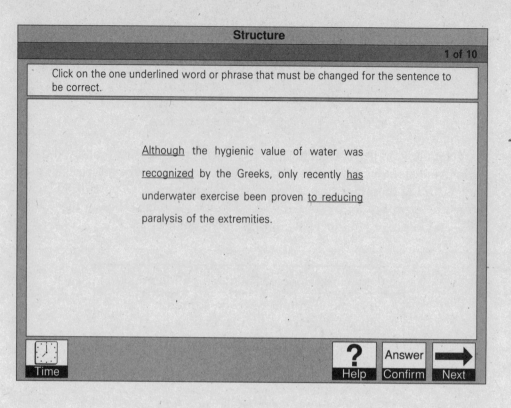

Click on the one underlined word or phrase that must be changed for the sentence to be correct.

Although the hygienic value of water was recognized by the Greeks, only recently has underwater exercise been proven to reducing paralysis of the extremities.

Time   Help   Answer Confirm   Next

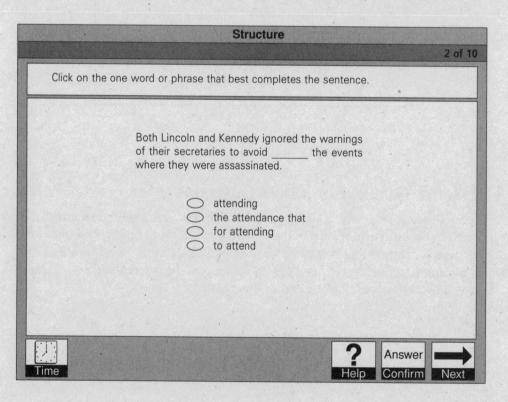

Click on the one word or phrase that best completes the sentence.

Both Lincoln and Kennedy ignored the warnings of their secretaries to avoid _____ the events where they were assassinated.

○ attending
○ the attendance that
○ for attending
○ to attend

Time   Help   Answer Confirm   Next

Click on the one underlined word or phrase that must be changed for the sentence to be correct.

A prosthetic leg <u>enables</u> a person <u>to function</u> without <u>the assistance</u> of a wheelchair or crutches; thus more people are able to avoid <u>to depend</u> on others.

?
Help

Answer
Confirm

Next

Time

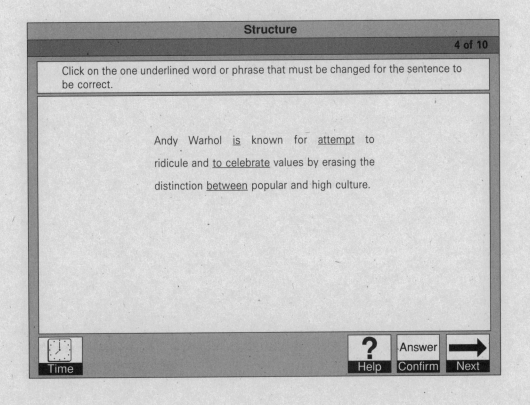

Click on the one underlined word or phrase that must be changed for the sentence to be correct.

Andy Warhol <u>is</u> known for <u>attempt</u> to ridicule and <u>to celebrate</u> values by erasing the distinction <u>between</u> popular and high culture.

?
Help

Answer
Confirm

Next

Time

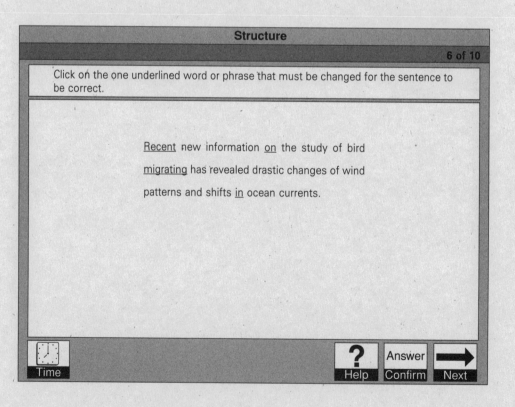

Structure

Click on the one word or phrase that best completes the sentence.

In addition to the constant threat of being replaced by younger, healthier athletes, professional football players risk _____ career-ending injuries on virtually every play.

○ to suffer
○ who suffer
○ suffering
○ suffering that which

Time

Help   Answer Confirm   Next

Structure

Click on the one underlined word or phrase that must be changed for the sentence to be correct.

<u>Recent</u> new information <u>on</u> the study of bird <u>migrating</u> has revealed drastic changes of wind patterns and shifts <u>in</u> ocean currents.

Time

Help   Answer Confirm   Next

Click on the one word or phrase that best completes the sentence.

In the early days of the New York transit system, passengers often were forced _____ hours before the trains arrived.

○ wait
○ them waiting
○ to wait
○ the wait that

Time Help Answer Confirm Next

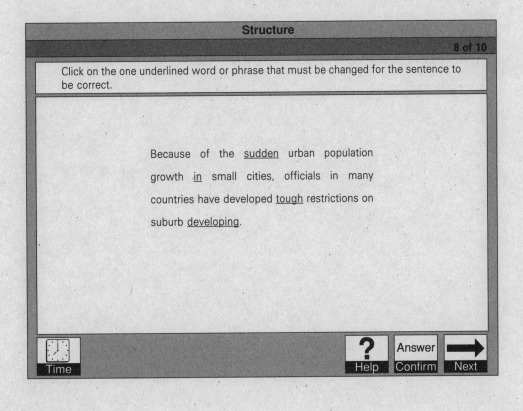

Click on the one underlined word or phrase that must be changed for the sentence to be correct.

Because of the <u>sudden</u> urban population growth <u>in</u> small cities, officials in many countries have developed <u>tough</u> restrictions on suburb <u>developing</u>.

Time Help Answer Confirm Next

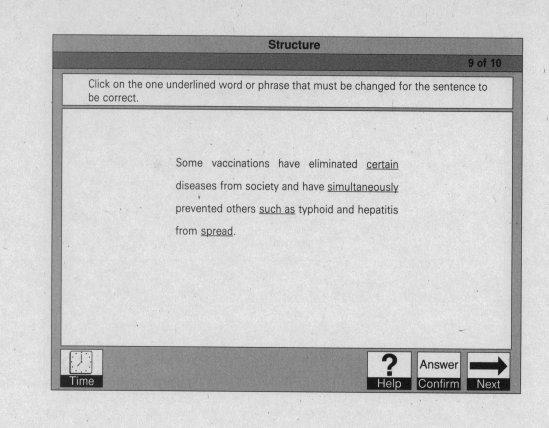

Click on the one underlined word or phrase that must be changed for the sentence to be correct.

Some vaccinations have eliminated <u>certain</u> diseases from society and have <u>simultaneously</u> prevented others <u>such as</u> typhoid and hepatitis from <u>spread</u>.

Time Help Answer Confirm Next

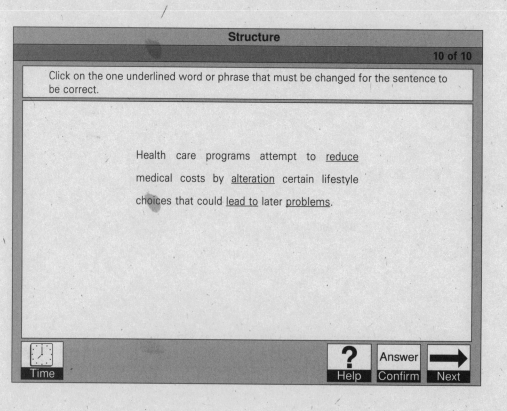

Click on the one underlined word or phrase that must be changed for the sentence to be correct.

Health care programs attempt to <u>reduce</u> medical costs by <u>alteration</u> certain lifestyle choices that could <u>lead to</u> later <u>problems</u>.

Time Help Answer Confirm Next

PREPOSITIONS

In the Structure section of the TOEFL CBT, ETS will test your basic knowledge of prepositions. You can expect three to five preposition questions per test. Preposition questions are some of the most difficult questions you will encounter on the TOEFL CBT. Prepositions are illogical and are inconsistent from one situation to another. Fortunately, your POE techniques will be extremely beneficial. Simply, if all other answer choices seem correct, and a preposition is underlined, chances are good that it will be the best answer choice.

Prepositions are only tested in Error Identification questions.

Prepositions that follow adjectives must be followed by an object, noun, or pronoun. Look at a typical TOEFL CBT preposition question:

> Doris Lessing has been <u>recognized</u> <u>from</u> her skill <u>as a</u> short-story writer and as <u>a</u> writer of nonfiction.

In the above example, ETS has substituted the incorrect preposition "from" for the correct preposition "for." ETS will test your knowledge of prepositions that follow adjectives. Following is a list of prepositions that ETS has used on recent exams. Try to memorize a few each day.

If a preposition is omitted, the words on either side are underlined.

Prepositions	
1. jealous of	16. associated with
2. characterized by	17. believe in
3. dedicated to	18. committed to
4. differ in	19. concerned about
5. benefit from	20. guilty of
6. given to	21. distinguished from
7. known for	22. escape from
8. serve as	23. excited about
9. rich with	24. furnished with
10. related to	25. interested in
11. on account of	26. prepared for
12. depend on	27. recover from
13. accused of	28. take advantage of
14. acquainted with	29. worried about
15. protect from	30. participate in

PRACTICE PREPOSITIONAL PHRASE QUESTIONS

The following exercises contain the sort of **prepositional phrase** questions most frequently found in the Structure section of the TOEFL CBT. Click on (in this case circle) the one underlined word or phrase that must be changed for the sentence to be correct. Answers to these questions can be found at the end of this chapter.

Click on the one underlined word or phrase that must be changed for the sentence to be correct.

William Penn, the <u>religious</u> and political leader <u>toward</u> the Quakers, established <u>friendly</u> relations <u>with</u> the indigenous tribes of the Pennsylvania region.

Time   Help   Answer Confirm   Next

Click on the one underlined word or phrase that must be changed for the sentence to be correct.

The Missouri Compromise was a piece of <u>legislation</u> that <u>admitted</u> Missouri <u>for</u> the United States as a state which <u>permitted</u> slavery.

Time   Help   Answer Confirm   Next

Click on the one underlined word or phrase that must be changed for the sentence to be correct.

Grandma Moses' <u>simple</u> paintings <u>in</u> American farm life struck the public's taste and became <u>widely</u> known <u>through</u> prints and Christmas cards.

Time | ? Help | Answer Confirm | → Next

Click on the one underlined word or phrase that must be changed for the sentence to be correct.

<u>At</u> most modern ski resorts, rangers are <u>fully</u> prepared <u>to assist</u> any skier stranded <u>if</u> snowstorms.

Time | ? Help | Answer Confirm | → Next

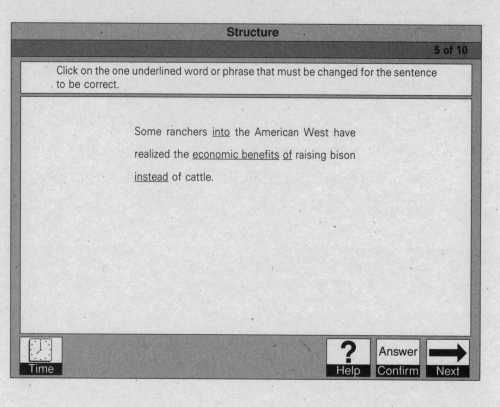

Click on the one underlined word or phrase that must be changed for the sentence to be correct.

Some ranchers <u>into</u> the American West have realized the <u>economic benefits</u> <u>of</u> raising bison <u>instead</u> of cattle.

Time   Help   Answer Confirm   Next

Click on the one underlined word or phrase that must be changed for the sentence to be correct.

<u>During</u> the early Italian Renaissance, <u>the</u> education of the artist had a <u>drastically</u> effect <u>on</u> the artistic quality of the masterpieces themselves.

Time   Help   Answer Confirm   Next

Click on the one underlined word or phrase that must be changed for the sentence to be correct.

Halophyte is the name given <u>into</u> any seed plant that <u>exhibits</u> the ability to grow in habitats <u>excessively</u> <u>rich in</u> salt.

Time   Help   Answer Confirm   Next

Click on the one underlined word or phrase that must be changed for the sentence to be correct.

The common zebra is <u>easy</u> prey to <u>its</u> faster predators, <u>but account of</u> its stripes, the predators are often <u>disoriented</u> and unable to focus.

Time   Help   Answer Confirm   Next

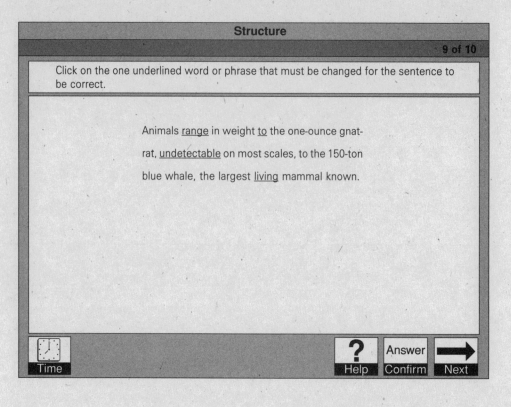

Click on the one underlined word or phrase that must be changed for the sentence to be correct.

Animals <u>range</u> in weight <u>to</u> the one-ounce gnat-rat, <u>undetectable</u> on most scales, to the 150-ton blue whale, the largest <u>living</u> mammal known.

Time Help Answer Confirm Next

Click on the one underlined word or phrase that must be changed for the sentence to be correct.

All mountain glaciers are in a <u>constant state</u> of motion as <u>various</u> weather conditions force the frozen masses <u>downward</u> one side of a valley, across the bottom, and up <u>the other</u> side.

Time Help Answer Confirm Next

CONJUNCTIONS

Conjunctions express a relationship between ideas. They connect different types of words and phrases: nouns with nouns, verbs with verbs, modifiers with modifiers, phrases with phrases, or clauses with clauses. On the TOEFL CBT, both conjunctions and conjunction patterns will be tested in both Sentence Completion and Error Identification question types.

There are two basic types of conjunctions; those that show *agreement* between ideas, and those that show *disagreement* between ideas. Conjunctions that show agreement give additional information that agrees with or further explains the idea in the main sentence. For example:

> Benjamin Franklin was a successful inventor **as well as** a politician and statesman.

In the above sentence, the conjunction "as well as" provides additional information that agrees with what is already stated or implied in the main sentence. Conjunctions that show disagreement between ideas contrast the idea in the main sentence. For example:

> **Although** petroleum is refined into industrial products such as plastic and synthetic fiber, it is primarily prized for its ability to combust.

In the above sentence, the conjunction "although" contradicts the idea that is stated or implied in the main sentence. Both types of conjunctions are tested in the TOEFL CBT. The following is a common list of conjunctions that show agreement and disagreement between ideas. Try to incorporate them into your vocabulary by practicing a few each day. Learning these conjunctions will not only improve your TOEFL CBT Structure score, but can also help in the Writing section of the TOEFL CBT, and improve your level of conversational English.

Agreement	Disagreement
such as	but
as well as	however
because	despite
also	although
in addition to	in spite of
as	whereas

On the TOEFL CBT, ETS usually tests your basic knowledge of conjunctions in the sentence completion type of question. ETS will try to confuse you by including articles, adverbs, and other parts of speech with conjunctions in the answer choices. Look at the example on the following page.

_____ the consumption of tobacco has dramatically decreased, smoking continues to be a widespread and costly health problem.

- ○ Despite
- ○ Although
- ○ Whereas
- ○ Neither

In this example, the main sentence states that "smoking continues to be a widespread and costly health problem." However, the dependent clause states that the consumption of tobacco has dramatically decreased. The disagreement of ideas between the main sentence and the dependent clause requires a conjunction of disagreement. The first answer choice, "Despite," can't begin a modifying phrase that contains a verb. The conjunction "Whereas" can't show contrast between the same subject. The conjunction "Neither" must be paired with "nor." Only the answer choice "Although" successfully competes conjunction requirements.

ETS also tests your basic knowledge of conjunction patterns. Conjunction patterns are fixed expressions that need to include all the words in the pattern in order to be correct. Look at several types of conjunction patterns typically found on the TOEFL CBT.

either . . . or	Paleontology, which deals with prehistoric life forms, can be treated as **either** a part of geology **or** biology.
neither . . . nor	Virus particles can **neither** function as a living cell **nor** survive for extended periods of time outside a host.
both . . . and	**Both** earthquakes **and** volcanoes require specific geological conditions.
not only . . . but also	In order to ensure ample food supplies, **not only** do some species of fish attack intruders in their hunting territories, **but** they **also** kill their own offspring.
such as	Early types of gunpowder were created with **such** materials **as** sulfur, saltpeter, and carbon in the form of charcoal.

Remember, when the negative "not only" acts as the subject, the auxiliary must immediately follow.

PRACTICE CONJUNCTION QUESTIONS

The following exercises contain the sort of **conjunction** questions most frequently found in the Structure section of the TOEFL CBT. Click on (in this case circle) the one word or phrase that best completes the sentence, or the one underlined word or phrase that must be changed for the sentence to be correct. Answers to these questions can be found at the end of this chapter.

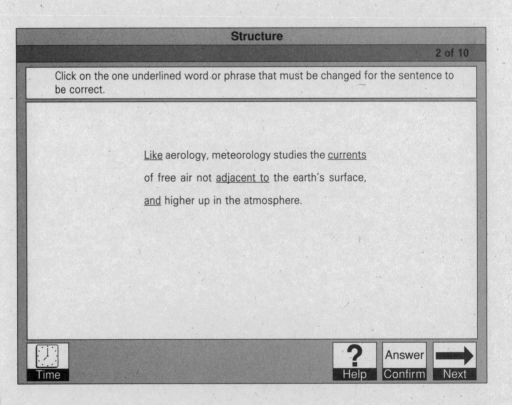

Click on the one word or phrase that best completes the sentence.

Researchers have discovered that listening to classical music can not only lower stress levels, _____ reduce blood pressure.

- ○ also
- ○ but also
- ○ not also
- ○ but not also

Time   Help   Answer Confirm   Next

Click on the one underlined word or phrase that must be changed for the sentence to be correct.

<u>Like</u> aerology, meteorology studies the <u>currents</u>

of free air not <u>adjacent to</u> the earth's surface,

<u>and</u> higher up in the atmosphere.

Time   Help   Answer Confirm   Next

Click on the one word or phrase that best completes the sentence.

As children grow from infancy to adolescence, _____ the immediate and the extended family play crucial roles in their cognitive development.

- ○ both
- ○ both of
- ○ and both
- ○ both of which

Time Help Answer Confirm Next

Click on the one underlined word or phrase that must be changed for the sentence to be correct.

<u>Despite</u> Alexander Pope was affected by such <u>handicaps</u> as paralysis and deafness, he translated classics and established himself as one of the greatest <u>poets</u> of the <u>eighteenth</u> century.

Time Help Answer Confirm Next

Click on the one word or phrase that best completes the sentence.

The cultural elite in certain ancient civilizations relied heavily upon papyrus to make everyday household objects _____.

○ that baskets and clothing are
○ such as baskets and clothing
○ if baskets and clothing
○ for baskets and clothing

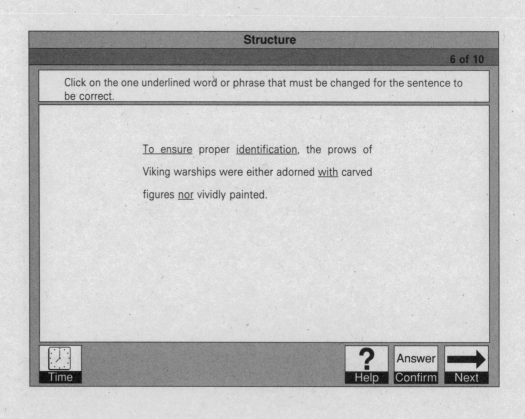

Click on the one underlined word or phrase that must be changed for the sentence to be correct.

To ensure proper identification, the prows of

Viking warships were either adorned with carved

figures nor vividly painted.

Click on the one word or phrase that best completes the sentence.

_____ most plants, which draw their nutrients from the soil, the Venus flytrap feeds upon insects trapped by its sticky leaves.

○ Whereas
○ Unlike
○ Although
○ In spite of

Time   Help   Answer Confirm   Next

Click on the one word or phrase that best completes the sentence.

_____ privacy extended to account holders, Switzerland plays an important role in international banking.

○ While the
○ The
○ Since the
○ Because of the

Time   Help   Answer Confirm   Next

Click on the one underlined word or phrase that must be changed for the sentence to be correct.

Although pilots heavily depend on numerous dials and monitors to flying large aircraft, their best defense against accidents is common sense.

Time | Help | Answer Confirm | Next

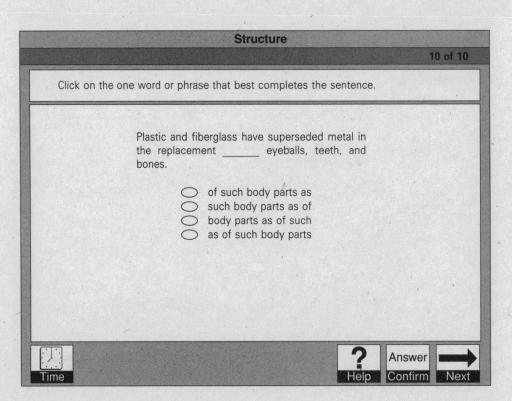

Click on the one word or phrase that best completes the sentence.

Plastic and fiberglass have superseded metal in the replacement _____ eyeballs, teeth, and bones.

- ○ of such body parts as
- ○ such body parts as of
- ○ body parts as of such
- ○ as of such body parts

Time | Help | Answer Confirm | Next

COMPARISONS AND SUPERLATIVES

Comparative adjectives compare the qualities of two nouns. If the adjective has only one syllable, the comparative form of the adjective is usually created by adding -*er* to the end of the adjective, and must be followed by "than." If the adjective has two syllables or more, the comparative form of the adjective is usually created by the preceding adverbs "more" or "less," and must also be followed by "than." There are exceptions to this "syllable" rule, but ETS will not test them.

Superlative adjectives show that a noun has a particular quality in the highest degree. If the adjective has one syllable, the superlative form of the adjective is usually created by adding -*est* to the end of the adjective. If the adjective has two syllables or more, the superlative form of the adjective is usually created by the preceding adverbs "most" or "least." There are exceptions to this "syllable" rule, but ETS will not test them.

Look at a list of adjectives in the comparative and superlative form:

low	lower	the lowest
abundant	more abundant	the most abundant
large	larger	the largest
terrible	less terrible	the least terrible
great	greater	the greatest
expensive	more expensive	the most expensive
long	longer	the longest
beautiful	less beautiful	the least beautiful

The adverbs "more," "less," "most," and "least" can never modify adjectives that end with -*er*, and -*est*. Look at a typical comparison/superlative question that frequently appears on the TOEFL CBT.

> Even though all rabbits are known to breed prolifically, the snowshoe rabbit actually has _____ than the cottontail does.
> - ◯ the longer the gestation period
> - ◯ its longer gestation period
> - ◯ the gestation period is longer
> - ◯ a longer gestation period

In this sentence, the first answer choice "the longer the gestation period" is part of a fixed comparative expression that needs another comparison to be complete. For example, "The bigger the apartment, the higher the rent." The second answer choice "its longer gestation period" incorrectly adds a possessive pronoun. The third answer choice "the gestation period is longer" creates an independent sentence. Only the fourth answer choice "a longer gestation period" completes the grammatical requirements for a correct comparative structure.

PRACTICE COMPARISON AND SUPERLATIVE QUESTIONS

The following exercises contain the sort of **comparison** and **superlative** questions most frequently found in the Structure section of the TOEFL CBT. Click on (in this case circle) the one word or phrase that best completes the sentence, or the one underlined word or phrase that must be changed for the sentence to be correct. Answers to these questions can be found at the end of this chapter.

Click on the one word or phrase that best completes the sentence.

Microwaves that once took up entire kitchen counters are now _____ to fit conveniently under cabinets and on cupboard shelves.

- ○ so tiny
- ○ as tiny as
- ○ tiny enough
- ○ tinier than

Time   Help   Answer Confirm   Next

Click on the one word or phrase that best completes the sentence.

Although headache pain is _____ back pain, both can interfere with ordinary daily activities.

- ○ more effectively controlled than
- ○ the effect is more than controlled
- ○ more than effectively controlled
- ○ controlled more than effectively

Time   Help   Answer Confirm   Next

Click on the one underlined word or phrase that must be changed for the sentence to be correct.

<u>Widely acknowledged</u> as one of <u>the hardiest</u> <u>shrub</u> in the New World, the rhododendron was <u>grown</u> in North America by pioneers settling the land east of the Mississippi River.

Time Help Answer Confirm Next

Click on the one word or phrase that best completes the sentence.

After silver, lead is the _____ found in nature.

○ most malleable element
○ element is most malleable
○ most malleable element that
○ element that most malleable

Time Help Answer Confirm Next

Click on the one word or phrase that best completes the sentence.

Francis Ellen Watkins Harper, because of her incredible writing skill, became known as _____ most influential black abolitionist writers.

- ⬭ who is one
- ⬭ one of the
- ⬭ what the
- ⬭ the only one that

Time Help Answer Confirm Next

Click on the one underlined word or phrase that must be changed for the sentence to be correct.

Of the 180 types of inborn errors of metabolism, the <u>most</u> harmful may cause death in <u>a</u> newborn baby or <u>result severe</u> physical or <u>mental</u> handicap.

Time Help Answer Confirm Next

Click on the one word or phrase that best completes the sentence.

The British Reform Bill of 1867 _____ the electorate by granting the right to vote to common working men.

○ doubling
○ more doubled
○ more than doubled
○ that doubled more

Click on the one underlined word or phrase that must be changed for the sentence to be correct.

Although K-2 is not the <u>most highest</u> peak in the Himalayas, professional climbers consider <u>it</u> the <u>most difficult</u> and dangerous mountain <u>to climb</u>.

Time Help Answer Confirm Next

Click on the one word or phrase that best completes the sentence.

The soybean, a plant native to China and Japan, has become _____ in the United States farming community.

○ one of the most popular crops
○ as one of most popular crops
○ only of the most popular crops
○ one popular crops most are in

Time   ?   Answer   Next
       Help Confirm

Click on the one word or phrase that best completes the sentence.

Dehydration occurs when _____ through perspiration or diarrhea than is replaced by fluid intake.

○ more water it is lost
○ losing more water
○ the loss of more water
○ more water is lost

Time   ?   Answer   Next
       Help Confirm

ANSWER KEY

Practice Subject Questions

1. There are
2. The most significant program
3. The scientific study
4. playwright Oscar Wilde distinguished
5. are diseases diagnosed
6. to discover
7. Many professional athletes gain
8. an earthworm bores
9. It is not easy
10. Drug addiction is
11. it was
12. hunting was probably the quickest
13. Collecting nectar
14. biofeedback programs help patients
15. they have

Practice Verb Questions

1. dates
2. incubate
3. produces
4. prescribes
5. is named
6. synthesize
7. have no
8. container
9. receive
10. disinfection

Practice Noun Questions

1. versatile
2. The discover
3. much
4. their
5. first gained national prominence
6. from bacteria
7. infectious
8. a greater range
9. live
10. structural

Practice Singular and Plural Questions

1. collection
2. area
3. symptom
4. site
5. type
6. formation
7. foot
8. Chameleon
9. whales
10. theory

Practice Article Questions

1. a
2. an
3. a
4. a
5. A
6. is important
7. The archaeology
8. After beginning
9. for
10. many a miles

Practice Pronoun Questions

1. him
2. artist
3. those
4. them
5. its
6. shield surface
7. its
8. of own
9. them
10. who

Practice Appositive Questions

1. a French landscape painter
2. the
3. a more adaptable animal
4. the cultivation of
5. microscopic parasites

Practice Adjective Questions

1. irritation
2. suddenly
3. be accomplished with
4. possibly
5. poison
6. ethnic unrest
7. recently
8. both
9. each of which
10. much
11. another
12. fast enough
13. four-inched
14. often inhabit moist places
15. century sixteenth

Practice Adverbial Questions

1. inaccurate
2. narrowly defeated
3. rather
4. eventual
5. completely by surprise when
6. so
7. easy
8. since
9. heavily
10. rather

Practice Subordination Questions

1. have no use
2. since
3. which portrayed
4. which it
5. what
6. they contain
7. praised
8. certainly
9. for
10. which attaches

Practice Noun Clause Questions

1. when glaciers covered the area
2. eliminating
3. when clouds form on the horizon
4. where
5. are the elements
6. what is perceived
7. what is now Arizona
8. when exposed to air
9. whether the driver
10. they want

Practice Passive/Active Modifier Questions

1. making
2. known
3. was constructed
4. stationed
5. discovering
6. accused
7. acts
8. facing
9. for
10. engineering

Practice Gerund/Infinitive Questions

1. to reducing
2. attending
3. to depend
4. attempt
5. suffering
6. migrating
7. to wait
8. developing
9. spread
10. alteration

Practice Prepositional Phrase Questions

1. toward
2. for
3. in
4. if
5. into
6. drastically
7. into
8. but account of
9. to
10. downward

Practice Conjunction Questions

1. but also
2. and
3. both
4. Despite
5. such as baskets and clothing
6. nor
7. Unlike
8. Because of the
9. to flying
10. of such body parts as

Practice Comparison and Superlative Questions

1. tiny enough
2. more effectively controlled than
3. shrub
4. most malleable element
5. one of the
6. result severe
7. more than doubled
8. most highest
9. one of the most popular crops
10. more water is lost

PART ◆IV

Reading

Reading

THE BASICS

Only the Listening and Structure sections are computer adaptive.

After the 10-minute break that follows the Structure section, you should feel well rested and completely relaxed. The TOEFL CBT Reading section will require all of your remaining brainpower. Luckily, this section is *not* computer adaptive, meaning the difficulty of a question is not based on how you answered the previous questions first. This also means that you can skip questions and go back to them later. Therefore, you will be able to focus on the easier questions and skip the more time-consuming questions, saving them for last. The Reading section contains four or five passages, each 250 to 350 words in length. Each passage is followed by 10 to 13 questions, for a total of approximately 44 to 55 questions. When each new passage appears, it appears by itself, centered on the screen. You will have to click on the "Proceed" button to see the first question. We recommend that you click on "Proceed" as soon as the passage pops up—don't read the entire passage first! We'll explain why later.

Once you've clicked on "Proceed," the passage will come up with the first question. The passages will appear on the left side of the screen and the questions on the right side of the screen, one at a time. ETS makes the Reading section just a little harder by selecting font sizes and passage lengths that will not fit on your screen. This means that you may have to scroll down or up to see the rest of the passage. For the sake of clarity, the examples we have printed in this book show entire passage on one screen. Be aware that most of the passages you will see on the real test will not fit on the screen and will require that you scroll. The computer screen looks something like this:

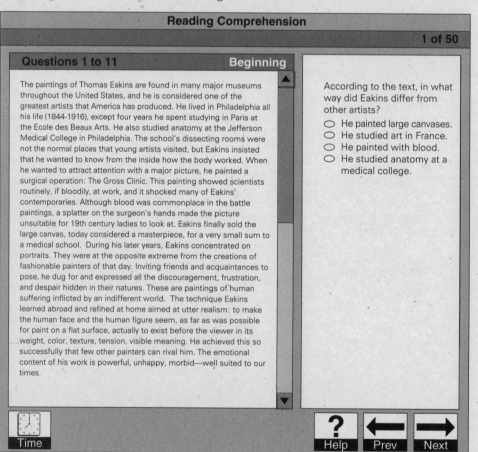

You have 70 to 90 minutes to complete this section. Seventy to 90 minutes seems like a long time, but you will be surprised by how quickly it passes. Fortunately, The Princeton Review has developed several time-saving techniques to help you work as efficiently as possible and make the most of your brainpower and time.

Move through the tutorials as quickly as possible.

THE TUTORIAL

The mandatory tutorial begins by explaining once again how to scroll—that is, how you can see more of the reading passage that isn't on the screen. If you feel comfortable with line scrolling, speed line scrolling, and page scrolling, don't waste your brainpower! Move through the tutorials as quickly as possible. If you think you need extra work on this technique, by all means, review.

Next, the tutorial explains the icons you need to know in order to move from one question to another. In the lower left-hand corner of the computer screen, you will see two icons, "Next" and "Prev." Simply click on the "Next" icon to jump to the next question. Click on the "Prev" icon to jump to the previous question. If at any time you need help, click on the "Help" icon located to the left of the "Prev" icon. Remember, time is running while you are in "Help." Fortunately, you will not need to click on "Help" after completing this book. Find the icons in the example below:

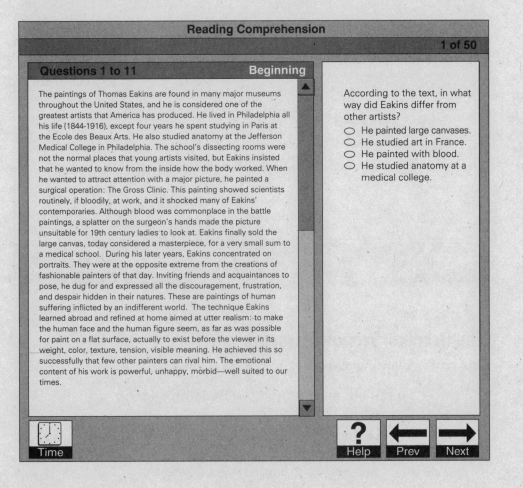

At this point, ETS familiarizes you with the type of questions you will encounter on the Reading section:

- Select one of four choices (just like the paper-and-pencil format)
- Click on a word, phrase, or sentence
- Add a sentence

Once again, work through this part of the tutorial as quickly as possible. You will have already learned how to handle these question types by the time you finish this chapter.

When you are finished with the tutorial, the TOEFL CBT Reading section finally begins. The first thing you can do to save yourself some time and brainpower on this section is learn the directions. As you can see, reading these directions can waste a lot of time! Read them once, before the test, and learn them. A short sample passage and a couple of examples might follow the directions. *Don't read them!* Get straight to work!

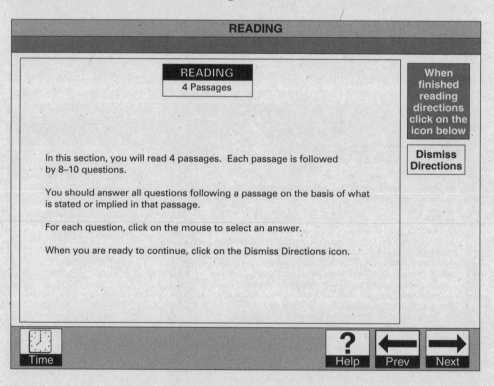

> You should immediately click on the "Dismiss Directions" icon and begin working on the Reading section.

THE READING SECTION PASSAGES

Answer the following question:

Points are awarded on the Reading section of the TOEFL CBT for

(A) reading the passage carefully and understanding every word

(B) answering the questions correctly

Of course the correct answer is (B). Although it seems like a pretty silly question, most test takers approach the Reading section as if they get points just for reading and understanding the passage. When you take the TOEFL CBT, you can bet that a lot of the other students in the room will waste most of their allotted time reading and rereading the passages, trying to comprehend every word. In fact, ETS will instruct you on the computer screen to read the entire passage before clicking on the "Proceed" icon. *Don't read the passage!*

TOEFL CBT reading passages are about science, humanities, and social studies, but they differ from the reading you do in school and for pleasure. They contain *no* information that you want to remember for your career or lifestyle. They only contain the answers to the questions ETS asks you.

TOEFL CBT reading material is carefully edited by ETS personnel, who make sure that all of the reading passages are:

1. **Boring** and difficult to concentrate on. ETS wants boring passages; it is much easier to understand an interesting passage.

2. **Dense**, containing many unimportant details. The answers to the questions are hidden among all the complicated details and perplexing vocabulary. This makes the answers extremely difficult to find.

3. **Poorly constructed**, lacking transitional phrases that make passages clear and easy to understand. This interrupts the flow of the passage and confuses the reader.

Each TOEFL CBT passage can be up to 350 words long. ETS makes sure you don't have enough time to read all of the passages *and* answer all the questions. Believe it or not, even native English speakers find it extremely tough to complete all the passages and comprehend all of the new vocabulary and details. You don't receive any points for reading the passage; **you only get points for correctly answering the question**.

Saving Time = 1-1-1-L

Students who want to score as many points as possible use the proven time saving technique **1-1-1-L**. Instead of reading the entire passage, you should only read:

> 1— the first sentence of the **first** paragraph.
>
> 1— the first sentence of the **second** paragraph.
>
> 1— the first sentence of **each remaining** paragraph.
>
> L— the last sentence of the **last** paragraph.

Let's try it. Practice the above 1-1-1-L concept with the following example. Read the first sentence of each paragraph, and the last sentence of the last paragraph.

If you try to read the entire passage as ETS suggests, you will *not* be able to finish the test.

During the TOEFL CBT, you will have to scroll down to read the first sentences of the final few paragraphs.

Beginning

Despite the fact that too much fat can be harmful, a moderate fat intake is actually essential for the maintenance of good health. Some of the symptoms of fat deficiency include flaking skin, emaciation, reduced functioning of the immune system, and fertility problems. Recent studies have not only linked fat-free diets to an increase in stress and aggression, but also to a dramatic rise in eating disorders such as anorexia and bulimia. The consumption of fat indirectly decreases the total amount of food intake by producing a feeling of satiety that lasts much longer than the sensation of fullness produced by protein or carbohydrates.

Nutritionally, fat is valued as a source of energy. It contains much less oxygen than other nutrients and subsequently releases an enormous amount of energy due to its rapid oxidation. Medical experts recommend that at least two teaspoons of fat per day be consumed. Any less seriously inhibits the digestive system from absorbing fat-soluble vitamins such as A, D, E, and K, all of which play an essential role for having healthy hair, skin, teeth, and eyes. Children and adults both require these fat-soluble vitamins, without which physical developmental disorders and infertility occur respectively.

There are several theories to explain the method of fat absorption. One such theory holds that the epithelial cells in the lining of the small intestine directly absorb fat. Once the fat is broken down into glycerol, the fat is then indirectly absorbed into the lymphatic system or directly into the blood stream. Medical research indicates the possibility that saturated fats, like those found in red meat, dairy products, and tropical oils, actually raise the level of cholesterol that builds up as plaque on arterial walls and eventually contributes to the incidence of arteriosclerosis. However, some types of fat actually help to reduce harmful cholesterol levels. **Polyunsaturated fats such as corn, soybean, and sesame oil, and monounsaturated fats like chicken fat and olive oil, contribute to a lower blood cholesterol count.**

Time   **?** Help   ← Prev   → Next

Congratulations! You just saved yourself approximately 5 minutes of valuable time. Remember, the TOEFL CBT passages are filled with so many poorly constructed sentences, unnecessary details, and strange vocabulary that most of them are incomprehensible. Don't waste time reading the passage. You do not receive any points for reading the passage. You only get points for answering the questions.

After using the "1-1-1-L" technique, you should have some idea as to what the main idea of the passage is about. Go back to the previous bold sentences in the passage and circle the words that keep reappearing in the sentences you just read and then answer the following questions. Look for the correct answers at the end of this chapter.

Drill 1

1. What subject keeps reoccurring in the sentences? _____

2. How many times does it appear?_____

3. What do you think the main topic of the passage is and what does the author say about it? _____

Identifying the main topic of the passage not only helps you focus on what the questions are most likely going to be about, but it also better prepares you to click on the correct answers. In addition, as you answer the questions, you will gradually learn more and more about the topic of the passage. The key is to indirectly read the passage as you are hunting for the answers to the questions.

You indirectly read the passage as you answer the questions!

THE QUESTIONS

Now that you have some idea of what the passage is about, it is time to tackle the questions. You want to approach the questions as efficiently as possible. The most important thing you want to remember is that *all questions are created equal!* Each question is worth *one* point. You get just as many points for answering an easy question as you do a difficult one. Therefore, the precious time that you have is best spent working on the easier questions first. Difficult questions take much more time. *Reminder:* The Reading section is *linear*. This means that the questions do not disappear forever once you have answered them. You can skip the hard questions and return to answer them later.

Answer the easy questions first!

The first crucial step you need to take is to learn how to distinguish the easy questions from the hard ones.

There are three types of questions in Reading section:

Easy Questions: We'll call these questions "first-pass questions."

Medium Questions: We'll call these questions "second-pass questions."

Difficult Questions: We'll call these questions "third-pass questions."

Here, "pass" means to systematically work through or pass through the passage. As the various question types are introduced, we'll tell you which ones to do the first time you pass through the passage, the second time you pass through the passage, and the third time you pass through the passage.

There are basically nine (yes, nine) different types of questions in the TOEFL CBT Reading section. By labeling each TOEFL CBT question as first-pass (easy), second-pass (medium), or third-pass (difficult), you will be able to work more confidently and the correct answers will be easier to anticipate. Study the diagram below to see the different question types.

First-Pass Questions	Second-Pass Questions	Third-Pass Questions
Vocabulary Questions	Main Idea Questions	Infer/Imply Questions
Reference Questions	Conclusion Questions	Except/Not Questions
Detail Questions	Click on Sentence Questions	Black Square Questions

Categorizing all the different questions makes them less threatening. You will now be able to make some sense out of all the confusion. We will introduce, explain, and teach you specific strategy for each question type.

CHRONOLOGICAL ORDER

An essential strategy for the TOEFL CBT is chronological order. ETS arranges all the questions in the order in which they appear in the text. Always remember where you found the answer to the previous question to help you locate the next question. In other words, the answer to question 5 will be found in the text after the line where you found the answer to question 4. This time-saving strategy will drastically reduce the time you spend searching for the answer to the questions, and give you more time to click on the correct answer.

PACING

THE PASSAGES

There is no penalty for guessing!

Pacing is crucial when you are taking the TOEFL CBT. You want to avoid going too fast or too slow. ETS arranges the passages in a loose order of progressive difficulty. The writing, the vocabulary, and the syntax of the questions and answers tend to be more complex in the *last* passage than in the *first*. Due to this progression, it is logical to start at the beginning of the Reading section, answer the easy questions first, and save the more difficult questions for later.

Begin with the first passage, and answer the first-pass questions first, the second pass questions second, and then the third-pass questions third. Then continue to the second, third, and fourth passages and do the same thing. If at any time a question seems too difficult and is taking too much time, you can either skip it and come back at the very end of the test, or use POE, guess, and go on. But remember, *you have to pick an answer for every question.*

The information you learn from the passage as you answer the first-pass questions will make it easier to answer the second-pass questions. Likewise, the information you learn from the passage as you answer the first- and second-pass questions will make it easier to answer the third-pass questions.

It will take a lot of mouse clicking to become familiar with skipping some questions, and answering others. However, with practice, it will get easier.

If you try to answer the questions in the order ETS gives them, you will **NOT** be able to finish the test

Study the following flow-chart to fully understand the best way to attack the Reading section as a whole. Remember that you should always complete all of the questions for any given passage before moving on to the next passage. Also, please note that you may see five passages. If that is the case, follow the same procedure on the fifth passage that you did on the first four.

EASY ——————————→ MEDIUM ——————————→ DIFFICULT

Passage 1	Passage 2	Passage 3	Passage 4
STEP ONE	STEP ONE	STEP ONE	STEP ONE
1-1-1-L	1-1-1-L	1-1-1-L	1-1-1-L
STEP TWO	STEP TWO	STEP TWO	STEP TWO
1st pass questions	1st pass questions	1st pass questions	1st pass questions
STEP THREE	STEP THREE	STEP THREE	STEP THREE
2nd pass questions	2nd pass questions	2nd pass questions	2nd pass questions
STEP FOUR	STEP FOUR	STEP FOUR	STEP FOUR
3rd pass questions	3rd pass questions	3rd pass questions	3rd pass questions
STEP FIVE	STEP FIVE	STEP FIVE	STEP FIVE
Go to the next passage	Go to the next passage	Go to the next passage	Check work

Answer the first pass questions in the order in which they appear!

(Note: There may be as many as five passages. If so, just keep following this technique.)

FIRST-PASS QUESTIONS

- **Vocabulary in context (VIC) questions:** ask you for the meaning of a specific word in the passage.

- **Reference questions:** ask you what a specific pronoun or noun in the passage refers to.

- **Detail questions:** ask for a specific piece of information found in the passage.

First-pass questions are considered the easiest questions on the TOEFL CBT. They are easy to locate and take the least amount of time to answer. More than half of the questions on the TOEFL CBT will be first-pass. Immediately after using the 1-1-1-L technique, make your best effort to answer all the following first-pass questions in the order in which they come.

Vocabulary in Context

For VIC questions, you want to select the best synonym for a specific word or phrase in the passage. In other words, a VIC question is about the *definition* of a word. Look at the example on the following page.

Look for other vocabulary words in the surrounding sentences that function as clues.

Beginning

All animal life on the planet Earth depends on a sufficient supply of oxygen for its day-to-day survival. The trees that now just sporadically dot our landscapes, but once heavily **blanketed** the earth's surface, still are able to provide a large portion of the oxygen supply. Through a process of photosynthesis, trees take in carbon dioxide from the surrounding air and in return create a sizeable amount of oxygen. Ironically, human beings, who cut down large numbers of trees to create land, shelter, and energy, pose the most significant threat to the survival of the worldwide tree population.

But humans are not the only force that threatens the survival of these mighty members of the plant kingdom. Lightning, fire, volcanoes, and earthquakes occur without warning and not only rapidly destroy many square miles of old-growth forest in a matter of hours, but may also permanently prevent new trees from growing. Likewise, disease-causing fungi and insect pests can either eradicate certain types of trees or seriously weaken their branches.

After humans, however, the factor which most determines whether a particular species of tree will prosper in a given area is climate. In particular, the amount of rainfall and the range of temperatures that a region experiences strongly affect the distribution of tree species.

All species of trees have evolved from plants that flourished many centuries ago in the warm and wet tropical regions of the planet. As the distribution of trees has spread to other regions, the differing climates of these regions have effectively limited the types of trees that can live there. The greater the range of temperature and rainfall that a certain specie of tree can withstand, the more adaptable it is and therefore the wider the range of distribution.

Look at the word highlighted in the text. Click on the answer choice that is closest in meaning to the word **blanketed**
○ decorated
○ hid
○ warmed
○ covered

Time | Help | Prev | Next

Whenever you see a vocabulary in context question, you'll need to read *two* sentences: the one in which the word is contained, and the one that comes before it. Quickly focusing on other vocabulary within the two sentences will help you to determine the tone of the sentences. Understanding the tone will help you to comprehend the context. ETS will try to trick you by giving the literal definition of the word in the answer choices. In some questions the literal definition will be the correct answer. In other questions, however, a secondary definition is used. You might need to look for a second sense of the word. Here, you might know that the noun "blanket" is what you put on your bed. However, as a verb, it might have a different meaning. Focus on the other vocabulary words to help you avoid ETS's tricks and traps. In this example, focus on the vocabulary "sufficient" and "heavily." These words indicate a sense of adequacy and quantity. Also, the words "sporadically dot" in the same sentence give a sense of the opposite meaning to the words "heavily blanketed." Be sure to keep all these helpful context techniques in mind as you approach VIC questions.

The best approach to ensure that you choose the correct answer choice is to find your own word for the VIC word and then match it to the answer choice synonym. Follow these steps:

1. Read the sentence containing the VIC word and the sentence directly before it.

2. Think of your own word to substitute for the VIC word.

    *   Use the rest of the sentence to come up with something that logically fits.

    *   The word does not have to be fancy; meaning is what really matters.

    *   It can even be a word in your native language, as long as the meaning is right.

3. Go through the answer choices one by one, comparing them to your word.

4. Eliminate any choice that doesn't mean the same thing as your word.

5. Select the best answer from the remaining choices and move on.

Focusing on the word that should go into the sentence as a synonym for the VIC word prevents you from being distracted by the answer choices. Since you already know what word you're looking for before you even look at the answer choices, ETS's trap answers won't have any effect on you.

Let's take a look at this example. The sentence says that the trees now "sporadically dot" the landscape, but that it used to be different before. That means that a good word to fill in the blank would be an opposite of "sporadically dot," such as "covered."

Now let's go to the answer choices:

*   "Decorated" doesn't mean "covered." Eliminate it.

*   "Hid" could kind of mean "covered," but not really. Don't eliminate it until we find something better.

*   "Warmed" doesn't mean "covered." Eliminate it.

*   "Covered" obviously means "covered." This answer choice is much better that "hid," so eliminate "hid" and click on "covered."

Sometimes, the word you fill in for the VIC word will be one of the answer choices. Sometimes it won't be. Either way, this technique allows you to zero in on the correct answer choice with the fewest distractors.

Summary of the VIC strategy:

Step 1: Read the sentence in which the VIC word is contained as well as the sentence before it.

Step 2: Come up with a word of your own to substitute for the VIC word. Use the sentence to help you determine what a good word would be.

Step 3: Go through the answer choices one by one, comparing them to the word you came up with.

Step 4: Eliminate the three answer choices that aren't synonyms of your word.

Step 5: If more than one answer choice remains, click on the best one and move on.

Vocabulary in Context (Part 2)

In the TOEFL CBT, ETS has another method of testing VIC words. On the left side of the computer screen, you will see several sentences in bold text with the VIC word being tested highlighted. On the right side of the screen you will see a question similar to the following:

Look at the word greedy in the passage. Click on the word or phrase in the bold text that has the same meaning.

Rather than clicking on one of the four answer choices that ETS has provided, you must click on the word that "greedy" is synonymous (the same) or antonymous (the opposite) to in the bold text. Be careful! There are many "distractor" answer choices in these types of questions.

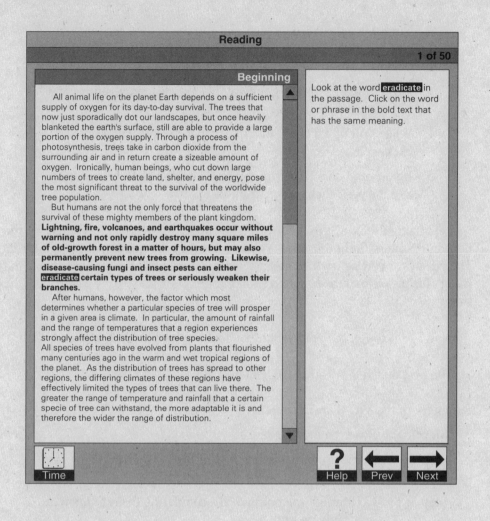

Beginning

All animal life on the planet Earth depends on a sufficient supply of oxygen for its day-to-day survival. The trees that now just sporadically dot our landscapes, but once heavily blanketed the earth's surface, still are able to provide a large portion of the oxygen supply. Through a process of photosynthesis, trees take in carbon dioxide from the surrounding air and in return create a sizeable amount of oxygen. Ironically, human beings, who cut down large numbers of trees to create land, shelter, and energy, pose the most significant threat to the survival of the worldwide tree population.

But humans are not the only force that threatens the survival of these mighty members of the plant kingdom. **Lightning, fire, volcanoes, and earthquakes occur without warning and not only rapidly destroy many square miles of old-growth forest in a matter of hours, but may also permanently prevent new trees from growing. Likewise, disease-causing fungi and insect pests can either eradicate certain types of trees or seriously weaken their branches.**

After humans, however, the factor which most determines whether a particular species of tree will prosper in a given area is climate. In particular, the amount of rainfall and the range of temperatures that a region experiences strongly affect the distribution of tree species.

All species of trees have evolved from plants that flourished many centuries ago in the warm and wet tropical regions of the planet. As the distribution of trees has spread to other regions, the differing climates of these regions have effectively limited the types of trees that can live there. The greater the range of temperature and rainfall that a certain specie of tree can withstand, the more adaptable it is and therefore the wider the range of distribution.

Look at the word eradicate in the passage. Click on the word or phrase in the bold text that has the same meaning.

Time

Help   Prev   Next

The strategies for this type of VIC question are similar to those for the first type of VIC question. First of all, since the answer is in the bold text, read the sentences that appear in bold and locate the VIC word. Once you've found it, follow the same steps you followed before:

1. Read the sentences in the passage that appear in bold and locate the VIC word.

2. Think of your own word to substitute for the VIC word.

    •   Use the rest of the sentence to come up with something that logically fits.

    •   The word does not have to be fancy; meaning is what really matters.

    •   It can even be a word in your native language, as long as the meaning is right.

3. Compare your word to each word in the bolded section, one word at a time, looking for the word that does what the question asks (meaning the same or opposite).

   • Eliminate words right away like articles, prepositions and other words that are the wrong part of speech

4. When you find a word that does what the question asks for, click on it.

5. If you can't eliminate three answer choices, pick the one you like the best, click on it and move on.

Let's take a look at this example. The first bold sentence says that all the natural disasters (lightning, fire, volcanoes, and earthquakes) destroy forests. Then it says "likewise" (which means "in the same way") the fungi eradicate the trees. This means that the fungi do something in the same way — they "kill" the trees.

Now, go through the bold sentences, looking for a word that means "kill."

The best match is "destroy." Click on it.

Summary of the VIC (Part 2) strategy:

You will encounter 2 or 3 VIC questions in the Reading section.

Step 1:	Read the bold sentences.
Step 2:	Come up with a word of your own to substitute for the VIC word.
Step 3:	Go through the bold words, comparing them to the word you came up with.
Step 4:	Click on the word that best matches the meaning of your word.
Step 5:	If two words are similar to your word, click on the one you like best and move on.

Reference Questions

In the TOEFL CBT, reference questions ask you to determine what a pronoun or noun refers to. On the left side of the computer screen, you will see several sentences in bold text with the VIC reference word being tested highlighted. On the right side of the screen you will see a question similar to the following:

Look at the word **one** in the passage. Click on the word or phrase in the bold text that this word refers to.

Using your mouse, click on the noun in the bold text that the reference word is synonymous with. Although you have more than just four choices, the answer is in the bold text. Reference questions are easy to spot. Simply look for the questions that use the word "refer." Look at the following example:

For reference questions, the answer is in the bold text.

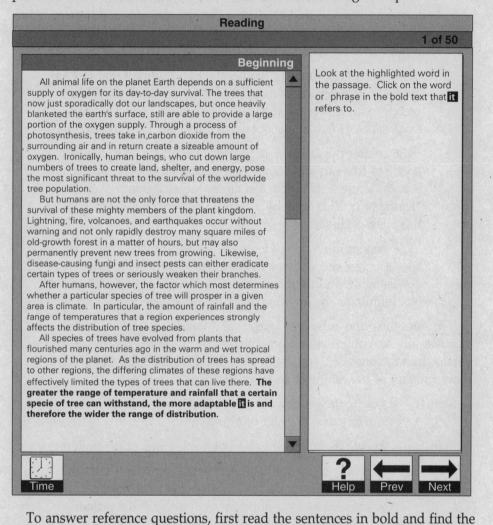

To answer reference questions, first read the sentences in bold and find the pronoun or noun being tested. Determine if the reference word is plural or singular. In this case, "it" is singular. Search for other singular nouns in the bold text. How many do you find?

The other singular nouns are:

- range of temperature
- specie of tree
- rainfall
- range of distribution

There are four possibilities. Mentally cross out the pronoun and plug the other singular nouns into the sentence to see if the sentence makes sense.

- "The greater the range of temperature and rainfall that a certain specie of tree can withstand, the more adaptable *the range of temperature* is and therefore the wider the range of distribution." No. This doesn't make sense. "The range of temperature" cannot adapt. Eliminate this answer choice.

- "The greater the range of temperature and rainfall that a certain specie of tree can withstand, the more adaptable *rainfall* is and therefore the wider the range of distribution." No. This doesn't make sense. "Rainfall" cannot adapt. Eliminate this answer choice.

- "The greater the range of temperature and rainfall that a certain specie of tree can withstand, the more adaptable *the specie of tree* is and therefore the wider the range of distribution." Yes. A "specie of tree" is adaptable and can be distributed. Click on this answer choice.

- "The greater the range of temperature and rainfall that a certain specie of tree can withstand, the more adaptable *the range of distribution* is and therefore the wider the range of distribution." No. Eliminate any answer choice that illogically repeats itself.

VIC questions and reference questions should take you no more than 30 seconds to do. As you practice, you will get faster! If the questions take longer than one minute, guess and go on, or save them for the third pass.

In summary of the reference question strategy:

A pronoun must agree in number and gender with the noun to which it refers.

Step 1: Locate the pronoun in the bold passage and determine if it refers to a singular or plural noun.

Step 2: Locate the other singular or plural nouns in the bold text.

Step 3: Mentally cross out the pronoun and replace it with the other possible noun choices and read the complete sentence. Does the noun correctly replace the pronoun?

Step 4: Using POE, eliminate answer choices that don't make sense or aren't consistent with the surrounding sentences and click on the best possible answer choice.

Detail Questions

Detail questions ask you for specific facts contained in the passage. You'll need to read the question to see what information is required, then go to the passage to find it. There are at least two detail questions for each passage. Although detail questions are phrased in various ways, the strategy to finding the answer is the same: Use chronological order and "lead words."

Lead Words

The best way to find the answers to detail questions is by using "lead words" together with chronological order. The lead word is the most specific word or phrase in the question. It tells you what the question is about, which in turn tells you where to look in the passage. Lead words are often nouns or noun phrases, and tend to be mentioned only once in the passage. Once you locate the lead word, simply scan the passage in order to locate it. The answer to the question will be near the location of the lead word.

Some hints for identifying lead words:

1. It's all right to be looking for more than one word, but more than three words is too many.

2. Words with capital letters, numbers, and abbreviations are particularly easy to spot in a passage (for example, 1776, Warren G. Harding, UNICEF, and so forth).

3. If the question itself doesn't have any lead words, check out the answers. They might contain words or numbers that contain great lead words.

Chronological Order

Earlier in the chapter we mentioned that you should think of the Reading section as an open-book test. The answers to all of the questions exist right there in the passage in front of you. Furthermore, the location of any particular answer within the passage is often indicated by where the question falls within the group of questions for that passage. The answers to the first question or two will be early in the passage. The answers to subsequent questions will follow, generally in order.

On detail questions you can easily use this knowledge to increase your efficiency and save a little time. Once you select a lead word from the question, go back to the passage to find that lead word. Start looking right after the spot in the passage where you found the answer to the previous question. The information you need to answer the question will usually appear within a few lines of the lead word. After you have found the information, put the answer into your own words. Next, go to the answer choices and click on the one that best paraphrases your answer. A paraphrase is simply a restatement of the same information in other words. Just as we did in VIC questions, if you go to the answer choices armed with what you think is the correct answer, you will be less likely to fall for a "distractor" answer put there by ETS to attract your attention.

In summary of the detail question strategy:

Step 1:   Read the question and identify the lead word.

Step 2:   Using chronological order, look for the lead word in the passage.

Step 3:   Once the lead word has been located, read the sentence in which it is contained.

Step 4:   If you've found the answer to the question, click on the answer choice that is closest to the answer you found in the passage.

Step 5:   If you haven't found the information in the text, and you think you might have chosen a poor lead word, try a different one. However, if you think you have chosen a good lead word, the question is probably very difficult. Save it for the third pass, or guess and move on.

Drill 2

Directions: Circle the lead words in the sample questions below. Answers to these questions can be found at the end of this chapter.

1. According to the passage, vitamin C can be found in . . .

2. Why was Rosa Parks arrested in 1955?

3. The "wings" of the manta ray are used for . . .

4. President Bush's committee is mentioned as an example of a bipartisan group that . . .

5. According to the passage, why was Karl XII of Sweden considered not typical of Swedish kings?

6. As described in the passage, the function of the legislative branch of the United States government is . . .

7. Why are snapping turtles in danger of becoming extinct?

8. Which of the following is most likely to cause a sudden climatic change?

Summary of first-pass question techniques:

1. After **1-1-1-L**, go to the first question. If it is a first pass type, do it. If not, skip it and come back to it later.

2. **VIC**—Put your own word in for the VIC word, then look for an answer choice that means the same thing.

3. **VIC II**—Come up with your own word for the VIC II word using the rest of the sentence in which it appears. Compare your word to every other word in the bolded paragraph until you find the one does what the question asks (meaning the same or opposite).

4. **Reference**—Locate the nouns in the bolded section. Replace them with the pronoun indicated in the question until you find one that matches in both number and gender.

5. **Detail**—Take lead words from the question or answer choices back to the passage to find the location of the correct answer. Chronological order will help you to start in the right place.

6. Use rigorous **POE** to eliminate as many answer choices as possible. Guess if you have to and move on.

Drill 3

Use all the strategies you have learned so far to answer the first-pass questions about the passage. Click on (in this case circle) the best answer. Answers to these questions can be found at the end of this chapter.

Questions 1 to 8   **Beginning**

Without regular supplies of some hormones, the human capacity to behave would be seriously impaired. The absence of others would cause immediate death. The most abundant hormones act to modify moods and affect actions. The most **minute** amounts of hormones can suppress appetite, alter aggressive or submissive attitudes, and change reproductive and parental behavior. Early in life, hormones accelerate the development of bodily form and may even define an individual's personality characteristics. Later in life, the changing hormonal outputs of some endocrine glands and the body's changing sensitivity to them bolster immunity and hasten the aging phenomena.

Up to the beginning of the present century, communication within the body and the consequent integration of behavior were considered the primary province of the nervous system. The emergence of endocrinology as a separate discipline can be traced to the experiments of Dr. William Bayliss and Dr. Ernest Starling on the hormone secretin, which is secreted from cells in the intestinal walls when food enters the stomach. It then travels through the bloodstream and stimulates the pancreas to liberate digestive fluid. By stimulating these special stomach cells to secrete hormones that in turn regulate distant target organs and tissues, Bayliss and Starling demonstrated that chemical integration could occur without the participation of the nervous system.

The term hormone was first used with reference to secretin. Starling derived the term from the Greek word hormon, meaning to excite or set in motion. The term endocrine was introduced shortly thereafter. Endocrine is used to refer to glands that secrete products directly into the bloodstream such as the pancreas, thyroid, and pituitary glands. Because the lack of any one of them may cause serious disorders, many hormones are now produced synthetically and used in treatment where a deficiency exists. Insects also have a unique hormone ecdysone. Much like steroids stimulate muscle formation in humans, ecdysone strengthens the exoskeleton of insects while they metamorphose into the adult stage. Plants rely on a variety of hormones such as auxin, gibberellin, and cytokinin that assist in flower, tuber, bulb, and bud formation. Ethylene, a synthetic hormone used by horticulturists, is believed to accelerate the ripening of fruit.

Look at the word highlighted in the text. Click on the answer choice that is closest in meaning to the word **minute**.

○ beneficial
○ tiny
○ predetermined
○ short

Time

? Help   ← Prev   → Next

Questions 1 to 8   Beginning

   Without regular supplies of some hormones, the human capacity to behave would be seriously impaired. The absence of others would cause immediate death. The most abundant hormones act to modify moods and affect actions. The most minute amounts of hormones can suppress appetite, alter aggressive or submissive attitudes, and change reproductive and parental behavior. **Early in life, hormones accelerate the development of bodily form and may even define an individual's personality characteristics. Later in life, the changing hormonal outputs of some endocrine glands and the body's changing sensitivity to them bolster immunity and hasten the aging phenomena.**

   Up to the beginning of the present century, communication within the body and the consequent integration of behavior were considered the primary province of the nervous system. The emergence of endocrinology as a separate discipline can be traced to the experiments of Dr. William Bayliss and Dr. Ernest Starling on the hormone secretin, which is secreted from cells in the intestinal walls when food enters the stomach. It then travels through the bloodstream and stimulates the pancreas to liberate digestive fluid. By stimulating these special stomach cells to secrete hormones that in turn regulate distant target organs and tissues, Bayliss and Starling demonstrated that chemical integration could occur without the participation of the nervous system.

   The term hormone was first used with reference to secretin. Starling derived the term from the Greek word hormon, meaning to excite or set in motion. The term endocrine was introduced shortly thereafter. Endocrine is used to refer to glands that secrete products directly into the bloodstream such as the pancreas, thyroid, and pituitary glands. Because the lack of any one of them may cause serious disorders, many hormones are now produced synthetically and used in treatment where a deficiency exists. Insects also have a unique hormone ecdysone. Much like steroids stimulate muscle formation in humans, ecdysone strengthens the exoskeleton of insects while they metamorphose into the adult stage. Plants rely on a variety of hormones such as auxin, gibberellin, and cytokinin that assist in flower, tuber, bulb, and bud formation. Ethylene, a synthetic hormone used by horticulturists, is believed to accelerate the ripening of fruit.

Look at the word **hasten** in the passage. Click on the word or phrase in the bold text closest in meaning to **hasten**.

Time

Help   Prev   Next

Questions 1 to 8 — Beginning

Without regular supplies of some hormones, the human capacity to behave would be seriously impaired. The absence of others would cause immediate death. The most abundant hormones act to modify moods and affect actions. The most minute amounts of hormones can suppress appetite, alter aggressive or submissive attitudes, and change reproductive and parental behavior. Early in life, hormones accelerate the development of bodily form and may even define an individual's personality characteristics. Later in life, the changing hormonal outputs of some endocrine glands and the body's changing sensitivity to them bolster immunity and hasten the aging phenomena.

Up to the beginning of the present century, communication within the body and the consequent integration of behavior were considered the primary province of the nervous system. The emergence of endocrinology as a separate discipline can be traced to the experiments of Dr. William Bayliss and Dr. Ernest Starling on the hormone secretin, which is secreted from cells in the intestinal walls when food enters the stomach. It then travels through the bloodstream and stimulates the pancreas to liberate digestive fluid. By stimulating these special stomach cells to secrete hormones that in turn regulate distant target organs and tissues, Bayliss and Starling demonstrated that chemical integration could occur without the participation of the nervous system.

The term hormone was first used with reference to secretin. Starling derived the term from the Greek word hormon, meaning to excite or set in motion. The term endocrine was introduced shortly thereafter. Endocrine is used to refer to glands that secrete products directly into the bloodstream such as the pancreas, thyroid, and pituitary glands. Because the lack of any one of them may cause serious disorders, many hormones are now produced synthetically and used in treatment where a deficiency exists. Insects also have a unique hormone ecdysone. Much like steroids stimulate muscle formation in humans, ecdysone strengthens the exoskeleton of insects while they metamorphose into the adult stage. Plants rely on a variety of hormones such as auxin, gibberellin, and cytokinin that assist in flower, tuber, bulb, and bud formation. Ethylene, a synthetic hormone used by horticulturists, is believed to accelerate the ripening of fruit.

According to the passage, which of the following was believed prior to the experiments led by Dr. Bayliss and Dr. Starling?

○ Bodily behavior was controlled exclusively by the nervous system.
○ The endocrine glands stimulated chemical integration.
○ Intestinal glands regulated hormones.
○ Endocrinology was limited to stimulating the aging phenomena.

Time

Questions 1 to 8 — Beginning

Without regular supplies of some hormones, the human capacity to behave would be seriously impaired. The absence of others would cause immediate death. The most abundant hormones act to modify moods and affect actions. The most minute amounts of hormones can suppress appetite, alter aggressive or submissive attitudes, and change reproductive and parental behavior. Early in life, hormones accelerate the development of bodily form and may even define an individual's personality characteristics. Later in life, the changing hormonal outputs of some endocrine glands and the body's changing sensitivity to them bolster immunity and hasten the aging phenomena.

Up to the beginning of the present century, communication within the body and the consequent integration of behavior were considered the primary province of the nervous system. **The emergence of endocrinology as a separate discipline can be traced to the experiments of Dr. William Bayliss and Dr. Ernest Starling on the hormone secretin, which is secreted from cells in the intestinal walls when food enters the stomach. It then travels through the bloodstream and stimulates the pancreas to liberate digestive fluid.** By stimulating these special stomach cells to secrete hormones that in turn regulate distant target organs and tissues, Bayliss and Starling demonstrated that chemical integration could occur without the participation of the nervous system.

The term hormone was first used with reference to secretin. Starling derived the term from the Greek word hormon, meaning to excite or set in motion. The term endocrine was introduced shortly thereafter. Endocrine is used to refer to glands that secrete products directly into the bloodstream such as the pancreas, thyroid, and pituitary glands. Because the lack of any one of them may cause serious disorders, many hormones are now produced synthetically and used in treatment where a deficiency exists. Insects also have a unique hormone ecdysone. Much like steroids stimulate muscle formation in humans, ecdysone strengthens the exoskeleton of insects while they metamorphose into the adult stage. Plants rely on a variety of hormones such as auxin, gibberellin, and cytokinin that assist in flower, tuber, bulb, and bud formation. Ethylene, a synthetic hormone used by horticulturists, is believed to accelerate the ripening of fruit.

Look at the highlighted word in the passage. Click on the word or phrase in the bold text that **it** refers to.

Questions 1 to 8 | Beginning

Without regular supplies of some hormones, the human capacity to behave would be seriously impaired. The absence of others would cause immediate death. The most abundant hormones act to modify moods and affect actions. The most minute amounts of hormones can suppress appetite, alter aggressive or submissive attitudes, and change reproductive and parental behavior. Early in life, hormones accelerate the development of bodily form and may even define an individual's personality characteristics. Later in life, the changing hormonal outputs of some endocrine glands and the body's changing sensitivity to them bolster immunity and hasten the aging phenomena.

Up to the beginning of the present century, communication within the body and the consequent integration of behavior were considered the primary province of the nervous system. The emergence of endocrinology as a separate discipline can be traced to the experiments of Dr. William Bayliss and Dr. Ernest Starling on the hormone secretin, which is secreted from cells in the intestinal walls when food enters the stomach. It then travels through the bloodstream and stimulates the pancreas to liberate digestive fluid. By stimulating these special stomach cells to secrete hormones that in turn regulate distant target organs and tissues, Bayliss and Starling demonstrated that chemical integration could occur without the participation of the nervous system.

The term hormone was first used with reference to secretin. Starling derived the term from the Greek word hormon, meaning to excite or set in motion. The term endocrine was introduced shortly thereafter. Endocrine is used to refer to glands that secrete products directly into the bloodstream such as the pancreas, thyroid, and pituitary glands. Because the lack of any one of them may cause serious disorders, many hormones are now produced synthetically and used in treatment where a deficiency exists. Insects also have a unique hormone ecdysone. Much like steroids stimulate muscle formation in humans, ecdysone strengthens the exoskeleton of insects while they metamorphose into the adult stage. Plants rely on a variety of hormones such as auxin, gibberellin, and cytokinin that assist in flower, tuber, bulb, and bud formation. Ethylene, a synthetic hormone used by horticulturists, is believed to accelerate the ripening of fruit.

What could Bayliss and Starling conclude after their experiments on hormone secretion?

○ Hormones can be digested.
○ Certain hormones are dangerous to organs and tissues.
○ Only the stomach can secrete hormones.
○ Chemical integration is not entirely dependent on the nervous system.

Time

? Help

← Prev

→ Next

Questions 1 to 8 — Beginning

Without regular supplies of some hormones, the human capacity to behave would be seriously impaired. The absence of others would cause immediate death. The most abundant hormones act to modify moods and affect actions. The most minute amounts of hormones can suppress appetite, alter aggressive or submissive attitudes, and change reproductive and parental behavior. Early in life, hormones accelerate the development of bodily form and may even define an individual's personality characteristics. Later in life, the changing hormonal outputs of some endocrine glands and the body's changing sensitivity to them bolster immunity and hasten the aging phenomena.

Up to the beginning of the present century, communication within the body and the consequent integration of behavior were considered the primary province of the nervous system. The emergence of endocrinology as a separate discipline can be traced to the experiments of Dr. William Bayliss and Dr. Ernest Starling on the hormone secretin, which is secreted from cells in the intestinal walls when food enters the stomach. It then travels through the bloodstream and stimulates the pancreas to liberate digestive fluid. By stimulating these special stomach cells to secrete hormones that in turn regulate distant target organs and tissues, Bayliss and Starling demonstrated that chemical integration could occur without the participation of the nervous system.

The term hormone was first used with reference to secretin. Starling derived the term from the Greek word hormon, meaning to excite or set in motion. The term endocrine was introduced shortly thereafter. Endocrine is used to refer to glands that secrete products directly into the bloodstream such as the pancreas, thyroid, and pituitary glands. Because the **lack** of any one of them may cause serious disorders, many hormones are now produced synthetically and used in treatment where a deficiency exists. Insects also have a unique hormone ecdysone. Much like steroids stimulate muscle formation in humans, ecdysone strengthens the exoskeleton of insects while they metamorphose into the adult stage. Plants rely on a variety of hormones such as auxin, gibberellin, and cytokinin that assist in flower, tuber, bulb, and bud formation. Ethylene, a synthetic hormone used by horticulturists, is believed to accelerate the ripening of fruit.

Look at the word highlighted in the text. Click on the answer choice that is closest in meaning to the word **lack**.

- ○ abuse
- ○ excess
- ○ injury
- ○ absence

Time

Help   Prev   Next

Questions 1 to 8 — Beginning

Without regular supplies of some hormones, the human capacity to behave would be seriously impaired. The absence of others would cause immediate death. The most abundant hormones act to modify moods and affect actions. The most minute amounts of hormones can suppress appetite, alter aggressive or submissive attitudes, and change reproductive and parental behavior. Early in life, hormones accelerate the development of bodily form and may even define an individual's personality characteristics. Later in life, the changing hormonal outputs of some endocrine glands and the body's changing sensitivity to them bolster immunity and hasten the aging phenomena.

Up to the beginning of the present century, communication within the body and the consequent integration of behavior were considered the primary province of the nervous system. The emergence of endocrinology as a separate discipline can be traced to the experiments of Dr. William Bayliss and Dr. Ernest Starling on the hormone secretin, which is secreted from cells in the intestinal walls when food enters the stomach. It then travels through the bloodstream and stimulates the pancreas to liberate digestive fluid. By stimulating these special stomach cells to secrete hormones that in turn regulate distant target organs and tissues, Bayliss and Starling demonstrated that chemical integration could occur without the participation of the nervous system.

The term hormone was first used with reference to secretin. Starling derived the term from the Greek word hormon, meaning to excite or set in motion. The term endocrine was introduced shortly thereafter. Endocrine is used to refer to glands that secrete products directly into the bloodstream such as the pancreas, thyroid, and pituitary glands. Because the lack of any one of them may cause serious disorders, many hormones are now produced synthetically and used in treatment where a deficiency exists. Insects also have a unique hormone ecdysone. Much like steroids stimulate muscle formation in humans, ecdysone strengthens the exoskeleton of insects while they metamorphose into the adult stage. Plants rely on a variety of hormones such as auxin, gibberellin, and cytokinin that assist in flower, tuber, bulb, and bud formation. Ethylene, a synthetic hormone used by horticulturists, is believed to accelerate the ripening of fruit.

The author mentions ecdysone as a hormone that

- ○ helps insects harden their outer shells
- ○ inhibits the immune system
- ○ desensitizes insects' sense of smell
- ○ camouflages certain insects from predators

Time

? Help | ← Prev | → Next

Questions 1 to 8   **Beginning**

Without regular supplies of some hormones, the human capacity to behave would be seriously impaired. The absence of others would cause immediate death. The most abundant hormones act to modify moods and affect actions. The most minute amounts of hormones can suppress appetite, alter aggressive or submissive attitudes, and change reproductive and parental behavior. Early in life, hormones accelerate the development of bodily form and may even define an individual's personality characteristics. Later in life, the changing hormonal outputs of some endocrine glands and the body's changing sensitivity to them bolster immunity and hasten the aging phenomena.

Up to the beginning of the present century, communication within the body and the consequent integration of behavior were considered the primary province of the nervous system. The emergence of endocrinology as a separate discipline can be traced to the experiments of Dr. William Bayliss and Dr. Ernest Starling on the hormone secretin, which is secreted from cells in the intestinal walls when food enters the stomach. It then travels through the bloodstream and stimulates the pancreas to liberate digestive fluid. By stimulating these special stomach cells to secrete hormones that in turn regulate distant target organs and tissues, Bayliss and Starling demonstrated that chemical integration could occur without the participation of the nervous system.

The term hormone was first used with reference to secretin. Starling derived the term from the Greek word hormon, meaning to excite or set in motion. The term endocrine was introduced shortly thereafter. Endocrine is used to refer to glands that secrete products directly into the bloodstream such as the pancreas, thyroid, and pituitary glands. Because the lack of any one of them may cause serious disorders, many hormones are now produced synthetically and used in treatment where a deficiency exists. Insects also have a unique hormone ecdysone. Much like steroids stimulate muscle formation in humans, ecdysone strengthens the exoskeleton of insects while they metamorphose into the adult stage. Plants rely on a variety of hormones such as auxin, gibberellin, and cytokinin that assist in flower, tuber, bulb, and bud formation. Ethylene, a synthetic hormone used by horticulturists, is believed to accelerate the ripening of fruit.

Time

Which of the following is affected by the hormone ethylene?

○ Correcting digestive disorders
○ Bud and flower formation
○ Insect metamorphosis
○ Ripening fruits

? Help   **←** Prev   **→** Next

SECOND-PASS QUESTIONS

While you were answering the first-pass questions, you indirectly read the passage. You actually take in more information than you might think! Use that information to answer the second-pass questions.

Use the information from first-pass questions to answer the second-pass questions.

- **Main idea questions** ask you for the topic of either the entire passage or a specific paragraph.

- **Conclusion questions** ask you to select the statement that best summarizes the author's opinion.

- **Click-on sentence questions** ask you click on the sentence that answers a detail question.

Main Idea Questions

Main idea questions almost always appear *first!* This is a trap that ETS uses to force you to read the entire passage. If you answer this question first, not only will you lose an incredible amount of time reading and rereading the passage, but you will also most likely answer incorrectly! Skip this question for the second pass. Think about this: After using the 1-1-1-L technique, and after answering all of the first-pass questions (VIC, reference, and detail questions), you will know what the main idea of the passage or paragraph is.

The way to find the main topic of any passage is to ask yourself one simple question:

Which answer choice is repeated in the first-pass questions?

Whatever topic the detail questions and answers have in common is the main idea! Main idea questions are phrased as follows:

Which of the following statements best expresses the main idea of the passage?

What does the passage mainly discuss?

With which of the following subjects is the passage mainly concerned?

Which of the following assumptions about _____ is expressed in the passage?

What is the main topic of the passage?

Which of the following questions does the author answer in the first paragraph?

What is the main point of the first paragraph?

When answering main idea questions, bear in mind that the answer shouldn't introduce anything new.

In summary of the main idea question strategy:

Step 1:	Quickly 1-1-1-L the passage again (if necessary).
Step 2:	Consider what you learned from the first-pass questions and eliminate answer choices that introduce a new topic.
Step 3:	Eliminate answer choices that seem too specific.
Step 4:	Click on the answer choice mentioned in the majority of the first-pass questions.

Conclusion Questions

Conclusion questions almost always appear *last!* The strategy for conclusion questions is the same as main idea questions. After answering all the first-pass questions (VIC, reference, and detail questions), you will know enough about the passage to click on the conclusion the author most likely agrees with.

The way to find the conclusion of any passage is to ask yourself one simple question:

Which answer choice is referred to in the first-pass questions?

The best way to find the correct answer to a conclusion question on any TOEFL CBT passage is to ask yourself one simple question:

Which answer choice is referred to in the answers to the first-pass questions?

The first-pass questions will contain the important information that comprises the conclusion. Look for an answer choice that best paraphrases the information you got from the first-pass questions. Conclusion questions usually look something like this:

With which of the following conclusions would the author most likely agree?

The passage supports which of the following generalizations?

Which of the following statements is supported by the passage?

When answering conclusion questions, bear in mind that the answer shouldn't introduce anything new.

In summary of the conclusion question strategy:

Step 1:	Quickly 1-1-1-L the passage again (if necessary).
Step 2:	Consider what you learned from the first-pass questions and eliminate answer choices that introduce a new topic.
Step 3:	Eliminate answer choices that seem too specific.
Step 4:	Select the answer choice included in the majority of the first-pass questions.

Click-on Sentence Questions

In the TOEFL CBT, ETS has developed a new type of question called click-on sentence questions. Like detail questions, click-on sentence questions ask you for specific facts contained in the passage. There is at least one click-on sentence question for each passage. Unlike detail questions, the paragraph in which the answer is located is indicated with arrows. Therefore *no* hunting or lead words are necessary. The passage will be located on the left side of the screen. On the right side you will see a question similar to the following:

> Click on the sentence in paragraph 4 that explains why the electron microscope has become a necessity for laboratories.

The paragraph in which the answer is contained has a minimum of four sentences. First, read the question to see what information is required to correctly answer the question. Then, quickly read the sentences and click on the one that best answers the question asked. For example:

Reading

Questions 1 to ?   **Beginning**

➡️ In the world of health, there is a lesser known statistical discipline called "actuarial science," which is the life-blood of the insurance industry, particularly in the United States. Its principal aim is to make predictions about the health and life expectancy of the insured, based upon a meticulous study of statistics. By carefully identifying and analyzing the patterns in these numbers, actuaries can quite accurately determine the profitability of insuring various people to varying degrees. With this in mind, an insurance company is less likely to insure someone who is considered to be in an "at risk" category, than someone who is deemed more "insurable."

Click on the sentence in Paragraph 2 that explains the benefits insurance companies gain by analyzing actuaries.

Time   **?** **Help**   ⬅️ **Prev**   ➡️ **Next**

As you read the four sentences in Paragraph 2, be sure to ask yourself this question: "Does the information in this sentence explain the benefits insurance companies gain by analyzing actuaries?" In this case, sentence three best answers the question.

In summary of the click on sentence question strategy:

Step 1: Read the question closely and identify the information needed.

Step 2: Read the sentences in the paragraph indicated and eliminate those answer choices that do *not* answer the question.

Step 3: Click on the sentence that best answers the question.

Step 4: If you can't eliminate three answer choices, don't worry, just pick the one you like best and move on.

Use the information from first- and second-pass questions to answer the third-pass questions.

THIRD-PASS QUESTIONS

Third-pass questions should be left until last, because they almost always use paraphrases and synonyms. They take longer to answer and can't be answered by reading only one or two sentences. They generally appear in one of three forms:

- **Except/not questions** ask you for the information *not* found in the passage.

- **Infer/imply questions** ask for information based on what is indirectly stated or implied.

- **Black square questions** ask you to insert a sentence into the passage.

Except/Not Questions

Except/not questions are the easiest of the third-pass questions, but they can require a lot of time. The correct answer to an except/not questions is always the choice that *does not* answer the question. In other words, the right answer is the one that is *not* mentioned! You will encounter at least four except/not questions on the TOEFL CBT. To identify except/not questions, simply look for the words *EXCEPT* or *NOT* in the question. For example:

> All of the following are mentioned as predators
> of the gadfly EXCEPT
>
> ○　　birds
> ○　　spiders
> ○　　squirrels
> ○　　frogs

To answer except/not questions, use chronology to narrow down the area of text you need to search. Also, work backwards! Use the answer choices as lead words to find where they appear in the passage. Usually, the three answers are located together. If the answers are spread throughout the passage, chronology will not be helpful. In either case, the fourth answer will *not* be mentioned in the passage and will be the answer you need to click on.

In summary of the except/not question strategy:

Step 1:　　Read the question. As soon as you determine that it is an except/not question, save it until the third pass. Remember that except/not questions ask you to find the answer choice that does not appear in the passage.

Step 2:　　Using the answer choices as lead words and chronology, go back to the passage and locate the information from each question.

Step 3:　　Select the answer choice not mentioned in the text.

Step 4:　　As always, if you're not sure, guess and move on. Since this is a third-pass question, be sure to keep your eye on the clock.

Infer/Imply Questions

Infer/imply questions are difficult to answer and if you are having trouble, you should spend minimal time on them. They contain the words "infer," "imply," and "suggest," and request information not directly stated in the passage. Read the following infer/imply question types:

> It can be inferred from the passage that . . .
>
> The author implies that . . .
>
> The passage suggests that . . .
>
> Based on the information in the passage, what can be inferred about . . .

"Inferred" and "implied" both refer to information that must be true, but is not actually written in the passage. To answer infer/imply questions, concentrate on what the passage says! Avoid being distracted by what could *possibly* be true. The answers to infer/imply questions are paraphrases of the facts in the text. Ask yourself this question: "Does the answer choice paraphrase the details found in the passage?" If not, you can eliminate that answer.

For infer/imply questions, eliminate any answer choice that:

- Is not directly supported by the passage in the form of a paraphrase.

- Repeats information word for word from the passage. Remember that the best answer choice is usually a paraphrase of what was stated in the passage. Any choice that contains too many words from the passage is probably a trap answer.

- Introduces new material not found in the passage. Since you have already answered the first- and second-pass questions you should have a pretty good idea of what the author's main idea and conclusion are.

- Contains "extreme" words. Watch out for words like "always," "never," "must," "shall," and "so forth." These words are easy to prove wrong since it only takes one instance to refute them. Better answer choices use words like sometimes, often, may, and could.

- Violates common sense. Eliminate answer choices that are ridiculous, illogical, or just plain crazy.

Practice the above concepts with the example on the following page.

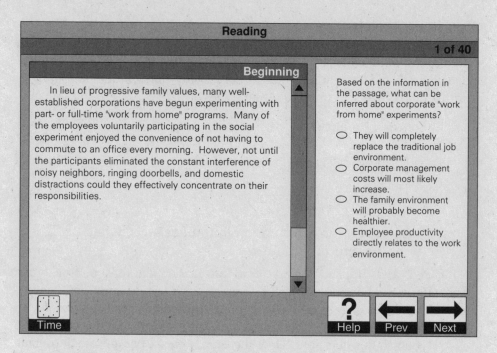

Beginning

In lieu of progressive family values, many well-established corporations have begun experimenting with part- or full-time "work from home" programs. Many of the employees voluntarily participating in the social experiment enjoyed the convenience of not having to commute to an office every morning. However, not until the participants eliminated the constant interference of noisy neighbors, ringing doorbells, and domestic distractions could they effectively concentrate on their responsibilities.

Based on the information in the passage, what can be inferred about corporate "work from home" experiments?

○ They will completely replace the traditional job environment.
○ Corporate management costs will most likely increase.
○ The family environment will probably become healthier.
○ Employee productivity directly relates to the work environment.

Time   Help   Prev   Next

- The first choice, "They will completely replace the traditional job environment," contains the extreme word "completely." Think about it! Eventually, will *everyone* work at home? No, this is illogical. Eliminate this answer choice.

- The subject of the second choice, "Corporate management costs will most likely increase," isn't mentioned at all in the passage. Eliminate all answer choices that introduce new subject matter.

- The third answer choice, "The family environment will probably become healthier," could be true, but it is *not* a paraphrase of the facts. Eliminate this answer choice.

- Only the fourth answer choice, "Employee productivity directly relates to the work environment," correctly paraphrases the statement, "However, not until the participants eliminated the constant interference . . . could they effectively concentrate on their responsibilities." Click on this answer choice.

Since infer/imply questions are third-pass questions, check your time. If time allows, spend a little more time finding the correct answer. However, if you have less than 5 or 10 minutes remaining, work quickly.

In summary of infer/imply question strategy:

Step 1: Read the question. As soon as you determine that it is an infer/imply question, save it until the third pass. Remember that correct answers to infer/imply questions must be true in light of what was stated in the passage.

Step 2: Using lead words and chronological order, locate the information referred to in the question. Check a line or two above, and a line or two below the lead word.

Step 3: Eliminate any answer choice that directly quotes the passage, is not a paraphrase, contradicts the main idea of the passage, includes "extreme" words, or violates common sense.

Step 4: From the remaining choices, click on the one that best paraphrases the text and answers the question asked. Since this is a third-pass question be sure to keep your eye on the clock.

ETS likes to make the correct answers difficult to find. Since the answers to infer/imply questions are always paraphrased, improving your paraphrasing skills will be extremely beneficial. Reminder: A paraphrase simply expresses the same idea with different words. To improve your paraphrasing techniques, complete the following drill.

Drill 4

Directions: Match the phrase on the left to its paraphrase on the right. Answers can be found at the end of this chapter.

1. determine optimal planting schedules

2. due to comprehensive adjustments

3. a primary reason for the victory

4. improvise a solution

5. introduction of a representative form of government

6. keep topsoil in place

7. a chronic shortage of

8. various emotional responses

9. roughly at the same time

10. a more conservative style

a. establishment of democracy

b. hinder erosion

c. find a new way to solve the problem

d. find the best time to sow seeds

e. almost simultaneously

f. because of drastic changes in

g. a more traditional approach

h. a major cause of its success

i. experience of different feelings

j. in dire need of

BLACK SQUARE QUESTIONS

In the TOEFL CBT test, ETS introduces a question type we call black square questions. In the passage on the left side of the computer screen, anywhere from 4 to 10 black boxes will appear. On the right side of the screen, a sentence will appear followed by the question, "Where would the sentence best fit in the passage? Click on the square ■ to add the sentence to the passage." When you point and click the mouse on a black square, the designated sentence will magically appear in place of it. If you click on another black square, the sentence will reappear there.

Because every black square is considered a possible answer choice, this question should be the very *last* you attempt to answer. As you approach this question type, remember the strategy for detail questions. Read the sentence you are required to insert, and select a lead word. Then, starting from the top of the text, quickly scan the text around the black squares for the lead word you have chosen. Once you have located the lead word, click on the black square to insert the sentence.

Read the sentences both before and after the sentence you just inserted. The sentence right before should contain information that introduces your new sentence. The following sentence should include information that continues the idea in your new sentence. If all three sentences flow with the text, you have correctly answered the question. Look at the following example:

> Answer black square questions last.

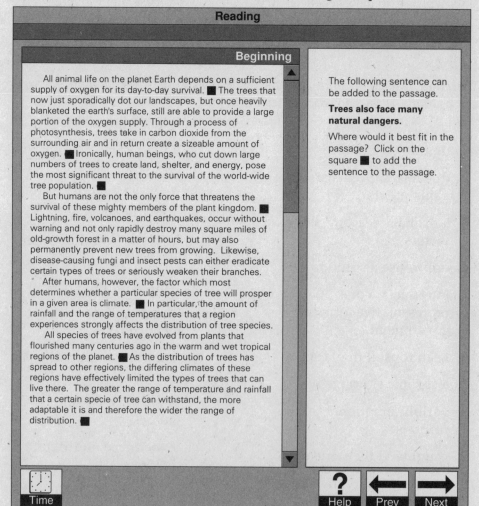

Read the sentence and select the lead word. Avoid the words that frequently appear in the text. The phrase "natural dangers" contains great lead words. Scan the text for "natural dangers," or for a paraphrase of it. In paragraph 2 you see a list of natural disasters: lightning, fire, volcanoes, and earthquakes. Click on the square in front of these natural disasters to insert the sentence. Reminder: Always read the sentence on either side of the inserted sentence to check for subject flow.

In summary of black square questions:

Step 1: Read the sentence that appears on the right side of your screen and select an appropriate lead word.

Step 2: From the top of the passage, scan the sentences around the black squares to locate your lead word.

Step 3: Click on the black square either before or after the sentence that contains the lead word.

Step 4: Read the sentences that precede and follow your answer to check for logical placement.

Summary of second- and third-pass question techniques:

1. After **1-1-1-L**, go to the first question. If it is a first pass type, do it. If it is a second- or third-pass question, skip it until the second or third pass.

Second Pass:

2. **Main Idea**—Consider what you learned when answering the first-pass questions. Eliminate answer choices that are too specific or not mentioned in the passage.

3. **Conclusion**—Consider what you learned when answering the first-pass questions. Eliminate answer choices that are too specific or not mentioned in the passage. Select the answer that includes information from the majority of the first-pass questions.

4. **Click on Sentence**—Read each of the sentences in the indicated section. Eliminate those that fail to answer the question asked.

Third Pass:

5. **Except/Not**—Use lead words from the answer choices and chronology to locate the information in the passage. Select the answer choice that is not mentioned in the text.

6. **Infer/Imply**—Use lead words and chronology to locate the information mentioned in the question. Using rigorous POE, select the choice that best paraphrases the information in the text.

7. **Black Square**—Use lead words to locate the correct black square. Read the sentences before and after the black square to check for logical placement.

8. **For all questions:** Be sure to use rigorous POE to eliminate answer choices you know are incorrect. Be careful not to spend too much time on any particular question. If you get bogged down, guess and move on.

Drill 5

Without answering any of the questions, look at the following passage and categorize each question presented according to type. After you determine the question type, indicate in which pass you will complete that particular question.

Drill 6

Use all the strategies you have learned to answer the following questions. Click on (in this case circle) the best answer. Answers to these questions can be found at the end of this chapter.

Questions 1 to 8 — Beginning

Although only a small portion of professional photographers have had any practical knowledge of daguerreotypes, they are nevertheless one of the most influential and notable inventions of the nineteenth century. Predecessors to photographs, daguerreotypes were perfected and subsequently popularized by Daguerre during the 1830s. The complicated process of development made use of copper plates upon which several thin coats of silver were applied. The faint layers so sensitized the plates that when exposed to natural light, various images gradually appeared. Unfortunately, prior to actually viewing the impressions, a sequence of complex procedures had to be strictly followed.

The final picture quality of daguerreotypes completely depended on the careful preparation of the plates, and great attention was placed on keeping the working area spotless. After being fastened to wooden blocks, the daguerreotypes were fastened to wooden blocks where they were thoroughly scoured with alcohol and squares of soft flannel. Since even one speck of dust would easily create a groove deep enough in the malleable plate surfaces to render the daguerreotypes worthless, they required extensive polishing until completely smooth.

Once the copper plates were buffed, they were relocated to a darkroom in order to be first soaked in trays and then in enclosed boxes filled with iodine and bromine respectively. Now that the plates were rendered sensitive to light by the thin layer of bromo-iodine on their surfaces, they were inserted into specialized holders and placed in cameras for exposure. Factors such as the quality of the lenses, natural sunlight, and subject matter all greatly influenced the exposure time required. Only through trial and error would daguerreotypists learn the correct amount of time essential for the likeness of the subject matter to be identically reproduced on the copper plates.

After what the daguerreotypists thought to be an adequate exposure time, the plates were taken to yet another darkroom. There they were alternately dipped in iron containers of heated mercury and immersed in vats of freezing water. The mercury vapors adhered the images to the plates and subsequently developed the pictures, whereas the water limited any possibility of the plates breaking up. The daguerreotypists meticulously applied hydrosulphite-soda to the plate surfaces to dissolve any remaining bromo-iodine not previously exposed to light. Finally, a thin solution of heated gold and chlorine was meticulously brushed over the plates. The gold served to accent the black and white hues in the final picture, and the chlorine brightened the finish. The daguerreotypes were then ready for display.

With which of the following topics is the author primarily concerned?

○ The increasing costs of daguerreotype development

○ The relation between daguerreotypes and modern-day photography

○ The effects photographic chemicals have on picture quality

○ The complicated process of daguerreotype development

Time   Help   Prev   Next

Questions 1 to 8   **Beginning**

Although only a small portion of professional photographers have had any practical knowledge of daguerreotypes, they are nevertheless one of the most influential and notable inventions of the nineteenth century. Predecessors to photographs, daguerreotypes were perfected and subsequently popularized by Daguerre during the 1830s. **The complicated process of development made use of copper plates upon which several thin coats of silver were applied. The faint `layers` so sensitized the plates that when exposed to natural light, various images gradually appeared.** Unfortunately, prior to actually viewing the impressions, a sequence of complex procedures had to be strictly followed.

The final picture quality of daguerreotypes completely depended on the careful preparation of the plates, and great attention was placed on keeping the working area spotless. After being fastened to wooden blocks, the daguerreotypes were fastened to wooden blocks where they were thoroughly scoured with alcohol and squares of soft flannel. Since even one speck of dust would easily create a groove deep enough in the malleable plate surfaces to render the daguerreotypes worthless, they required extensive polishing until completely smooth.

Once the copper plates were buffed, they were relocated to a darkroom in order to be first soaked in trays and then in enclosed boxes filled with iodine and bromine respectively. Now that the plates were rendered sensitive to light by the thin layer of bromo-iodine on their surfaces, they were inserted into specialized holders and placed in cameras for exposure. Factors such as the quality of the lenses, natural sunlight, and subject matter all greatly influenced the exposure time required. Only through trial and error would daguerreotypists learn the correct amount of time essential for the likeness of the subject matter to be identically reproduced on the copper plates.

After what the daguerreotypists thought to be an adequate exposure time, the plates were taken to yet another darkroom. There they were alternately dipped in iron containers of heated mercury and immersed in vats of freezing water. The mercury vapors adhered the images to the plates and subsequently developed the pictures, whereas the water limited any possibility of the plates breaking up. The daguerreotypists meticulously applied hydrosulphite-soda to the plate surfaces to dissolve any remaining bromo-iodine not previously exposed to light. Finally, a thin solution of heated gold and chlorine was meticulously brushed over the plates. The gold served to accent the black and white hues in the final picture, and the chlorine brightened the finish. The daguerreotypes were then ready for display.

Look at the highlighted word in the passage. Click on the word or phrase in the bold text that `layers` refers to.

Time

Help   Prev   Next

Questions 1 to 8   Beginning

Although only a small portion of professional photographers have had any practical knowledge of daguerreotypes, they are nevertheless one of the most influential and notable inventions of the nineteenth century. Predecessors to photographs, daguerreotypes were perfected and subsequently popularized by Daguerre during the 1830s. The complicated process of development made use of copper plates upon which several thin coats of silver were applied. The faint layers so sensitized the plates that when exposed to natural light, various images gradually appeared. Unfortunately, prior to actually viewing the impressions, a sequence of complex procedures had to be strictly followed.

The final picture quality of daguerreotypes completely depended on the careful preparation of the plates, and great attention was placed on keeping the working area spotless. After being fastened to wooden blocks, the daguerreotypes were fastened to wooden blocks where they were thoroughly scoured with alcohol and squares of soft flannel. **Since even one speck of dust would easily create a groove deep enough in the malleable plate surfaces to render the daguerreotypes worthless, they required extensive polishing until completely smooth.**

Once the copper plates were buffed, they were relocated to a darkroom in order to be first soaked in trays and then in enclosed boxes filled with iodine and bromine respectively. Now that the plates were rendered sensitive to light by the thin layer of bromo-iodine on their surfaces, they were inserted into specialized holders and placed in cameras for exposure. Factors such as the quality of the lenses, natural sunlight, and subject matter all greatly influenced the exposure time required. Only through trial and error would daguerreotypists learn the correct amount of time essential for the likeness of the subject matter to be identically reproduced on the copper plates.

After what the daguerreotypists thought to be an adequate exposure time, the plates were taken to yet another darkroom. There they were alternately dipped in iron containers of heated mercury and immersed in vats of freezing water. The mercury vapors adhered the images to the plates and subsequently developed the pictures, whereas the water limited any possibility of the plates breaking up. The daguerreotypists meticulously applied hydrosulphite-soda to the plate surfaces to dissolve any remaining bromo-iodine not previously exposed to light. Finally, a thin solution of heated gold and chlorine was meticulously brushed over the plates. The gold served to accent the black and white hues in the final picture, and the chlorine brightened the finish. The daguerreotypes were then ready for display.

Look at the word highlighted in the text. Click on the word that **they** refers to.

Time

Help   Prev   Next

Questions 1 to 8 — Beginning

Although only a small portion of professional photographers have had any practical knowledge of daguerreotypes, they are nevertheless one of the most influential and notable inventions of the nineteenth century. Predecessors to photographs, daguerreotypes were perfected and subsequently popularized by Daguerre during the 1830s. The complicated process of development made use of copper plates upon which several thin coats of silver were applied. The faint layers so sensitized the plates that when exposed to natural light, various images gradually appeared. Unfortunately, prior to actually viewing the impressions, a sequence of complex procedures had to be strictly followed.

The final picture quality of daguerreotypes completely depended on the careful preparation of the plates, and great attention was placed on keeping the working area spotless. After being fastened to wooden blocks, the daguerreotypes were fastened to wooden blocks where they were thoroughly scoured with alcohol and squares of soft flannel. Since even one speck of dust would easily create a groove deep enough in the malleable plate surfaces to render the daguerreotypes worthless, they required extensive polishing until completely smooth.

Once the copper plates were buffed, they were relocated to a darkroom in order to be first soaked in trays and then in enclosed boxes filled with iodine and bromine respectively. Now that the plates were rendered sensitive to light by the thin layer of bromo-iodine on their surfaces, they were inserted into specialized holders and placed in cameras for exposure. Factors such as the quality of the lenses, natural sunlight, and subject matter all greatly influenced the exposure time required. Only through trial and error would daguerreotypists learn the correct amount of time essential for the likeness of the subject matter to be identically reproduced on the copper plates.

After what the daguerreotypists thought to be an adequate exposure time, the plates were taken to yet another darkroom. There they were alternately dipped in iron containers of heated mercury and immersed in vats of freezing water. The mercury vapors adhered the images to the plates and subsequently developed the pictures, whereas the water limited any possibility of the plates breaking up. The daguerreotypists meticulously applied hydrosulphite-soda to the plate surfaces to dissolve any remaining bromo-iodine not previously exposed to light. Finally, a thin solution of heated gold and chlorine was meticulously brushed over the plates. The gold served to accent the black and white hues in the final picture, and the chlorine brightened the finish. The daguerreotypes were then ready for display.

Time

Look at the highlighted word in the text. Click on the following answer choice that is closest in meaning to the word malleable.

○ soft
○ unusual
○ persistent
○ flat

Help   Prev   Next

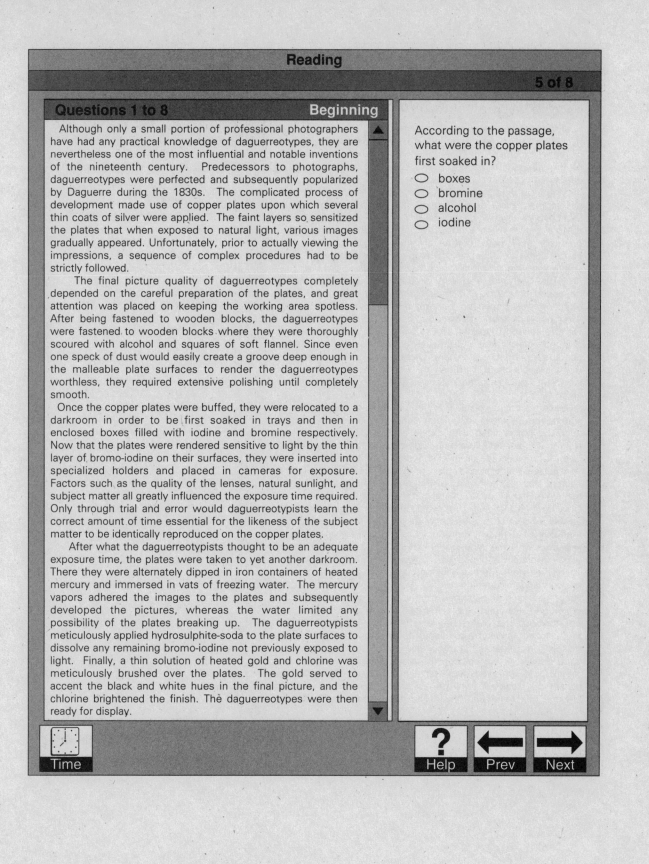

Questions 1 to 8   **Beginning**

Although only a small portion of professional photographers have had any practical knowledge of daguerreotypes, they are nevertheless one of the most influential and notable inventions of the nineteenth century. Predecessors to photographs, daguerreotypes were perfected and subsequently popularized by Daguerre during the 1830s. The complicated process of development made use of copper plates upon which several thin coats of silver were applied. The faint layers so sensitized the plates that when exposed to natural light, various images gradually appeared. Unfortunately, prior to actually viewing the impressions, a sequence of complex procedures had to be strictly followed.

The final picture quality of daguerreotypes completely depended on the careful preparation of the plates, and great attention was placed on keeping the working area spotless. After being fastened to wooden blocks, the daguerreotypes were fastened to wooden blocks where they were thoroughly scoured with alcohol and squares of soft flannel. Since even one speck of dust would easily create a groove deep enough in the malleable plate surfaces to render the daguerreotypes worthless, they required extensive polishing until completely smooth.

Once the copper plates were buffed, they were relocated to a darkroom in order to be first soaked in trays and then in enclosed boxes filled with iodine and bromine respectively. Now that the plates were rendered sensitive to light by the thin layer of bromo-iodine on their surfaces, they were inserted into specialized holders and placed in cameras for exposure. Factors such as the quality of the lenses, natural sunlight, and subject matter all greatly influenced the exposure time required. Only through trial and error would daguerreotypists learn the correct amount of time essential for the likeness of the subject matter to be identically reproduced on the copper plates.

After what the daguerreotypists thought to be an adequate exposure time, the plates were taken to yet another darkroom. There they were alternately dipped in iron containers of heated mercury and immersed in vats of freezing water. The mercury vapors adhered the images to the plates and subsequently developed the pictures, whereas the water limited any possibility of the plates breaking up. The daguerreotypists meticulously applied hydrosulphite-soda to the plate surfaces to dissolve any remaining bromo-iodine not previously exposed to light. Finally, a thin solution of heated gold and chlorine was meticulously brushed over the plates. The gold served to accent the black and white hues in the final picture, and the chlorine brightened the finish. The daguerreotypes were then ready for display.

According to the passage, what were the copper plates first soaked in?

○ boxes
○ bromine
○ alcohol
○ iodine

Time

? Help   ← Prev   → Next

Questions 1 to 8   **Beginning**

Although only a small portion of professional photographers have had any practical knowledge of daguerreotypes, they are nevertheless one of the most influential and notable inventions of the nineteenth century. Predecessors to photographs, daguerreotypes were perfected and subsequently popularized by Daguerre during the 1830s. The complicated process of development made use of copper plates upon which several thin coats of silver were applied. The faint layers so sensitized the plates that when exposed to natural light, various images gradually appeared. Unfortunately, prior to actually viewing the impressions, a sequence of complex procedures had to be strictly followed.

The final picture quality of daguerreotypes completely depended on the careful preparation of the plates, and great attention was placed on keeping the working area spotless. After being fastened to wooden blocks, the daguerreotypes were fastened to wooden blocks where they were thoroughly scoured with alcohol and squares of soft flannel. Since even one speck of dust would easily create a groove deep enough in the malleable plate surfaces to render the daguerreotypes worthless, they required extensive polishing until completely smooth.

Once the copper plates were buffed, they were relocated to a darkroom in order to be first soaked in trays and then in enclosed boxes filled with iodine and bromine respectively. Now that the plates were rendered sensitive to light by the thin layer of bromo-iodine on their surfaces, they were inserted into specialized holders and placed in cameras for exposure. Factors such as the quality of the lenses, natural sunlight, and subject matter all greatly influenced the exposure time required. Only through trial and error would daguerreotypists learn the correct amount of time essential for the likeness of the subject matter to be identically reproduced on the copper plates.

➡ After what the daguerreotypists thought to be an adequate exposure time, the plates were taken to yet another darkroom. There they were alternately dipped in iron containers of heated mercury and immersed in vats of freezing water. The mercury vapors adhered the images to the plates and subsequently developed the pictures, whereas the water limited any possibility of the plates breaking up. The daguerreotypists meticulously applied hydrosulphite-soda to the plate surfaces to dissolve any remaining bromo-iodine not previously exposed to light. Finally, a thin solution of heated gold and chlorine was meticulously brushed over the plates. The gold served to accent the black and white hues in the final picture, and the chlorine brightened the finish. The daguerreotypes were then ready for display.

Click on the sentence in Paragraph 4 that tells how the daguerreotypists kept the plates from disintegrating. Paragraph 4 is marked with an arrow (➡).

Time

? Help   ⬅ Prev   ➡ Next

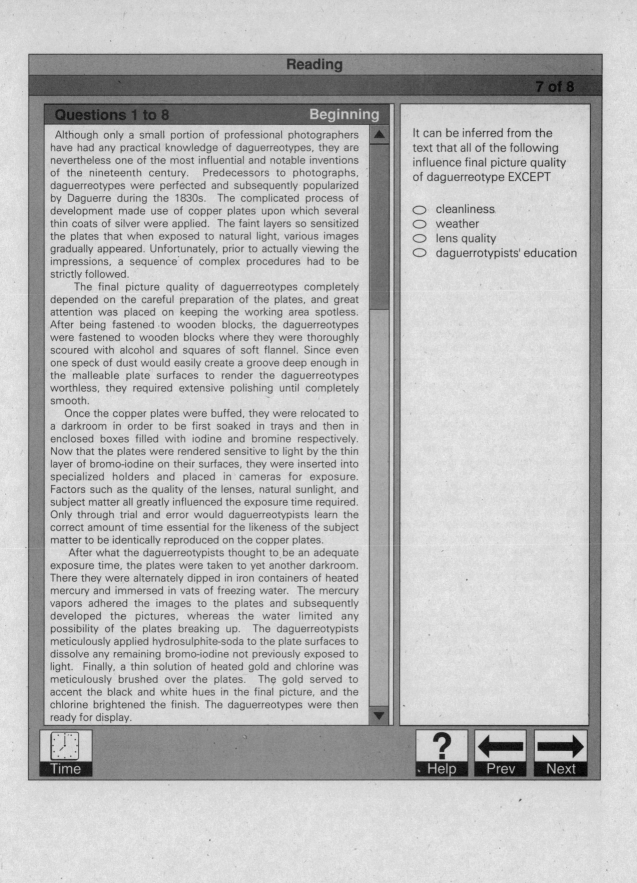

Questions 1 to 8   Beginning

Although only a small portion of professional photographers have had any practical knowledge of daguerreotypes, they are nevertheless one of the most influential and notable inventions of the nineteenth century. Predecessors to photographs, daguerreotypes were perfected and subsequently popularized by Daguerre during the 1830s. The complicated process of development made use of copper plates upon which several thin coats of silver were applied. The faint layers so sensitized the plates that when exposed to natural light, various images gradually appeared. Unfortunately, prior to actually viewing the impressions, a sequence of complex procedures had to be strictly followed.

The final picture quality of daguerreotypes completely depended on the careful preparation of the plates, and great attention was placed on keeping the working area spotless. After being fastened to wooden blocks, the daguerreotypes were fastened to wooden blocks where they were thoroughly scoured with alcohol and squares of soft flannel. Since even one speck of dust would easily create a groove deep enough in the malleable plate surfaces to render the daguerreotypes worthless, they required extensive polishing until completely smooth.

Once the copper plates were buffed, they were relocated to a darkroom in order to be first soaked in trays and then in enclosed boxes filled with iodine and bromine respectively. Now that the plates were rendered sensitive to light by the thin layer of bromo-iodine on their surfaces, they were inserted into specialized holders and placed in cameras for exposure. Factors such as the quality of the lenses, natural sunlight, and subject matter all greatly influenced the exposure time required. Only through trial and error would daguerreotypists learn the correct amount of time essential for the likeness of the subject matter to be identically reproduced on the copper plates.

After what the daguerreotypists thought to be an adequate exposure time, the plates were taken to yet another darkroom. There they were alternately dipped in iron containers of heated mercury and immersed in vats of freezing water. The mercury vapors adhered the images to the plates and subsequently developed the pictures, whereas the water limited any possibility of the plates breaking up. The daguerreotypists meticulously applied hydrosulphite-soda to the plate surfaces to dissolve any remaining bromo-iodine not previously exposed to light. Finally, a thin solution of heated gold and chlorine was meticulously brushed over the plates. The gold served to accent the black and white hues in the final picture, and the chlorine brightened the finish. The daguerreotypes were then ready for display.

It can be inferred from the text that all of the following influence final picture quality of daguerreotype EXCEPT

○ cleanliness
○ weather
○ lens quality
○ daguerrotypists' education

Time

Help   Prev   Next

Questions 1 to 8   Beginning

Although only a small portion of professional photographers have had any practical knowledge of daguerreotypes, they are nevertheless one of the most influential and notable inventions of the nineteenth century. ■Predecessors to photographs, daguerreotypes were perfected and subsequently popularized by Daguerre during the 1830s. The complicated process of development made use of copper plates upon which several thin coats of silver were applied. The faint layers so sensitized the plates that when exposed to natural light, various images gradually appeared. ■Unfortunately, prior to actually viewing the impressions, a sequence of complex procedures had to be strictly followed.

The final picture quality of daguerreotypes completely depended on the careful preparation of the plates, and great attention was placed on keeping the working area spotless. ■After being fastened to wooden blocks, the daguerreotypes were fastened to wooden blocks where they were thoroughly scoured with alcohol and squares of soft flannel. Since even one speck of dust would easily create a groove deep enough in the malleable plate surfaces to render the daguerreotypes worthless, they required extensive polishing until completely smooth.■

Once the copper plates were buffed, they were relocated to a darkroom in order to be first soaked in trays and then in enclosed boxes filled with iodine and bromine respectively. Now that the plates were rendered sensitive to light by the thin layer of bromo-iodine on their surfaces, they were inserted into specialized holders and placed in cameras for exposure. Factors such as the quality of the lenses, natural sunlight, and subject matter all greatly influenced the exposure time required. ■Only through trial and error would daguerreotypists learn the correct amount of time essential for the likeness of the subject matter to be identically reproduced on the copper plates.

After what the daguerreotypists thought to be an adequate exposure time, the plates were taken to yet another darkroom. ■There they were alternately dipped in iron containers of heated mercury and immersed in vats of freezing water. The mercury vapors adhered the images to the plates and subsequently developed the pictures, whereas the water limited any possibility of the plates breaking up. ■ The daguerreotypists meticulously applied hydrosulphite-soda to the plate surfaces to dissolve any remaining bromo-iodine not previously exposed to light. Finally, a thin solution of heated gold and chlorine was meticulously brushed over the plates. The gold served to accent the black and white hues in the final picture, and the chlorine brightened the finish. ■ The daguerreotypes were then ready for display.

The following sentence can be added to the passage.

Without these two chemicals, the final pictures would appear flat and dull.

Where would it best fit in the passage? Click on the square ■ to add the sentence to the passage.

Time   ? Help   ← Prev   → Next

SUMMARY

Passage Strategy

- Move through the tutorial as quickly as possible.

- Click on "Proceed" as soon as each passage comes up so you can see the first question.

- 1-1-1-L the passage. Don't read the entire text! This is crucial.

- Answer the first-pass questions first, the second-pass questions next, and the third-pass questions last in passage 1, then go to passage 2 and do the same thing until the last passage. (See diagram on page 295.)

- Keep your eye on the time.

- Never get stuck on one question.

- Use process of elimination (POE) and common sense to reduce answer choice possibility.

- Answer every question! If you absolutely can't find the answer, *guess!*

Question Strategy

First-Pass Questions

1. **VIC**—Put your own word in for the VIC word, then match it to the answer choice that means the same thing.

2. **Reference**—What does the pronoun refer to? What else do you know about that thing? Remember, pronouns must agree in number and gender with the nouns they replace.

3. **Detail**—Use chronological order and lead words to find the information.

Second-Pass Questions

1. **Main Idea**—Consider what is mentioned in the first-pass questions.

2. **Conclusion**—Select the answer choice mentioned in the majority of the first-pass questions.

3. **Click on Sentence**—Read sentences indicated and POE the answer choices that fail to answer the question.

Third-Pass Questions

1. **Except/Not**—Using chronology and the answer choices as lead words, locate the information in the text. Click on the answer *not* mentioned.

2. **Infer/Imply**—Using chronology and lead words, locate the information that the question refers to. Click on the answer choice that best paraphrases the text.

3. **Black Square**—Use lead words to locate the correct black square.

Helpful Hints

1. Memorize the different question types and whether they are first-, second-, or third-pass questions.

2. Have confidence! Familiarize yourself with a computer and a mouse *before* taking the TOEFL CBT. You want to "fast forward" through these tutorials.

3. The first-, second-, and third-pass questions are not fixed. It depends on what you feel. If you see a third-pass question that seems easy, go ahead and click on the correct answer. If you see a first-pass question that seems difficult, go ahead and skip it. Use the method to your advantage!

4. Avoid reading the entire passage: Use 1-1-1-L. If you don't, you will *not* be able to finish!

ANSWER KEY

Drill 1

1. fat
2. 8 times
3. fat; you need some

Drill 2

1. vitamin C
2. Rosa Parks or 1955
3. wings (Because the passage is probably about manta rays, those words will appear many times in the passage, and thus are not good choices for lead words.)
4. bipartisan
5. Karl XII
6. legislative branch
7. snapping turtles (or, if the passage is about snapping turtles, try *extinct*)
8. sudden climatic change

Drill 3

1. tiny

2. accelerate

3. Bodily behavior was controlled mainly by the nervous system.

4. secretin

5. Chemical integration is not entirely dependent on the nervous system.

6. absence

7. helps insects harden their outer shells

8. ripening fruits

Drill 4

1. d.

2. f.

3. h.

4. c.

5. a.

6. b.

7. j.

8. i.

9. e.

10. g.

Drill 5

1. Main Idea; Second Pass

2. Reference; First Pass

3. Reference; First Pass

4. VIC; First Pass

5. Detail; First Pass

6. Click on Sentence; Second Pass

7. Infer/Imply; Third Pass

8. Black Square; Third Pass

Drill 6

1. the complicated progress of daguerreotype development

2. coats

3. daguerreotypes

4. soft

5. iodine

6. The mercury vapors adhered the images to the plates and subsequently developed the pictures, whereas the water limited any possibility of the plates breaking up.

7. daguerrotypists' education

8. The last black square

PART V

Writing

7 Writing

THE BASICS

Formerly known as the Test of Written English (TWE), the Writing section of the TOEFL CBT consists of a *mandatory* essay you must write based on a simple topic given to you by ETS. It is the last section of the TOEFL CBT, and you are given 30 minutes to complete it.

Since the essay asks for your opinion and the topics are very general, you do *not* need any specialized knowledge to write the essay. In fact, all of the potential essay topics are listed both in the TOEFL CBT Bulletin and at www.toefl.org. There is no point in memorizing them, but it never hurts to read through some of the topics to get an idea of what you will see on your test. On the day of the exam, you have the option of either *writing* the essay by hand, or *typing* the essay into the computer. If you choose to write your essay, the test proctor will give you several sheets of scratch paper and an official test booklet in which to write your final essay. If you choose to type your essay, you will also receive several sheets of scratch paper, and the computer will then lead you through a tutorial for the Writing section.

SHOULD I WRITE OR TYPE MY ESSAY?

If possible, you should type your essay.

If you are at all familiar with a standard keyboard and have some basic knowledge about word processing, you should absolutely choose the option to type your essay. Typing your essay will *drastically* improve your score in two essential ways. First, you will be able to cut, paste, and move sentences around, which will no doubt improve the organization and content of your essay. In addition, typing your paper will look a hundred times neater than if you write it, and neatness is taken into consideration when your essay is graded.

If you are unfamiliar with a keyboard, have never typed before, or have no knowledge about a basic word processing program, then of course it would be to your benefit to write your essay by hand. Your final score will be lower, however, due to content and the neatness factor. Keep in mind that if your ultimate goal is to go to a university or college, it will be to your advantage to be proficient in both typing and word processing. In other words, if you are computer illiterate and want to attend an American university, take a computer class and learn the basics, or have a friend explain word processing to you and then practice, practice, and practice some more!

THE TUTORIAL

ETS begins the Writing section of the TOEFL CBT with a tutorial. It teaches you how to highlight, cut and paste, and undo text. ETS also informs you how to move around the text using the page up, page down, home, end, and arrow keys. If you are familiar with any word processing program, you will have no problem completing this tutorial. Move through it as quickly as possible. If you are *not* familiar with a word processing program, or are unable to type on a standard keyboard, don't waste your time and energy trying to learn 10 minutes before the Writing section. It is impossible to learn how to type or become comfortable with word processing in that short amount of time. You want to spend your 30 minutes composing your essay, not familiarizing yourself with cutting and pasting. The tutorial will teach you basic skills, but it will not teach you speed or efficient typing. If this is your situation, you should handwrite your essay.

SCORING

According to ETS, your essay will be separately scored and evaluated by two "qualified" readers. (How ETS defines "qualified" remains a mystery.) If the ratings given by the "qualified" readers differ by more than one point, a third "qualified" reader will be called in to make a final grading decision. In any event, your essay could receive a score (from excellent to poor) of 6.0, 5.5, 5.0, 4.5, 4.0, 3.5, 3.0, 2.5, 2.0, 1.5, or 1. If you choose *not* to write your essay or write on a topic not given by ETS, or if you write in your native language, or you write a profanity directed at ETS, you will receive a big, fat 0. We recommend that you *not* choose any of these last four options due to the fact that your Writing section score is combined with your Structure section score to yield your final Structure score. In other words:

> **1/2 Structure section score + 1/2 Writing section score =**
> **Final Structure score**

Look at the following TOEFL CBT scoring guide that the "qualified" readers refer to. Any essay that is given a score of:

6—**effectively** addresses the essay, is **well** organized and developed, **clearly** uses support, and **effectively** demonstrates a variety of vocabulary and sentence structure.

5—**generally** addresses the essay, is **generally** well organized and developed, **generally** uses support, and demonstrates **some** variety of vocabulary and sentence structure.

4—**adequately** addresses the essay topic, is **adequately** organized and developed, **adequately** uses support, and **adequately** demonstrates a variety of vocabulary and sentence structure, either of which may contain **occasional** errors.

3—**inadequately** addresses the essay topic, is **inadequately** organized and developed, **inadequately** uses support, and contains **inappropriate** vocabulary and sentence structure, either of which contain **many** errors.

2—is seriously **disorganized** and **underdeveloped**, contains **little** detail and support, and demonstrates **serious problems** with vocabulary and sentence structure.

1—is **incoherent**, **underdeveloped**, contains **no** detail and support, and contains **severe** and **consistent errors**.

0—is **blank, off topic** written in **a language other than English,** or consists of **random** words and phrases.

DIRECTIONS

Learn the directions before you take the real TOEFL CBT!

After you begin the TOEFL CBT Writing section, the directions appear on the screen. The clock is running, so dismiss the directions immediately to see the essay topic.

WRITING THE ESSAY

Each language has it own stylistic rules for writing an essay. English is no different. To maximize your score, you should follow American English rules for writing a successful essay. ETS holds that the writing section gives you the "opportunity to demonstrate your ability to write in English." They also state that "this includes the ability to generate and organize ideas, to support those ideas with examples or evidence, and to compose in standard written English a response to an assigned topic." That's a lot to accomplish in 30 minutes. In fact, it seems difficult to complete. However, The Princeton Review has developed effective and efficient techniques to help you crack the Writing Section on the TOEFL CBT.

APPEARANCE

Graders spend less than two minutes reading your essay; you must pay attention to its appearance!

Keep in mind that your essay is read and graded in less than two minutes. The first thing readers do is glance at the layout of your essay on the page. What they see at first glance is what sticks in their minds the most. For that reason you need to pay close attention to how your essay looks.

Tips for an attractive essay:

- **Write neatly**. If you decide to write your essay rather than type it, you must write neatly. Nothing will make a "qualified" reader less happy than handwriting that's difficult to decipher. It's better to have a mediocre, legible essay than one that's brilliant but hard to read.

- **Length**. Make sure the essay is at least 200 words. If your essay is too short, regardless of the quality of what you write, the reader will start off by thinking, "This person couldn't come up with 200 words in English."

- **Indentation**. If you choose to type your essay, keep in mind that the tab key will not work during the Writing section of the TOEFL CBT. Therefore, you must manually hit the space bar 5 times to indent your paragraphs. For handwritten essays, indents at the beginning of each paragraph make your essay look structured and well planned.

BODY

Now you need to keep in mind what the essay reader is looking for in terms of content. Most importantly, the reader does **not** care *what* you say, but *how* you say it. In other words, the reader isn't wondering if your examples, details, and evidence are true or false, he only looks for complete English sentences that support your opinion. Feel free to be as creative as you want! Personal examples and stories do *not* have to be true; they can be completely made up and invented. Nothing needs to be true! Nor does the reader care if you actually agree or disagree with the essay topic questions! He is only examining your sentence structure, grammar, vocabulary, and (most importantly) whether you support your points with specific examples.

> The reader does not care *what* you say, just *how* you say it.

Look at the following tips to help construct a great essay:

- **Short and simple**. The longer your sentences, the more likely it is that they contain some kind of error. No sentence should exceed two lines in length.

- **Tense and Person**. Decide if you want to write in the past or present tense. Write in the first person ("I"). This makes the essay more personal to the reader.

- **Grammar**. Use grammatical structures you are comfortable with. If you're not sure whether a sentence structure you'd like to use is okay in English, don't use it. You can probably do just as well by splitting that sentence into two sentences.

- **Vocabulary**. Only use words and phrases you know. Being overly ambitious with your vocabulary will only lead to improper usage. A few advanced vocabulary words or idioms are a fantastic way to spruce up your essay; just make sure you know what they mean.

- **Spelling**. If you're not sure of the spelling of a word, don't use it. You can probably think of a great synonym to replace it. Words from your native language might have the same meaning as English words, but the spelling could be different. The computer you will use on the TOEFL CBT Writing section will *not* have a spell check function.

- **Punctuation**. Make sure that all sentences have periods at the end and that all lists are separated by commas. Avoid trying to use colons, semicolons, or other advanced forms of punctuation unless you're sure of their correct usage.

- **Repetition.** Avoid repeating yourself. As you read your essay, any adjective or verb that appears more than once or twice should be replaced by a synonym.

PACING

In the Writing section of the TOEFL CBT, you have 30 minutes to read the essay topic and write an essay. In order to complete the Writing section, break it down into the following 5-minute intervals:

Minutes **1–5**: Read the essay topic, choose a side, and write the outline on the provided scratch paper.

Minutes **6–10**: Write the *introduction* paragraph.

Minutes **11–15**: Write the *first support* paragraph.

Minutes **16–20**: Write the *second support* paragraph

Minutes **21–25**: Write the *conclusion* paragraph.

Minutes **26–30**: Reread your essay and make any final corrections.

Keep an eye on the clock to allow only 5 minutes for each section. Try not to fall behind. Four mediocre paragraphs will score higher than two well-developed ones. Do *not* continue after your 30 minutes is up. Any students caught writing after the official 30 minutes is over will forfeit their entire TOEFL CBT exam and *no* refund will be made.

1. The Essay Question

First, you must read and understand the essay question. Essay questions are very general and cover a wide range of topics including sports, pollution, technology, or entertainment. They will *not* include topics on current political events, historical figures, or any details or facts. The questions do *not* require any specific knowledge. The following are some typical essay questions found on the Writing section of the TOEFL CBT.

> Your university has enough money to build either a new sports stadium or a new library. Which project should your university build: a sports stadium or a library? Use specific reasons and examples to support your opinion.

Do you agree or disagree with the following statement? Sometimes it is acceptable to tell a lie. Use specific reasons and details to support your answer.

Some people are perfectionists. Others do only what is necessary to complete their responsibilities. Compare these two attitudes. Which attitude do you agree with? Support your choice with specific examples.

2. Choosing Your Side

All TOEFL CBT essay questions ask for your *opinion*, so you must choose a side. The first thing you must do is decide which opinion you would like to support, or whether you agree or disagree with the statement. Once you have chosen a side, do *not* change. There is *no* right correct side to choose, and ETS does *not* care which side you choose. Therefore, pick the one you're most comfortable with; more importantly, pick the side that appears the easiest to support.

There is no "right" or "wrong" answer to a Writing topic!

3. Outlining the Essay

The first five minutes (or less if possible) should be spent quickly preparing a rough outline. ETS will *not* see this outline, so it doesn't matter how neat it is. Outlines help you organize your thoughts and prepare you for efficient writing. Think of it this way: If you were driving your car to a new and unfamiliar place, would you leave your house without a map? No, you wouldn't. If you did, you would waste time just driving around trying to find your destination. The same idea applies for the TOEFL CBT Writing section. Your essay needs to be focused, concise, and well organized. An outline provides the map necessary for a well-written essay. It will help you organize your thoughts, keeping you from aimlessly wandering around.

An outline must include the following **four** essential paragraphs:

Paragraph I: <u>Introduction</u>: The initial presentation of the essay and your *opinion statement* (whether you agree or disagree with the essay question).

Paragraph II: <u>Support #1</u>: Reasons, details, and examples to support your opinion statement.

Paragraph III: <u>Support #2</u>: Reasons, details, and examples to *further* support your opinion statement.

Paragraph IV: <u>Conclusion</u>: The *restatement* of your opinion statement, plus a brief *summary* of the essay.

Each above listed point is just *one* paragraph, which consists of 4 to 6 sentences each, so you have to write a minimum of 16 to 24 sentences in 20 minutes. (Remember, the first five minutes are spent writing an outline and the last five are spent checking over the essay.) This amounts to approximately one sentence per minute. This is possible to accomplish! Breaking the TOEFL CBT essay down and thinking about it in this way makes it seem much more feasible to complete.

Ask the test proctors for paper.

Step 1: First, focus on writing the opinion statement. This is your opinion about the essay question and is the backbone of your essay.

Step 2: Next, think of a sentence that supports your opinion statement and have one personal example or specific detail to illustrate it.

Step 3: Next, think of another sentence that supports your opinion statement, and have another personal example or specific detail to illustrate it. If you ever have trouble thinking of a personal example or specific detail, *make it up!*

Step 4: Finally, summarize and restate your opinion statement for the conclusion.

Look at an example outline:

Topic: Some people believe that everyone should have the opportunity to attend a college or university. Others suggest that university education be reserved for the smartest and best high school students. Which belief do you agree with? Use specific reasons and details to explain your answer.

For the topic above, your outline might look something like this:

Paragraph I: <u>Introduction</u>: Education should be for everyone, not just for those individuals who are naturally smart.

Paragraph II: <u>Support #1</u>: Few students mentally develop at the same rates.

   A) Specific detail: A poor high school student becomes the top university graduate.

Paragraph III: <u>Support #2</u>: Academic institutions are for more than just memorizing facts and data.

   A) Personal experience: Being elected to the student government.

Paragraph IV: <u>Conclusion</u>: Every student should be able to decide for herself whether or not she wants more education.

Don't worry about using complete sentences for your outline. No one will ever see your outline. Its purpose is to keep your essay directed and focused as you write. Make sure to limit yourself to 5 (or fewer) minutes to write your outline. If you need more time than that, your plans for your essay are too ambitious. Now that you have written your outline, the next 20 minutes will be spent filling in the details with complete sentences in order to complete your essay. Remember, your essay only needs to have about 16 to 24 sentences.

Now that you have seen an example of how to write an outline, try writing some on your own. Remember that ETS will never see your outline.

Drill 1

Spend the first 5 minutes writing the outline.

Directions: Read the essay topics and write outlines. Follow the guidelines for writing outlines. Give yourself 5 minutes to complete each outline.

Topic 1:   Certain high schools require that students study foreign languages. Other schools let students study whatever subjects they like. Which of these two policies do you think a school should adopt? Give specific reasons and examples to support your opinion.

I   Introduction:

_____

II   Support #1:

_____

   A) Specific detail:

_____

III   Support #2:

_____

   A) Personal experience:

_____

IV   Conclusion:

_____

Topic 2:   There are many types of pollution in this world. Pick one type of pollution and tell what you have done to try to reduce it. Be sure to use specific examples and details in your answer.

I   Introduction:

_____

II   Support #1:

_____

A) Specific detail:

_____

III Support #2:

_____

A) Personal experience:

_____

IV   Conclusion:

_____

Topic 3:   In the past decades, computers have had a tremendous effect on our society. Some experts state that people are relying upon computers too much. Others believe we should rely on computers even more. Which of these two statements do you agree with? Give specific reasons and examples to support your opinion.

I   Introduction:

_____

II   Support #1:

_____

A) Specific detail:

_____

III Support #2:

_____

A) Personal experience:

_____

IV   Conclusion:

_____

4. Writing the Essay

Once you have finished practicing writing outlines, the next step is expanding them into essay form. Look at the standard English essay diagram for writing a composition:

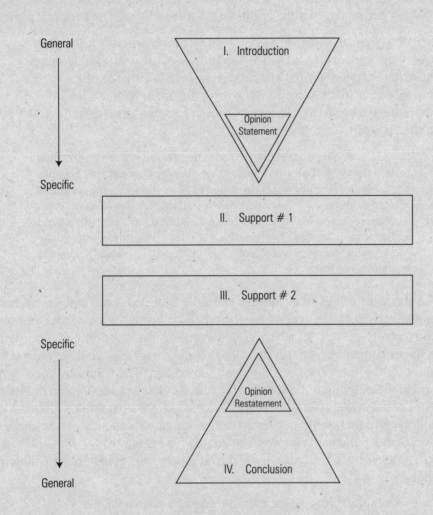

With a few adjustments, your outline will fit neatly within this standard English essay diagram. Begin with the introduction.

The Introduction

The introduction is the first interaction the "qualified" readers have with your essay. Therefore, it has to grab the readers' attention and prepare them for what is to follow. The introduction can be anywhere from three to four sentences in length. It begins with a general statement and gradually becomes more specific as it leads your reader to your opinion statement. Reread the previous topic.

Topic: Some people believe that everyone should have the opportunity to attend a college or university. Others suggest that higher education be reserved for the smartest and best high school students. Which belief do you agree with? Use specific reasons and details to explain your answer.

How would you feel if a government official suddenly informed you that you couldn't attend the college of your dreams because you weren't smart or bright enough? Everything you had worked for in the past 12 years was down the drain. If higher education were reserved for only the smartest and best students, this would be your dilemma. Personally, I believe education should be available for everyone, not just for those individuals who are naturally smart.

The above introduction introduces the topic to be discussed in the main body of the essay. Notice how general the introduction begins. It asks a question that anybody could answer. Gradually, it becomes more specific and eventually gives the opinion statement. In an introductory paragraph, your opinion statement should be the very *last* sentence. Remember, ETS wants to know your opinion of the essay topic. Be sure to give one. By stating your opinion in the last sentence of the introduction, the reader knows exactly what will be discussed in the following paragraphs: personal details, specific facts, and examples as to why you think education should be available for everyone.

> **The last sentence of your introduction should be your opinion statement**

To successfully write your own introduction, ask yourself the following questions:

- Does the introduction grab the reader's attention?

- Does it begin with a general statement and gradually become more specific?

- Is my opinion statement located in the last sentence of the introduction?

Now that you have seen an example of how to write an introduction, try writing some on your own. Remember, ETS doesn't care *what* you write, they only care *how* you write it.

Drill 2

Directions: Reread the following topics and write **introductions** for each. Follow the guidelines for writing introductions. Give yourself 5 minutes to write each introduction. You may refer to the outlines that you have already written. If at all possible, complete this drill on a computer using a word-processing application. Just be sure to disable any high level functions such as spelling check or grammar check if you can. On the real TOEFL CBT, the word processor will not do much beyond cut and paste. If you have no access to a computer, simply write out your answers on a sheet of paper or in the book.

Topic 1:   Certain high schools require that students study foreign languages. Other schools let students study whatever subjects they like. Which of these two policies do you think a school should adopt? Give specific reasons and examples to support your opinion.

_____

_____

_____

_____

_____

_____

Topic 2:   There are many types of pollution in this world. Pick one type of pollution and tell what you have done to try to reduce it. Be sure to use specific examples and details in your answer.

_____

_____

_____

_____

_____

_____

Topic 3: In the past decades, computers have had a tremendous affect on our society. Some experts state that people are relying upon computers too much. Others believe we should rely on computers even more. Which of these two statements do you agree with? Give specific reasons and examples to support your opinion.

The Support

All the TOEFL CBT essay topics have *one* thing in common. They all ask for specific details and examples to support your opinion. If you write a terrific essay with a lot of hard vocabulary and grammatical structures, yet you fail to mention any specific details or examples, your final score will be limited. The paragraph following the introduction must give the first reason that supports your opinion statement. The third paragraph must give an additional reason that supports your opinion statement. In both paragraphs, specific examples must follow. In your basic essay, opinions without specific support mean *nothing*.

Look at an example. Reread the previous topic and the introduction.

Topic 4: Some people believe that everyone should have the opportunity to attend a college or university. Others suggest that higher education be reserved for the smartest and best high school students. Which belief do you agree with? Use specific reasons and details to explain your answer.

How would you feel if a government official suddenly informed you that you couldn't attend the college of your dreams because you weren't smart or bright enough? Everything you had worked for in the past 12 years was down the drain. If higher education were reserved for only the smartest and best students, this would be your dilemma. Personally, I believe education should be available for everyone, not just for those individuals who are naturally smart.

Generally speaking, few students mentally develop at the same rate. Some high school students might reach their intellectual peak at 17, while others might reach it at 21. To be honest, I was a mediocre high-school student at best. I seldom applied myself, and quite frankly, was bored with the dull high-school subjects such as mathematics, science, and history. However, once I was accepted into the university, I could select my own classes such as theatre production, videotape editing, and graphic design. Not only did my grades hit A level, but I also grew excited about what I was studying. In fact, I graduated in the top 10 students of my class.

I also believe that academic institutions are for more than just memorizing facts and data. It is possible to interact with other cultures, learn how to manage your stress, and become involved in various organizations. I was elected president of my freshman class. In addition to completing my studies, I also organized fund raising events, led class activities, and spoke publicly. To my surprise, these experiences were much more rewarding and valuable than my classes were.

Notice that the first sentence in paragraphs two and three above repeat the general sentences from the outline. Now all you need to do is fill in the specific details. The two support paragraphs must back up your opinion statement by providing personal details, specific facts, and examples. Remember, the personal details, specific facts, and examples do *not* need to be true. They only have to support your opinion statement. In the above case, none of the facts are true, yet the argument sounds convincing.

To successfully write your own support paragraphs, ask yourself the following questions:

- Is the general sentence from the outline the first sentence of my paragraph?

- Do the paragraphs contain personal details, specific facts, and examples?

- Do the personal details, specific facts, and examples support my opinion statement?

Now that you have seen an example of how to write support paragraphs, try writing some on your own. Remember, ETS doesn't care *what* you write, they only care *how* you write it.

Drill 3

Directions: Reread the following topics and write two **support paragraphs** for each. Follow the guidelines for writing support paragraphs. Give yourself *10 minutes* to write both paragraphs. You may refer to your outlines and introduction you have already written. As mentioned before, do these drills on a computer if possible. The closer you can simulate the real test-taking experience in your practice, the better.

Topic 1: Certain high schools require that students study foreign languages. Other schools let students study whatever subjects they like. Which of these two policies do you think a school should adopt? Give specific reasons and examples to support your opinion.

_____

_____

_____

_____

_____

_____

_____

_____

_____

_____

_____

_____

Topic 2:   There are many types of pollution in this
world. Pick one type of pollution and tell what you have
done to try to reduce it. Be sure to use specific
examples and details in your answer.

_____

_____

_____

_____

_____

_____

_____

_____

_____

_____

_____

_____

_____

_____

Topic 3:   In the past decades, computers have had a tremendous affect on our society. Some experts state that people are relying upon computers too much. Others believe we should rely on computers even more. Which of these two statements do you agree with? Give specific reasons and examples to support your opinion.

_____

_____

_____

_____

_____

_____

_____

_____

_____

_____

_____

_____

_____

_____

The Conclusion

The conclusion is the last opportunity to demonstrate to the ETS "qualified" readers that you can compose an essay in response to a general topic. While the introduction begins with a general tone and develops a specific opinion statement, the conclusion is the opposite. It begins with a specific statement, working its way toward a more general close to the essay. The very first sentence should be the **opinion restatement**. In other words, summarize your original opinion statement. Do *not* simply repeat it word for word. It needs to be rewritten to convey the same message. The opinion restatement has already been written in the outline. Simply return to the outline and make it the first sentence. The next three to four sentences should summarize the points you have mentioned in the support paragraphs.

Look at an example. Reread the previous essay topic, the introduction, and the main support paragraphs.

Topic: Some people believe that everyone should have the opportunity to attend a college or university. Others suggest that higher education be reserved for the smartest and best high school students. Which belief do you agree with? Use specific reasons and details to explain your answer.

How would you feel if a government official suddenly informed you that you couldn't attend the college of your dreams because you weren't smart or bright enough? Everything you had worked for in the past 12 years would be down the drain. If higher education were reserved for only the smartest and best students, this would be your dilemma. Personally, I believe education should be available for everyone, not just for those individuals who are naturally smart.

Generally speaking, few students mentally develop at the same rate. Some high school students might reach their intellectual peak at 17, while others might reach it at 21. To be honest, I was a mediocre high-school student at best. I seldom applied myself, and quite frankly, was completely bored with the dull high-school subjects such as mathematics, science, and history. However, once I was accepted into the university, I could easily select my own classes such as theatre production, videotape editing, and graphic design. Not only did my grades hit A level, but I also grew excited about what I was studying. In fact, I graduated in the top 10 students of my class.

I also believe that academic institutions are for more than just memorizing facts and data. It is possible to personally interact with other cultures, learn how to better manage your stress, and become involved in various organizations. I was president of my class. In addition to completing my studies, I also organized fund raising events, led class activities, and spoke publicly. To my surprise, these experiences were much more rewarding and valuable than my classes were.

In conclusion, every student should be able to decide for himself whether he desires more education or not. As one who wasn't academically strong in high school, I improved my grades in college and even surpassed my classmates. I also developed important skills outside of the classroom. Given all this, one could say that I am living proof why a student must have control over his own educational destiny.

Notice that the first sentence of the conclusion repeats the opinion restatement from the outline. All that is then needed are two or three more sentences to summarize the points in the two middle support passages. Try to end the conclusion with a strong statement declaring why you believe what you do about the essay topic. Convince the ETS "qualified" readers that you are confident in your assertions. A strong argument equals a strong score. A weak argument equals a weak score.

To successfully write your own conclusion, ask yourself the following questions:

- Does the conclusion begin with the opinion restatement and gradually become more general?

- Does the conclusion summarize the details of the two middle supporting paragraphs?

- Does the conclusion end with a strong statement?

Now that you have seen an example of how to write a conclusion, try writing some on your own. Again, ETS doesn't care *what* you write, they only care *how* you write it.

Drill 4

Directions: Reread the following topics and write **conclusions** for each. Follow the guidelines for writing conclusions. Give yourself five minutes to write each conclusion. You may refer to the outlines, introductions, and main support paragraphs that you have already written. As mentioned before, do these drills on a computer if possible. The closer you can simulate the real test-taking experience in your practice, the better.

Topic 1:   Certain high schools require that students study foreign languages. Other schools let students study whatever subjects they like. Which of these two policies do you think a school should adopt? Give specific reasons and examples to support your opinion.

_____

_____

_____

_____

_____

_____

_____

_____

Topic 2: There are many types of pollution in this world. Pick one type of pollution and tell what you have done to try to reduce it. Be sure to use specific examples and details in your answer.

_____

_____

_____

_____

_____

_____

_____

Topic 3: In the past decades, computers have had a tremendous affect on our society. Some experts state that people are relying upon computers too much. Others believe we should rely on computers even more. Which of these two statements do you agree with? Give specific reasons and examples to support your opinion.

_____

_____

_____

_____

_____

_____

_____

5. Checking Your Work

The last five minutes of the Written section of the TOEFL CBT should be spent rereading your essay to check for mistakes. Since many of you will be typing your essay, any errors can be corrected with a few simple clicks of the mouse. This is one more reason why you should type the essay rather than hand-write it. Look over our checklist to help find the most common essay errors.

Grammar

- Do the subject and verb agree in each sentence?
- Do the pronouns agree with what they refer to?
- Do you vary your sentence structure?

Spelling

- Are the plural words in the plural form?
- Have you confused your native language's spelling with the English spelling?

Punctuation

- Is there a period at the end of every sentence?
- Do commas separate items in a list?
- Does each sentence begin with a capital letter?
- Are proper names capitalized?

Diction (word choice)

- Are the nouns, adjectives, and adverbs in the correct form?
- Are your prepositions correct?
- Do any sentences begin with the word "and"? If so, eliminate and rewrite.

Making a Good Essay Better

Although you will become a better writer as you compose more essays, there are some basic tricks that can initially help you improve your essay.

Easy Verbs and Adjectives

Too often, students will continually repeat the same verbs and adjective over and over. In order to impress your ETS "qualified" reader and raise your score, try to replace such verbs as "go," "take," "make,""walk," "tell," "see," "is," "am," "are," "was," "were," etc. with more descriptive words and phrases such as "attend," "run," "grab," "create," "hurry," "inform," and "observe," to name just a few. Adjectives such as "big," "little," "fast," "fat," "fun," "ugly," "beautiful" can also be replaced by more descriptive adjectives such as "enormous", "minute," "speedy," "obese," "exciting," "hideous," "gorgeous," etc. The English language is full of descriptive vocabulary words.

Modifiers

A modifier is any word that gives additional information to another word. Every verb and adjective can be modified by an adverb. Likewise, every noun can be modified by an adjective. A boring *subject + verb + object* sentence can be made more exciting by adding some modifiers.

Linking Words

Linking words and phrases help essays flow. They connect each paragraph and sentence with the next one. Ideas blend together and make the essay more cohesive. Some common linking words and phrases that should be practiced are:

as far as I'm concerned	however
in my opinion	for the most part
to be honest	for instance
to my surprise	for example
fortunately	what's more
unfortunately	furthermore
personally	on the contrary
I believe	nevertheless
definitely	moreover
by all means	in addition
apparently	in conclusion
perhaps	in fact
clearly	in that case
frankly	lastly
honestly	although
generally speaking	on the contrary
at first	on the whole
finally	even though

Keep these linking words and phrases in mind while writing your essay as well as while checking it. Paragraphs and sentences that flow together will absolutely increase your score.

For example, take a sentence from the example essay on higher education.

> I was president of my class.

To make this sentence more interesting, first change the verb.

> I was selected as president of my class.

Now add some modifiers

> I was randomly selected as president of my freshman class.

Now add some linking words

> Fortunately, I was randomly selected as president of my freshman class.

The original sentence has drastically improved. It has become longer, more developed, more interesting and informative, and much more "essay-friendly."

Drill 5

Directions: Practice changing verbs, adding modifiers, and adding linking words to the following sentences. Because there is no one correct answer, practice rewriting each sentence using different verbs, modifiers, and linking words. As mentioned before, do these drills on a computer if possible. The closer you can simulate the real test-taking experience in your practice, the better.

It is important to concentrate while studying.

_____

_____

_____

_____

_____

_____

The professor went to the cafeteria, but it was closed.

_____

_____

_____

_____

_____

Some of the classes were cancelled, but the student
went anyway.

_____

_____

_____

_____

_____

_____

A computer is a tool that helps students improve their
grades.

_____

_____

_____

_____

_____

Supervisors get their employees by putting
advertisements in the newspaper.

_____

_____

_____

_____

_____

In order to go to college, a student must take a special exam.

_____

_____

_____

_____

_____

Two people share a room on most college campuses.

_____

_____

_____

_____

_____

New students have many problems when they go to college.

_____

_____

_____

_____

_____

SUMMARY OF WRITING SECTION STRATEGY

Spend 5 minutes on each of the following:

1. Read the question, choose a side, and write your outline.

2. Write the **introduction** paragraph.

3. Write the **first support** paragraph.

4. Write the **second support** paragraph.

5. Write the **conclusion** paragraph.

6. Reread, correct, and edit your essay as necessary.

TOEFL CBT Practice Topics

Directions: For the following topics, use what you have learned to demonstrate your ability to write in English. Give yourself 30 minutes to complete each essay. If possible, practice on a computer. If you don't have access to a computer, write legibly by hand on the lines provided. Either way, remember that at the real TOEFL CBT, the proctor will give you blank paper on which to outline your essay.

Essay Topic #1

Writing

Some say that the world would be a better place now if the automobile had never been invented. Do you agree or disagree with this statement? Use specific examples and details to support your answer.

Cut

Paste

Undo

Time

Help

Answer Confirm

Next

Essay Topic #2

Writing

Some people say that the best way to raise children is to encourage them to be independent thinkers. Others disagree and say that children need to be taught discipline in order to become successful. Which statement do you agree with? Use specific examples and details to support your answer.

Cut

Paste

Undo

Time

? Help

Answer Confirm

→ Next

Essay Topic #3

Some people would rather live in rural areas. Others most definitely believe urban living is better. Which do you prefer? Use specific examples and details to support your answer.

Cut

Paste

Undo

Time

? Help

Answer Confirm

Next

Essay Topic #4

What are some important qualities of a good professor or teacher? Use specific details and examples to explain why these qualities are important.

Cut

Paste

Undo

Time

? Help

Answer Confirm

Next

Essay Topic #5

Do you agree or disagree with the following statement?
Education should be free. Use specific reasons and examples
to support your answer.

Cut

Paste

Undo

Time

? Help

Answer
Confirm

Next

PART ◆ VI

Taking the Test

HOW TO TAKE THE PRINCETON REVIEW TOEFL CBT DIAGNOSTIC EXAM

You should plan to take the diagnostic exam at the end of this book only after reading through all of the other chapters and completing all of the drills. Be sure to review the test-taking tips for each section of the TOEFL CBT before you sit down to take the test. If you have access to the Internet, be sure to complete the TOEFL CBT tests at The Princeton Review website before you take the real test.

When taking the diagnostic exam, your goal should be to approximate actual test conditions as closely as possible. Because the diagnostic exam is a paper version of the TOEFL CBT, it is impossible for you to point and click a mouse. Therefore, use a pen or pencil to circle the correct answer. To help better prepare yourself, practice clicking on the "Next" and "Answer Confirm" icons by circling them with your pen or pencil. Remember, once you click on the "Answer Confirm" icon, you will never see that question again. Therefore, answer the questions in the order they appear, and do NOT change an answer once you have circled the "Answer Confirm" icon. To take The Princeton Review diagnostic test, you will need:

- A quiet room
- A compact-disc player (preferably a Walkman or CD player that requires headphones)
- A pen or a pencil
- A watch
- Approximately three hours and fifteen minutes of uninterrupted time.

When you are ready to begin, remember the following:

1. Adjust the volume on your compact-disc player before the actual questions begin.

2. Use only the amount of time actually allotted for each section.

3. Take the entire test in one sitting.

4. Circle your answer choices (since you will be unable to "click" on them as on the actual TOEFL CBT). Remember to also circle the "Next" and "Answer Confirm" icons in the Listening and Structure sections.

5. If possible, complete the Writing section on computer.

6. Do not score the test until you have read the next couple of pages and until you have at least an hour to spend examining your results.

EVALUATING YOUR PERFORMANCE

Use the answer key that appears after the test to determine your score. Make sure to correct and study your performance carefully. Try to do it within 24 hours of taking the test, or you'll have a hard time remembering why you chose one answer over another. When looking at your performance on the diagnostic, don't just settle for counting up the number of wrong and right answers and looking up the vocabulary words you didn't know. Pay special attention to all of the following:

1. "STUPID" MISTAKES

We use the term *stupid mistakes* to refer to the mistakes you make on questions you *know* you should have been able to answer correctly. In other words, if the correct answer seems obvious now and you can't understand why you chose the answer you did, and you find yourself saying, "Wow, that was really stupid of me," you've run across a "stupid" mistake.

Interestingly enough, you'll find that "stupid" mistakes usually aren't stupid at all; they're more often due to simple *carelessness*, and they usually happen for one of two reasons:

> **Reason 1: Impatience.** "Haste makes waste," the saying in English goes—you probably have a similar saying in your native language. You'll probably find that you got some questions wrong because you didn't bother to read through all of the answer choices before choosing your answer.

> **Reason 2: Misunderstanding the question.** Sometimes even native speakers have to read a question two or three times before understanding what the question is actually asking. Why should you expect understand everything the first time you read it? Many students get questions wrong just because they are answering the wrong question.

It's important to figure out *why* you got any wrong answer wrong, especially when you make a "stupid" mistake. It will help you learn to avoid that type of mistake in the future.

2. "LUCKY" GUESSES

Sometimes the only thing more surprising than mysterious wrong answers (such as the stupid mistakes discussed above) are all those questions you answer correctly and are not sure *why*. Most students tend to attribute these right answers to plain, old-fashioned good luck. That may be true for some of them. After all, if you guess on four questions, the odds are you will get one of them right and the other three wrong. However, that probably doesn't explain all of the questions you answer correctly, even though you didn't think you knew the answer. Chances are you were using the test-taking strategies from this book without even realizing it, the most important of which is POE.

The best way to recognize questions on which you used POE effectively is to look for questions you answered correctly to which you did not "know" the answer. Try to remember why you chose the answer you selected, then apply that same reasoning to other questions on the other practice tests and the real questions on the real TOEFL CBT.

3. Other "Wrong" Answers

Some wrong answers are due to carelessness, but some can be attributed to information you just didn't know or remember. When you look over your test, make sure that the wrong answer you chose isn't one you could have eliminated using POE. Did you pick a silly answer in the Listening section just because you missed the statement? Did you choose an answer with poor syntax in the Structure section? Try to discover if you could have eliminated an answer or two before guessing.

4. Pacing Problems

To determine if you had problems with time, ask yourself the following questions:

- Were you unable to finish any of the sections?

If so, then you probably spent too much time answering one or more questions. ETS gives you plenty of time on the TOEFL CBT, but don't linger over questions. Choose and move on.

- Did you run out of time before getting to the last passage on the Reading section?

If so, you may have spent too much time on a couple of questions. Remember, don't get bogged down on any one question! Skip the third-pass questions, and save them for last. Use chronology to find the information you need and use POE to eliminate any answer choices.

On the other hand, it's possible that you rushed through the test and answered too carelessly.

- Did you finish any section or sections with more than one minute of the allotted time left over?

If so, you need to slow down and spend more time answering the questions. There's no prize given for finishing the TOEFL CBT early, and rushing to finish can hurt your score.

WHAT SHOULD YOU DO NOW?

If you have some time before you are scheduled to take the actual TOEFL CBT, you can use the results of your diagnostic test to help decide if you need any additional preparation. You can order a CD-ROM from ETS with a form provided in the TOEFL CBT Bulletin. Just make sure you leave plenty of time for the materials to arrive.

We do not recommend any test materials published by anyone other than ETS. Many of the examples in non-ETS publications contain problems that are poorly written or that just don't appear on real TOEFL CBT exams, leading you to waste time studying things that won't help you on the test. Try to schedule your use of the materials so that you have a full-length TOEFL CBT exam (either ours or ETS's) to take sometime in the week before the test.

The Week Before the Test

Here's a list of *dos* and *don'ts* for the week before the test:

- *Don't* try to learn any new material the week before the TOEFL CBT. You can't learn much vocabulary or grammar in that amount of time. You're better off practicing the test-taking tips.

- *Do* make sure you know exactly how to get to your test center. You don't want to be late, or feel rushed to get there. Getting lost is one way to really hurt your self-confidence on a day when you need to remain calm and in control. Take a practice trip to the test site so you can see how long it takes.

- *Don't* study at all on the day before the test. The most helpful thing you can do is relax; at most, maybe see a movie or watch television, in English if you can, and go to sleep early.

- *Do* make sure that you know, well in advance, everything that you need to take with you to the test.

By the time the actual test day rolls around, you won't be worrying about any minor details, and you'll be able to focus completely on the test.

The Day of the Test

Wake up a little earlier than you have to. Give yourself time to eat a light breakfast and try to make time to do some "warm-up" questions of each type. Then make sure you have the following items with you before you leave for the test:

- Identification: Check your TOEFL CBT Bulletin for a list of acceptable forms of identification.

- Your confirmation number.

- Names of institutions to which you want your scores to be sent.

- A TOEFL CBT Voucher, if you have one.

- A positive attitude.

When you're finished, go home and forget about the TOEFL CBT. It takes about 15 days for your scores to arrive. (Remember, your 30-minute essay needs grading!) You can wait with confidence because you've mastered a skill that won't help you anywhere else in your life—the skill of taking the TOEFL CBT. Won't it be nice to forget it?

The Princeton Review
TOEFL CBT Diagnostic
Exam and Answers

You may only take 60 minutes to answer the following 50 questions. Do not take more than 60 minutes to complete this section. When you are ready to begin, play Track 7 of the CD. Transcriptions for these drills can be found in the Appendix. You should only refer to them after you complete the exercises. Remember, on the real test you will only hear the passage once and you will not see anything in writing.

Listening

Listening

Listening
50 questions

Question Directions – Part A

In the first part, you will hear short conversations between two people. Each conversation is followed by a question about it.

Each question in this part has four answer choices. Select the best answer to each question. Answer the questions on the basis of what is stated or implied by the speakers.

During the questions, you can refer to these directions again by clicking on the Help icon. To change the volume, click on the Volume icon.

You cannot click on any icons during a conversation.

When you are ready to continue, click on the Dismiss Directions icon.

When finished reading directions click on the icon below

Dismiss Directions

Time | Volume | Help | Answer Confirm | Next

Listening

Listening

Listening

What does the woman imply about John?

- He's probably seen the play before.
- He should be able to buy tickets for the game.
- He intended to see the play another time.
- He probably isn't interested in seeing the play.

Time

Volume Help Answer Confirm Next

Listening

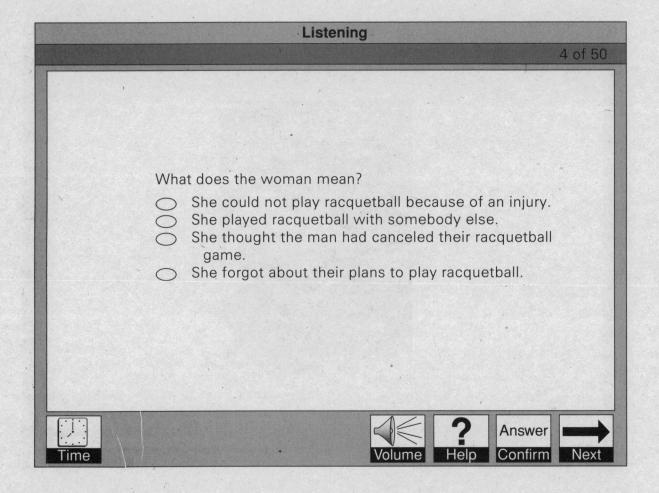

What does the woman mean?

○ She could not play racquetball because of an injury.
○ She played racquetball with somebody else.
○ She thought the man had canceled their racquetball game.
○ She forgot about their plans to play racquetball.

Time

Volume Help Answer Confirm Next

Listening

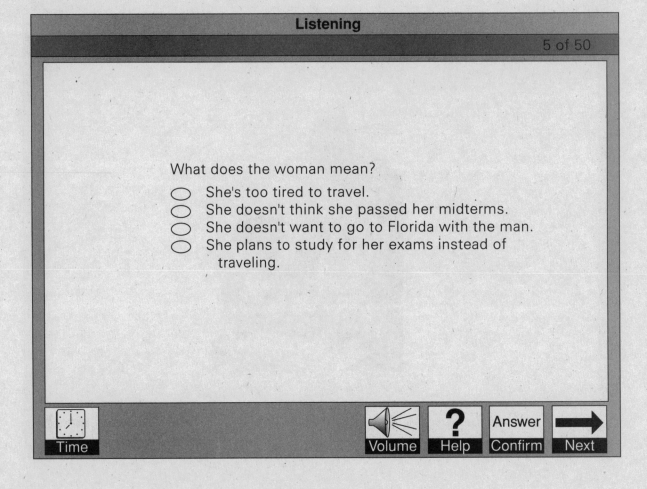

What does the woman mean?

○ She's too tired to travel.
○ She doesn't think she passed her midterms.
○ She doesn't want to go to Florida with the man.
○ She plans to study for her exams instead of
    traveling.

Time

Volume   Help   Answer Confirm   Next

Listening

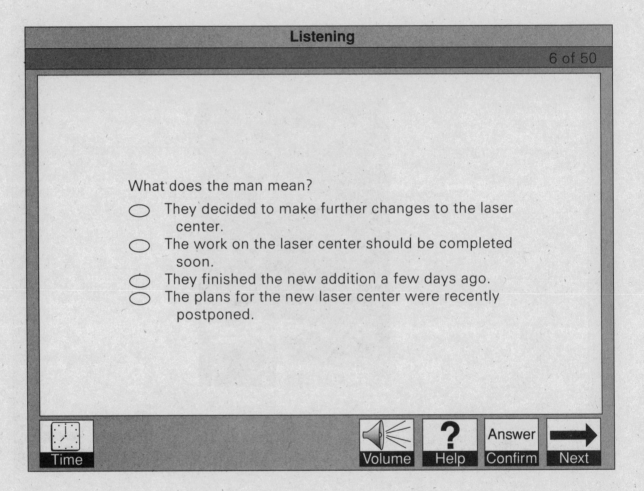

What does the man mean?

○ They decided to make further changes to the laser center.

○ The work on the laser center should be completed soon.

○ They finished the new addition a few days ago.

○ The plans for the new laser center were recently postponed.

Time   Volume Help Answer Confirm Next

Listening

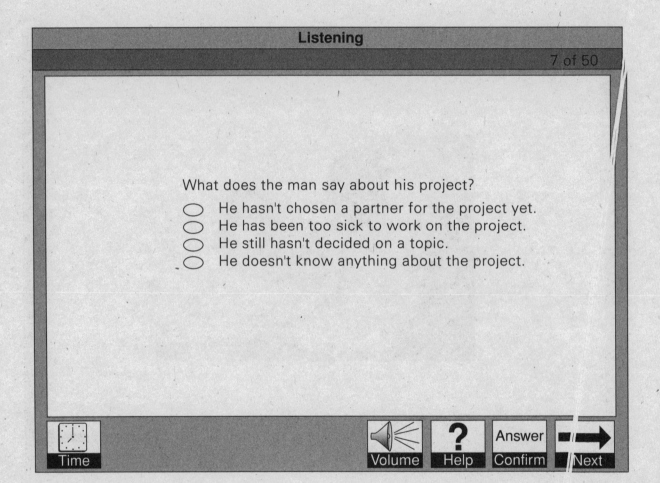

What does the man say about his project?

- ○ He hasn't chosen a partner for the project yet.
- ○ He has been too sick to work on the project.
- ○ He still hasn't decided on a topic.
- ○ He doesn't know anything about the project.

Time | Volume | Help | Answer Confirm | Next

Listening

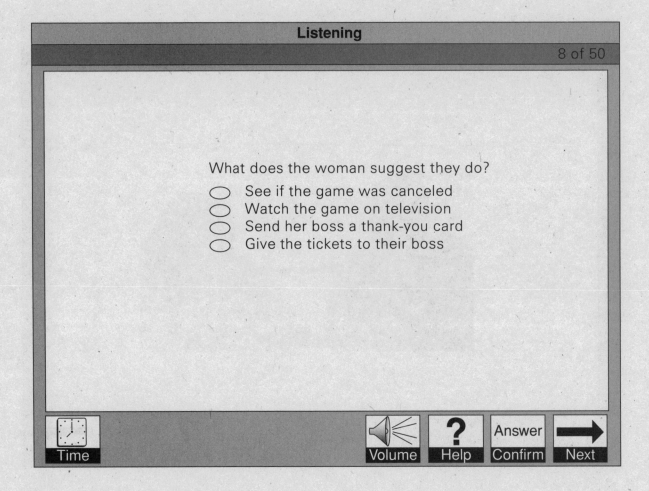

What does the woman suggest they do?

- ○ See if the game was canceled
- ○ Watch the game on television
- ○ Send her boss a thank-you card
- ○ Give the tickets to their boss

Time

Volume

? Help

Answer Confirm

→ Next

Listening

What does the woman mean?

○ David has no interest in the movie.
○ David will not go to the movie.
○ David has already seen the movie.
○ David is almost done studying.

Time   Volume   Help   Answer Confirm   Next

Listening

What does the man mean?

- ◯ He would prefer to take a taxi.
- ◯ The bus rates were recently raised.
- ◯ The bus frequently comes late.
- ◯ Taxis are cheaper than buses.

Time   Volume   Help   Answer Confirm   Next

Listening

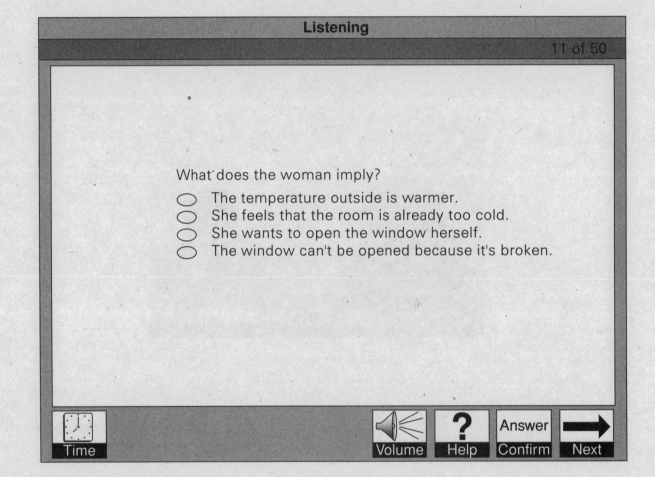

What does the woman imply?

○ The temperature outside is warmer.
○ She feels that the room is already too cold.
○ She wants to open the window herself.
○ The window can't be opened because it's broken.

Time

Volume Help Answer Confirm Next

Listening

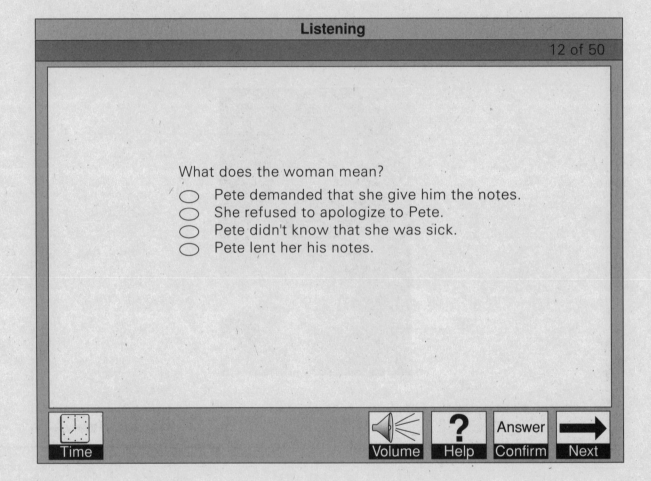

What does the woman mean?

○ Pete demanded that she give him the notes.
○ She refused to apologize to Pete.
○ Pete didn't know that she was sick.
○ Pete lent her his notes.

Time

Volume

Help

Answer Confirm

Next

Listening

Listening

What does the man mean?

○ The woman should learn how to paint.
○ The museum has very few twentieth-century
   sculptures.
○ The twentieth-century painting collection is also small.
○ The woman forgot to mention the paintings.

Time   Volume   Help   Answer Confirm   Next

Listening

What does the woman imply?

○ It was unnecessary to take the journalism classes.
○ The journalism classes were easier than she expected.
○ The man should have taken the journalism classes also.
○ The journalism classes helped her with her new position.

Time   Volume   Help   Answer Confirm   Next

Listening

What does the woman mean?

- He has always excelled in debate.
- Her speech skills need improvement.
- It is difficult for her to debate topics.
- He doesn't have the right skills for debate.

Time

Volume Help Answer Confirm Next

Listening

What does the woman imply?

○ The disk could be among some other disks.
○ She saw his disk on the shelf.
○ The man shouldn't have touched her computer.
○ The man should call the computer center.

Time   Volume   Help   Answer Confirm   Next

Listening

Question Directions – Part B

In this part, there are several talks and conversations. Each talk or conversation is followed by several questions.

The conversations and talks are about a variety of topics. You do not need special knowledge of the topics to answer the questions correctly. Rather, you should answer each question on the basis of what is stated or implied by the speakers in the conversation or talk.

During the questions, you can refer to these directions again by clicking on the Help icon. To change the volume, click on the Volume icon.

You cannot click on any icons during a talk or conversation.

When you are ready to continue, click on the Dismiss Directions icon.

When finished reading directions click on the icon below

Dismiss Directions

Time | Volume | Help | Answer Confirm | Next

Listening

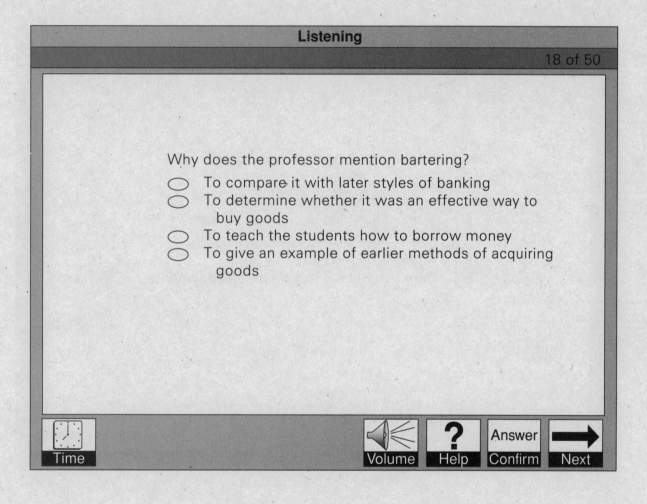

Why does the professor mention bartering?

⬭ To compare it with later styles of banking
⬭ To determine whether it was an effective way to buy goods
⬭ To teach the students how to borrow money
⬭ To give an example of earlier methods of acquiring goods

Time Volume Help Answer Confirm Next

Listening

What were the problems of using gold as money?

Click on 2 answers.

☐ It only had value in certain cultures.
☐ It was dangerous to carry.
☐ It was too heavy.
☐ Bankers refused to accept it as payment.

Time

Volume   Help   Answer Confirm   Next

According to the passage, for which of the following purposes do humans most likely cut down trees?

Click on 2 answers.

- ☐ Farming
- ☐ Furniture
- ☐ Shelter
- ☐ Firewood

Time   Volume   ? Help   Answer Confirm   → Next

Listening

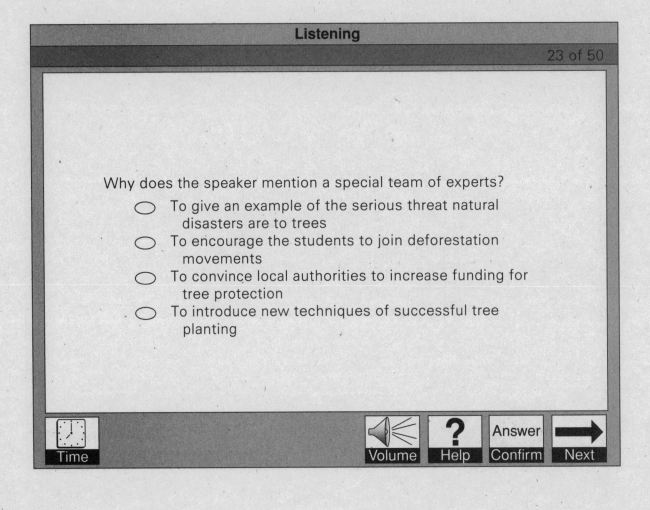

Based on the professor's lecture, match the following threats to trees with the degree of severity.

Click on a phrase. Then click on the space where it belongs. Use each phrase only once.

Humans
Insects and disease
Natural disasters

Most severe threat	Severe threat	Least severe threat

Time

Volume Help Answer Confirm Next

Listening

Based on the professor's description, match the following cooking techniques to the society in which they were used.

Click on a phrase. Then click on the space where it belongs. Use each phrase only once.

Brazier method
Tribal method
Manor method

Hunting and gathering	Southern colonial	Pompeii

Time   Volume   Help   Answer Confirm   Next

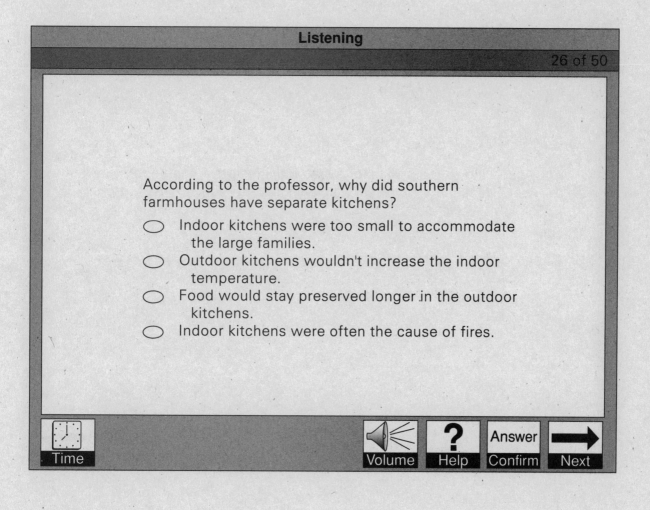

According to the professor, why did southern farmhouses have separate kitchens?

○ Indoor kitchens were too small to accommodate the large families.

○ Outdoor kitchens wouldn't increase the indoor temperature.

○ Food would stay preserved longer in the outdoor kitchens.

○ Indoor kitchens were often the cause of fires.

Listening

According to the professor, what activities other than cooking were done in the northern colonial kitchens?

Click on 2 answers.

- ☐ Bathing
- ☐ Painting
- ☐ Sewing
- ☐ Construction

Time Volume Help Answer Confirm Next

Listening

What is the purpose of the lecture?

- ◯ To persuade the students to stop smoking
- ◯ To explain newly accepted research on smoking
- ◯ To gain support for anti-smoking legislation
- ◯ To inform the students of the side effects of smoking

Time   Volume   Help   Answer Confirm   Next

Listening

What is true about smoking during pregnancy?

- The infants are born earlier than expected.
- The birth weight is substantially higher.
- The infants are more likely to have asthma as adults.
- It interferes with the babies' ability to digest food.

Time

Volume

Help

Answer Confirm

Next

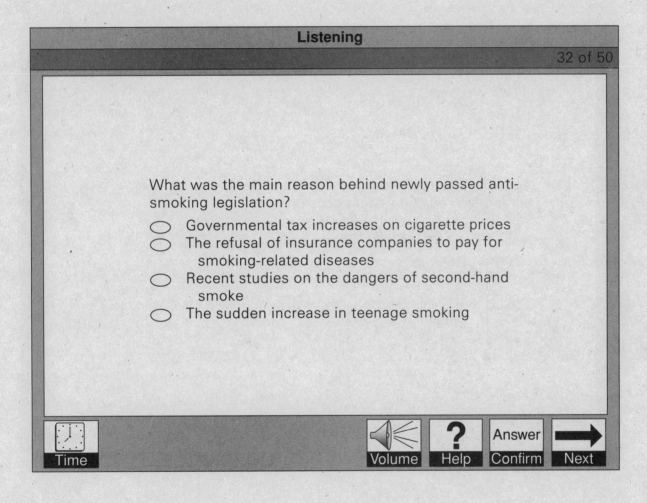

Listening

According to the lecture, which of the following does the autonomic nervous system control?

Click on 2 answers.

- ☐ Heart rate
- ☐ Muscular movement
- ☐ Circulation
- ☐ Speech

Time   Volume   Help   Answer Confirm   Next

What is true regarding nicotine and habitual cigarette smokers?

- ⬭ They have difficulty digesting it.
- ⬭ They need more to bring about the same effects.
- ⬭ It decreases their ability to concentrate.
- ⬭ It makes them more tired.

Time   Volume   Help   Answer Confirm   Next

Listening

What is the main idea of the lecture?

- ◯ Why butterflies are more popular than moths
- ◯ The effects of pesticides on moth populations
- ◯ The physical differences between butterflies and moths
- ◯ The survival techniques of moths

Time

Volume

Help

Answer Confirm

Next

According to the professor, why are moths less likely to be seen than butterflies?

- ⬭ Moths are active during the night.
- ⬭ Butterflies are larger than moths.
- ⬭ There are more butterflies than moths.
- ⬭ Moths are faster than butterflies.

Time   Volume   **?** Help   Answer Confirm   ➡ Next

Listening

What does the professor say about the antennae of moths?

- They are thin and smooth.
- They resemble the antennae of wasps.
- They are long and straight.
- They are knobby and feathery.

Time   Volume   Help   Answer Confirm   Next

According to the passage, what do moths imitate in order to camouflage themselves?

Click on 2 answers.

☐ Flowers
☐ Leaves
☐ Antennae
☐ Sticks

Time

Volume

Help

Answer Confirm

Next

Listening

The professor briefly explains a process. Summarize the process by putting the events in order.

Click on a sentence. Then click on the space where it belongs. Use each sentence only once.

The larvae release a highly offensive smell.

Thousands of larvae begin to wiggle and squirm.

The caterpillars weave a communal silk tent.

A predator threatens the larvae.

1 [_____]   3 [_____]

2 [_____]   4 [_____]

Time   Volume   Help   Answer Confirm   Next

What does the professor say about the monkey moth?

- ◯ Its legs detach from its body.
- ◯ It has a horrible taste.
- ◯ It is in danger of extinction.
- ◯ The predator cannot catch it.

Time

Volume

Help

Answer Confirm

Next

Listening

What does the professor mainly discuss?

- ⬭ The types of joints of highly evolved creatures
- ⬭ The symptoms of arthritic joints
- ⬭ The reasons why joints are so important to mammals
- ⬭ How various joints differ from each other

Time

Volume

Help

Answer Confirm

Next

Based on the professor's description, classify the following types of joints.

Click on a phrase. Then click on the space where it belongs. Use each phrase only once.

Ball-and-socket joint
Hinge joint
Pivot joint

Neck	Shoulder	Elbow

Time

Volume

? Help

Answer Confirm

→ Next

Listening

According to the professor, what is true about the ball-and-socket joint?

- It is the most delicate of all the joints.
- It is most likely to be affected by arthritis.
- It is the most common type of joint.
- It allows the greatest range of movement.

Time

Volume

Help

Answer Confirm

Next

Listening

Listening

According to the lecture, why is information lost from the short-term memory?

- ◯ It disappears into an unknown section of the brain.
- ◯ It is replaced by newer information.
- ◯ It is transferred into the long-term memory.
- ◯ It is blocked by short-term memory inhibitors.

Time   Volume   Help   Answer Confirm   Next

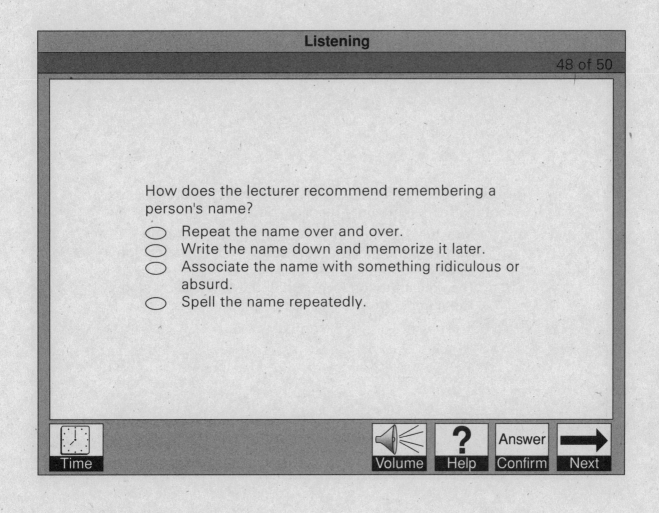

How does the lecturer recommend remembering a person's name?

- ○ Repeat the name over and over.
- ○ Write the name down and memorize it later.
- ○ Associate the name with something ridiculous or absurd.
- ○ Spell the name repeatedly.

Listening

49 of 50

According to the lecture, what is the most important factor affecting memory recollection?

○ How full the memory is of unimportant material
○ How well the material was stored in the association stage
○ The concentration level during the registration stage
○ The number of memory self-help books read

Time · Volume · Help · Answer Confirm · Next

What are two disturbances that could possibly affect the recall stage?

Click on 2 answers.

☐ Medicine
☐ Fatigue
☐ Age
☐ Disuse

Time

Volume

? Help

Answer Confirm

➡ Next

```
┌─────────────────────────────────────────────────────────────────────┐
│                            Structure                                  │
├─────────────────────────────────────────────────────────────────────┤
│                                                                       │
│  ┌─────────────────────────────────┐          ┌───────────────────┐  │
│  │            Structure             │          │      When         │  │
│  │          20 Question             │          │     finished      │  │
│  └─────────────────────────────────┘          │     reading        │  │
│                                                 │    directions     │  │
│  This section is designed to measure your       │   click on the    │  │
│  ability to recognize language that is          │    icon below     │  │
│  appropriate for standard written English.      └───────────────────┘  │
│  There are two types of questions in this       ┌───────────────────┐  │
│  section.                                       │     Dismiss       │  │
│  In the first type of question, there are       │    Directions     │  │
│  incomplete sentences. Beneath each sentence    └───────────────────┘  │
│  there are four words or phrases. You will                           │
│  click on the one word or phrase that best                           │
│  completes the sentence.                                             │
│    ┌──────────────────────────────────────────┐                     │
│    │  Example:  Geysers have often been        │                     │
│    │            compared to volcanoes____they  │                     │
│    │            both emit hot liquids below    │                     │
│    │            the Earth's surface.           │                     │
│    │                        due to             │                     │
│    │                        because            │                     │
│    │                        in spite of        │                     │
│    │                        regardless         │                     │
│    └──────────────────────────────────────────┘                     │
│  The second type of question has four underlined words or phrases.   │
│  You will click on the one underlined word or phrase that must be    │
│  changed for the sentence to be correct.                             │
│    ┌──────────────────────────────────────────┐                     │
│    │  Example:  Guppies are sometimes call     │                     │
│    │            rainbow fish because of the    │                     │
│    │            males' bright colors.          │                     │
│    └──────────────────────────────────────────┘                     │
│  Now begin working on the Structure questions. When you are ready    │
│  to continue, click on the Dismiss Directions icon.                  │
│                                                                       │
│  ┌──────┐                         ┌───┐ ┌────────┐ ┌──────────┐      │
│  │ 🕐   │                         │ ? │ │ Answer │ │    →     │      │
│  │ Time │                         │Help││Confirm│ │   Next   │      │
│  └──────┘                         └───┘ └────────┘ └──────────┘      │
└─────────────────────────────────────────────────────────────────────┘
```

You may only take 16 minutes to answer the folowing 20 questions. Do not take more than 16 minutes to complete this section.

Structure

Click on the word or phrase that best completes the sentence.

After hydrogen, oxygen is the _____ in the atmosphere of the Earth.

- ⃝ element is most plentiful
- ⃝ most plentiful element that
- ⃝ element that most plentiful
- ⃝ most plentiful element

Time   **?** Help   Answer Confirm   ➡ Next

Click on the word or phrase that best completes the sentence.

Born in 1961, Diana, the princess of Wales, <u>founded a number of</u> non-profit <u>organization</u> before <u>losing</u> her life on a well-traveled expressway in Paris, France.

Time   **?** Help   Answer Confirm   ➡ Next

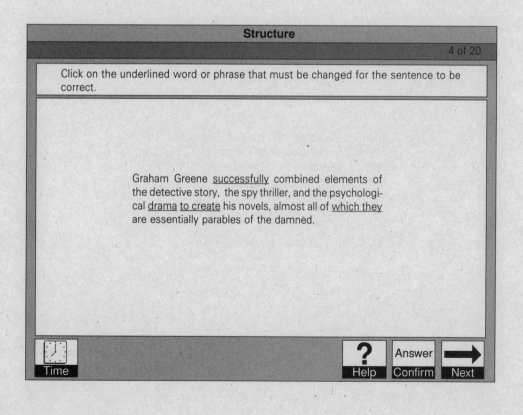

Click on the word or phrase that best completes the sentence.

Aluminum's extreme malleability, durability, and conductivity make _____ for high-tension electrical power transmission.

○ it useful
○ it a useful
○ it is of useful
○ it uses

Time · ? Help · Answer Confirm · Next

Click on the underlined word or phrase that must be changed for the sentence to be correct.

Graham Greene <u>successfully</u> combined elements of the detective story, the spy thriller, and the psychological <u>drama</u> <u>to create</u> his novels, almost all of <u>which they</u> are essentially parables of the damned.

Time · ? Help · Answer Confirm · Next

Structure

Click on the underlined word or phrase that must be changed for the sentence to be correct.

Long before instruments were solely associated with creating music, they played an essential role in many ceremonies, included both religious and pagan.

Click on the word or phrase that best completes the sentence.

According to some psychologists, the objective of parenting is to help children learn what _____ to know in order to live a mentally healthy and well-balanced life as adults.

- ○ they are needed
- ○ they need
- ○ it is needed
- ○ do they need

Structure

7 of 20

Click on the underlined word or phrase that must be changed for the sentence to be correct.

Hawaii's variety of <u>untamed</u> volcanic ranges and pristine beaches <u>attract</u> many tourists who <u>enjoy</u> diverse <u>wilderness</u>.

Time | ? Help | Answer Confirm | Next

Structure

8 of 20

Click on the underlined word or phrase that must be changed for the sentence to be correct.

<u>Many</u> undergraduate linguistic majors are shocked <u>to realize</u> that <u>much</u> of the English vernacular originates from the <u>language native</u> of the American Indians.

Time | ? Help | Answer Confirm | Next

Structure

Click on the word or phrase that best completes the sentence.

One of the principles held by modern-day educators is that a math teacher need not tell a student _____ about solving complex mathematical equations.

- ○ that going
- ○ to go how
- ○ which going
- ○ how to go

Time   Help   Answer Confirm   Next

Click on the word or phrase that best completes the sentence.

Historically, the knife is perhaps the earliest form of a weapon, _____ its availability varied depending on the geographical area.

- ○ whereas
- ○ despite
- ○ although
- ○ unlike

Time   Help   Answer Confirm   Next

Click on the underlined word or phrase that must be changed for the sentence to be correct.

The common white potato <u>closely</u> <u>resembles</u> a fruit, <u>but account</u> of several botanical features <u>it</u> is considered a part of the vegetable family.

Time   ? Help   Answer Confirm   Next

Click on the word or phrase that best completes the sentence.

With age, veins and arteries lose their elasticity and ability to quickly transport blood throughout the body, _____ them less efficient.

- ○ and to make
- ○ makes
- ○ which it makes
- ○ thereby making

Time   ? Help   Answer Confirm   Next

Structure

Click on the underlined word or phrase that must be changed for the sentence to be correct.

Electricity, at first considered a luxury seventy years <u>ago</u>, is now viewed as a <u>necessary</u> to human survival and <u>plays</u> an essential role <u>in</u> modern-day progress.

Time | Help | Answer Confirm | Next

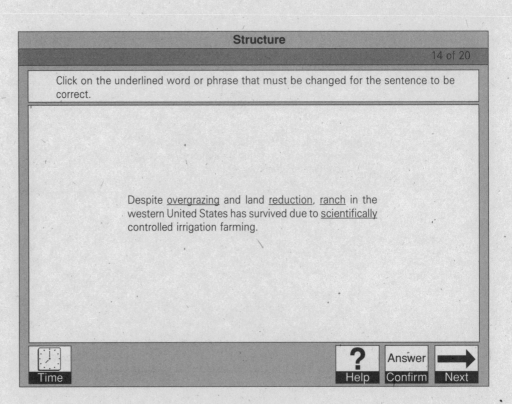

Click on the underlined word or phrase that must be changed for the sentence to be correct.

Despite <u>overgrazing</u> and land <u>reduction</u>, <u>ranch</u> in the western United States has survived due to <u>scientifically</u> controlled irrigation farming.

Time | Help | Answer Confirm | Next

Click on the word or phrase that best completes the sentence.

_____ 500 artificial satellites orbiting the earth, and although they were all initially designed for communication, only 75 percent are actually functioning.

○ About
○ There are about
○ If there are about
○ It is about

Time ? Help Answer Confirm Next →

Click on the word or phrase that best completes the sentence.

A recently released study has concluded that not only _____ who live under high-powered electrical lines more likely to contract leukemia, but they are also less likely to respond to treatment.

○ they are children
○ children
○ are children
○ do some children

Time ? Help Answer Confirm Next →

Structure

Click on the underlined word or phrase that must be changed for the sentence to be correct.

<u>Even though</u> grapevines do not produce <u>any</u> fruit during the winter, they require <u>a such</u> dormant cold spell in order <u>to bear</u> grapes in the upcoming season.

Time   ? Help   Answer Confirm   → Next

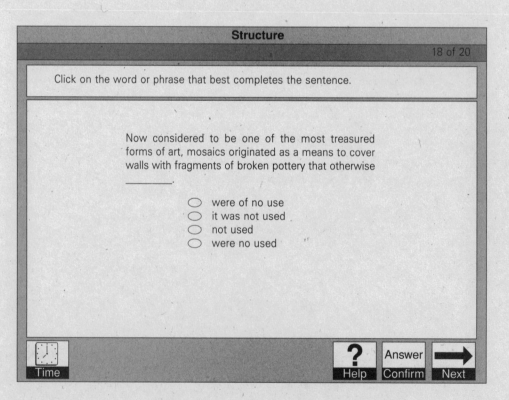

Click on the word or phrase that best completes the sentence.

Now considered to be one of the most treasured forms of art, mosaics originated as a means to cover walls with fragments of broken pottery that otherwise _____.

   ◯ were of no use
   ◯ it was not used
   ◯ not used
   ◯ were no used

Time   ? Help   Answer Confirm   → Next

Click on the underlined word or phrase that must be changed for the sentence to be correct.

Dmitri Shostakovich's music <u>is</u> usually <u>rich</u> and well composed, often <u>incorporates</u> many crescendos <u>to gradually</u> increase the fullness of tone.

Time   Help   Answer Confirm   Next

Click on the underlined word or phrase that must be changed for the sentence to be correct.

Protection against <u>dirt</u> and disease, <u>prevent</u> from adhesion, and lubrication <u>are</u> several of the <u>many</u> functions of eyelids for humans.

Time   Help   Answer Confirm   Next

Reading

READING

READING

5 Passages

In this section, you will read 5 passages. Each passage is followed by 8–10 questions.

You should answer all questions following a passage on the basis of what is stated or implied in that passage.

For each question, click on the mouse to select an answer.

When you are ready to continue, click on the Dismiss Directions icon.

When finished reading directions click on the icon below

Dismiss Directions

Time

? Help

Answer Confirm

Next

You may only take 90 minutes to answer the following 49 questions. Do not take more than 90 minutes to complete this section.

Reading

Beginning

Early studies of anatomy were hampered by the authorities' disapproval of dissections, and by the lack of refrigeration. By the 1500s in Europe the collected knowledge about the human body had been codified and was the exclusive domain of the Doctors of Physick, a group of scholars who went to great lengths to prevent medical information from spreading. To this end, the Doctors stored their knowledge in obscure languages such as Greek, Latin, and Arabic. The Doctors, by not allowing the works of anatomy to be translated into common tongues, remained invincible to intellectual assaults by laymen. Not only did Doctors of Physick refuse to supplement the bodily lore they learned at the university with practical observations, but they also charged ludicrous amounts to treat their patients.

The doctors generally prescribed two different treatments for disease, blood lettings for those with physical disorders, and point-branding for those in need of psychiatric care. The treatments involved using leeches and needles, respectively, and often caused patients to end up worse off than they were prior to treatment. Given these conditions, the common people opted to patronize the village apothecary, who was typically a local grocer selling ineffectual herbal remedies.

Protected by an imposing guild system, the citadel of medicine was finally cracked by Paracelsus, a rogue physician of the sixteenth century. Paracelsus was a self-taught medicine man who instructed his own students at the University of Basal in a local dialect instead of Latin, and actually burned copies of books on the traditional principles of medicine. Teaching only from his own experience as a doctor who had treated hundreds of patients, he enraged his fellow professors by freely disseminating the safeguarded wisdom of his profession among the common man. This not only violated the Hippocratic oath, in which the Doctor of Physick swore to guard his professional knowledge, but it also eventually proved detrimental to Paracelsus' career.

In 1528, Paracelsus was thrown out from the University, but the damage to medical tradition had already been done. The works of Paracelsus were published after his death, and among other things they completely altered the European notion of disease, overturning the then-popular opinion that disease was caused by unbalanced "humors" within a patient's body. But this was just the beginning of the far-reaching impact Paracelsus had on Western medicine.

When finished reading the passage, click on the icon below

Proceed

Time

? Help

← Prev

→ Next

Beginning

Early studies of anatomy were hampered by the authorities' disapproval of dissections, and by the lack of refrigeration. By the 1500s in Europe the collected knowledge about the human body had been codified and was the exclusive domain of the Doctors of Physick, a group of scholars who went to great lengths to prevent medical information from spreading. To this end, the Doctors stored their knowledge in obscure languages such as Greek, Latin, and Arabic. The Doctors, by not allowing the works of anatomy to be translated into common tongues, remained invincible to intellectual assaults by laymen. Not only did Doctors of Physick refuse to supplement the bodily lore they learned at the university with practical observations, but they also charged ludicrous amounts to treat their patients.

The doctors generally prescribed two different treatments for disease, blood lettings for those with physical disorders, and point-branding for those in need of psychiatric care. The treatments involved using leeches and needles, respectively, and often caused patients to end up worse off than they were prior to treatment. Given these conditions, the common people opted to patronize the village apothecary, who was typically a local grocer selling ineffectual herbal remedies.

Protected by an imposing guild system, the citadel of medicine was finally cracked by Paracelsus, a rogue physician of the sixteenth century. Paracelsus was a self-taught medicine man who instructed his own students at the University of Basal in a local dialect instead of Latin, and actually burned copies of books on the traditional principles of medicine. Teaching only from his own experience as a doctor who had treated hundreds of patients, he enraged his fellow professors by freely disseminating the safeguarded wisdom of his profession among the common man. This not only violated the Hippocratic oath, in which the Doctor of Physick swore to guard his professional knowledge, but it also eventually proved detrimental to Paracelsus' career.

In 1528, Paracelsus was thrown out from the University, but the damage to medical tradition had already been done. The works of Paracelsus were published after his death, and among other things they completely altered the European notion of disease, overturning the then-popular opinion that disease was caused by unbalanced "humors" within a patient's body. But this was just the beginning of the far-reaching impact Paracelsus had on Western medicine.

What is the main topic?
- ○ The overthrow of established medical tradition
- ○ The ethical questions encountered by ancient doctors
- ○ The archaic notion of bodily humors
- ○ The university system in the sixteenth century

Time

? Help

← Prev

→ Next

Reading

Beginning

Early studies of anatomy were [hampered] by the authorities' disapproval of dissections, and by the lack of refrigeration. By the 1500s in Europe the collected knowledge about the human body had been codified and was the exclusive domain of the Doctors of Physick, a group of scholars who went to great lengths to prevent medical information from spreading. To this end, the Doctors stored their knowledge in obscure languages such as Greek, Latin, and Arabic. The Doctors, by not allowing the works of anatomy to be translated into common tongues, remained invincible to intellectual assaults by laymen. Not only did Doctors of Physick refuse to supplement the bodily lore they learned at the university with practical observations, but they also charged ludicrous amounts to treat their patients.

The doctors generally prescribed two different treatments for disease, blood lettings for those with physical disorders, and point-branding for those in need of psychiatric care. The treatments involved using leeches and needles, respectively, and often caused patients to end up worse off than they were prior to treatment. Given these conditions, the common people opted to patronize the village apothecary, who was typically a local grocer selling ineffectual herbal remedies.

Protected by an imposing guild system, the citadel of medicine was finally cracked by Paracelsus, a rogue physician of the sixteenth century. Paracelsus was a self-taught medicine man who instructed his own students at the University of Basal in a local dialect instead of Latin, and actually burned copies of books on the traditional principles of medicine. Teaching only from his own experience as a doctor who had treated hundreds of patients, he enraged his fellow professors by freely disseminating the safeguarded wisdom of his profession among the common man. This not only violated the Hippocratic oath, in which the Doctor of Physick swore to guard his professional knowledge, but it also eventually proved detrimental to Paracelsus' career.

In 1528, Paracelsus was thrown out from the University, but the damage to medical tradition had already been done. The works of Paracelsus were published after his death, and among other things they completely altered the European notion of disease, overturning the then-popular opinion that disease was caused by unbalanced "humors" within a patient's body. But this was just the beginning of the far-reaching impact Paracelsus had on Western medicine.

Look at the highlighted word in the passage. Click on the word or phrase in the **bold** text that is closest in meaning to .

Time

Help Prev Next

Beginning

Early studies of anatomy were hampered by the authorities' disapproval of dissections, and by the lack of refrigeration. By the 1500s in Europe the collected knowledge about the human body had been codified and was the exclusive domain of the Doctors of Physick, a group of scholars who went to great lengths to prevent medical information from spreading. To this end, the Doctors stored their knowledge in obscure languages such as Greek, Latin, and Arabic. The Doctors, by not allowing the works of anatomy to be translated into common tongues, remained invincible to intellectual assaults by laymen. Not only did Doctors of Physick refuse to supplement the bodily lore they learned at the university with practical observations, but they also charged ludicrous amounts to treat their patients.

The doctors generally prescribed two different treatments for disease, blood lettings for those with physical disorders, and point-branding for those in need of psychiatric care. The treatments involved using leeches and needles, respectively, and often caused patients to end up worse off than they were prior to treatment. Given these conditions, the common people opted to patronize the village apothecary, who was typically a local grocer selling ineffectual herbal remedies.

Protected by an imposing guild system, the citadel of medicine was finally cracked by Paracelsus, a rogue physician of the sixteenth century. Paracelsus was a self-taught medicine man who instructed his own students at the University of Basal in a local dialect instead of Latin, and actually burned copies of books on the traditional principles of medicine. Teaching only from his own experience as a doctor who had treated hundreds of patients, he enraged his fellow professors by freely disseminating the safeguarded wisdom of his profession among the common man. This not only violated the Hippocratic oath, in which the Doctor of Physick swore to guard his professional knowledge, but it also eventually proved detrimental to Paracelsus' career.

In 1528, Paracelsus was thrown out from the University, but the damage to medical tradition had already been done. The works of Paracelsus were published after his death, and among other things they completely altered the European notion of disease, overturning the then-popular opinion that disease was caused by unbalanced "humors" within a patient's body. But this was just the beginning of the far-reaching impact Paracelsus had on Western medicine.

According to the passage, why did the doctors use languages such as Greek, Latin, and Arabic?

- ○ They were languages spoken by the laymen.
- ○ They allowed the doctors to publish documents.
- ○ They were the languages Socrates spoke.
- ○ They kept the common people from understanding medicine.

Time

Help

Prev

Next

Reading

Beginning

Early studies of anatomy were hampered by the authorities' disapproval of dissections, and by the lack of refrigeration. By the 1500s in Europe the collected knowledge about the human body had been codified and was the exclusive domain of the Doctors of Physick, a group of scholars who went to great lengths to prevent medical information from spreading. To this end, the Doctors stored their knowledge in obscure languages such as Greek, Latin, and Arabic. The Doctors, by not allowing the works of anatomy to be translated into common tongues, remained invincible to intellectual assaults by laymen. Not only did Doctors of Physick refuse to supplement the bodily lore they learned at the university with practical observations, but they also charged **ludicrous** amounts to treat their patients.

The doctors generally prescribed two different treatments for disease, blood lettings for those with physical disorders, and point-branding for those in need of psychiatric care. The treatments involved using leeches and needles, respectively, and often caused patients to end up worse off than they were prior to treatment. Given these conditions, the common people opted to patronize the village apothecary, who was typically a local grocer selling ineffectual herbal remedies.

Protected by an imposing guild system, the citadel of medicine was finally cracked by Paracelsus, a rogue physician of the sixteenth century. Paracelsus was a self-taught medicine man who instructed his own students at the University of Basal in a local dialect instead of Latin, and actually burned copies of books on the traditional principles of medicine. Teaching only from his own experience as a doctor who had treated hundreds of patients, he enraged his fellow professors by freely disseminating the safeguarded wisdom of his profession among the common man. This not only violated the Hippocratic oath, in which the Doctor of Physick swore to guard his professional knowledge, but it also eventually proved detrimental to Paracelsus' career.

In 1528, Paracelsus was thrown out from the University, but the damage to medical tradition had already been done. The works of Paracelsus were published after his death, and among other things they completely altered the European notion of disease, overturning the then-popular opinion that disease was caused by unbalanced "humors" within a patient's body. But this was just the beginning of the far-reaching impact Paracelsus had on Western medicine.

Look at the highlighted word in the text. Click on the answer choice that is closest in meaning to the word **ludicrous**.

- ⭘ practical
- ⭘ dangerous
- ⭘ sharp
- ⭘ ridiculous

Time

Help Prev Next

Beginning

Early studies of anatomy were hampered by the authorities' disapproval of dissections, and by the lack of refrigeration. By the 1500s in Europe the collected knowledge about the human body had been codified and was the exclusive domain of the Doctors of Physick, a group of scholars who went to great lengths to prevent medical information from spreading. To this end, the Doctors stored their knowledge in obscure languages such as Greek, Latin, and Arabic. The Doctors, by not allowing the works of anatomy to be translated into common tongues, remained invincible to intellectual assaults by laymen. Not only did Doctors of Physick refuse to supplement the bodily lore they learned at the university with practical observations, but they also charged ludicrous amounts to treat their patients.

The doctors generally prescribed two different treatments for disease, blood lettings for those with physical disorders, and point-branding for those in need of psychiatric care. The treatments involved using leeches and needles, respectively, and often caused patients to end up worse off than they were prior to treatment. Given these conditions, the common people opted to patronize the village apothecary, who was typically a local grocer selling ineffectual herbal remedies.

Protected by an imposing guild system, the citadel of medicine was finally cracked by Paracelsus, a rogue physician of the sixteenth century. Paracelsus was a self-taught medicine man who instructed his own students at the University of Basal in a local dialect instead of Latin, and actually burned copies of books on the traditional principles of medicine. Teaching only from his own experience as a doctor who had treated hundreds of patients, he enraged his fellow professors by freely disseminating the safeguarded wisdom of his profession among the common man. This not only violated the Hippocratic oath, in which the Doctor of Physick swore to guard his professional knowledge, but it also eventually proved detrimental to Paracelsus' career.

In 1528, Paracelsus was thrown out from the University, but the damage to medical tradition had already been done. The works of Paracelsus were published after his death, and among other things they completely altered the European notion of disease, overturning the then-popular opinion that disease was caused by unbalanced "humors" within a patient's body. But this was just the beginning of the far-reaching impact Paracelsus had on Western medicine.

According to the text, which of the following were used by doctors to treat those with mental disorders?
- ○ leeches
- ○ needles
- ○ blood letting
- ○ herbal remedies

Time

Help | Prev | Next

Reading

Beginning

Early studies of anatomy were hampered by the authorities' disapproval of dissections, and by the lack of refrigeration. By the 1500s in Europe the collected knowledge about the human body had been codified and was the exclusive domain of the Doctors of Physick, a group of scholars who went to great lengths to prevent medical information from spreading. To this end, the Doctors stored their knowledge in obscure languages such as Greek, Latin, and Arabic. The Doctors, by not allowing the works of anatomy to be translated into common tongues, remained invincible to intellectual assaults by laymen. Not only did Doctors of Physick refuse to supplement the bodily lore they learned at the university with practical observations, but they also charged ludicrous amounts to treat their patients.

The doctors generally prescribed two different treatments for disease, blood lettings for those with physical disorders, and point-branding for those in need of psychiatric care. The treatments involved using leeches and needles, respectively, and often caused patients to end up worse off than they were prior to treatment. Given these conditions, the common people opted to patronize the village apothecary, who was typically a local grocer selling ineffectual herbal remedies.

Protected by an imposing guild system, the citadel of medicine was finally cracked by Paracelsus, a rogue physician of the sixteenth century. Paracelsus was a self-taught medicine man who instructed his own students at the University of Basal in a local dialect instead of Latin, and actually burned copies of books on the traditional principles of medicine. Teaching only from his own experience as a doctor who had treated hundreds of patients, he enraged his fellow professors by freely disseminating the safeguarded wisdom of his profession among the common man. This not only violated the Hippocratic oath, in which the Doctor of Physick swore to guard his professional knowledge, but it also eventually proved detrimental to Paracelsus' career.

In 1528, Paracelsus was thrown out from the University, but the damage to medical tradition had already been done. The works of Paracelsus were published after his death, and among other things they completely altered the European notion of disease, overturning the then-popular opinion that disease was caused by unbalanced "humors" within a patient's body. But this was just the beginning of the far-reaching impact Paracelsus had on Western medicine.

It can be inferred from the passage that the Doctors of Physick

○ only worked with the upper class

○ performed dissections for ceremonial purposes

○ learned what they could from their everyday practice

○ often were of no help to their patients

Time

Beginning

Early studies of anatomy were hampered by the authorities' disapproval of dissections, and by the lack of refrigeration. By the 1500s in Europe the collected knowledge about the human body had been codified and was the exclusive domain of the Doctors of Physick, a group of scholars who went to great lengths to prevent medical information from spreading. To this end, the Doctors stored their knowledge in obscure languages such as Greek, Latin, and Arabic. The Doctors, by not allowing the works of anatomy to be translated into common tongues, remained invincible to intellectual assaults by laymen. Not only did Doctors of Physick refuse to supplement the bodily lore they learned at the university with practical observations, but they also charged ludicrous amounts to treat their patients.

The doctors generally prescribed two different treatments for disease, blood lettings for those with physical disorders, and point-branding for those in need of psychiatric care. The treatments involved using leeches and needles, respectively, and often caused patients to end up worse off than they were prior to treatment. Given these conditions, the common people **opted** to patronize the village apothecary, who was typically a local grocer selling ineffectual herbal remedies.

Protected by an imposing guild system, the citadel of medicine was finally cracked by Paracelsus, a rogue physician of the sixteenth century. Paracelsus was a self-taught medicine man who instructed his own students at the University of Basal in a local dialect instead of Latin, and actually burned copies of books on the traditional principles of medicine. Teaching only from his own experience as a doctor who had treated hundreds of patients, he enraged his fellow professors by freely disseminating the safeguarded wisdom of his profession among the common man. This not only violated the Hippocratic oath, in which the Doctor of Physick swore to guard his professional knowledge, but it also eventually proved detrimental to Paracelsus' career.

In 1528, Paracelsus was thrown out from the University, but the damage to medical tradition had already been done. The works of Paracelsus were published after his death, and among other things they completely altered the European notion of disease, overturning the then-popular opinion that disease was caused by unbalanced "humors" within a patient's body. But this was just the beginning of the far-reaching impact Paracelsus had on Western medicine.

Look at the highlighted word in the text. Click on the answer choice that is closest in meaning to the word **opted**.

- ○ chose
- ○ loved
- ○ refused
- ○ planned

Time

? Help

← Prev

→ Next

Reading

Beginning

Early studies of anatomy were hampered by the authorities' disapproval of dissections, and by the lack of refrigeration. By the 1500s in Europe the collected knowledge about the human body had been codified and was the exclusive domain of the Doctors of Physick, a group of scholars who went to great lengths to prevent medical information from spreading. To this end, the Doctors stored their knowledge in obscure languages such as Greek, Latin, and Arabic. The Doctors, by not allowing the works of anatomy to be translated into common tongues, remained invincible to intellectual assaults by laymen. Not only did Doctors of Physick refuse to supplement the bodily lore they learned at the university with practical observations, but they also charged ludicrous amounts to treat their patients.

The doctors generally prescribed two different treatments for disease, blood lettings for those with physical disorders, and point-branding for those in need of psychiatric care. The treatments involved using leeches and needles, respectively, and often caused patients to end up worse off than they were prior to treatment. Given these conditions, the common people opted to patronize the village apothecary, who was typically a local grocer selling ineffectual herbal remedies.

Protected by an imposing guild system, the citadel of medicine was finally cracked by Paracelsus, a rogue physician of the sixteenth century. Paracelsus was a self-taught medicine man who instructed his own students at the University of Basal in a local dialect instead of Latin, and actually burned copies of books on the traditional principles of medicine. Teaching only from his own experience as a doctor who had treated hundreds of patients, he enraged his fellow professors by freely disseminating the safeguarded wisdom of his profession among the common man. This not only violated the Hippocratic oath, in which the Doctor of Physick swore to guard his professional knowledge, but it also eventually proved detrimental to Paracelsus' career.

In 1528, Paracelsus was thrown out from the University, but the damage to medical tradition had already been done. The works of Paracelsus were published after his death, and among other things they completely altered the European notion of disease, overturning the then-popular opinion that disease was caused by unbalanced "humors" within a patient's body. But this was just the beginning of the far-reaching impact Paracelsus had on Western medicine.

According to the passage, what can be concluded about Paracelsus' medical education?

○ He graduated from the University of Basal.

○ He educated himself about medicine.

○ He was disliked by his university professors.

○ He kept his medical knowledge to himself.

Time   Help   Prev   Next

Beginning

Early studies of anatomy were hampered by the authorities' disapproval of dissections, and by the lack of refrigeration. By the 1500s in Europe the collected knowledge about the human body had been codified and was the exclusive domain of the Doctors of Physick, a group of scholars who went to great lengths to prevent medical information from spreading. To this end, the Doctors stored their knowledge in obscure languages such as Greek, Latin, and Arabic. The Doctors, by not allowing the works of anatomy to be translated into common tongues, remained invincible to intellectual assaults by laymen. Not only did Doctors of Physick refuse to supplement the bodily lore they learned at the university with practical observations, but they also charged ludicrous amounts to treat their patients.

The doctors generally prescribed two different treatments for disease, blood lettings for those with physical disorders, and point-branding for those in need of psychiatric care. The treatments involved using leeches and needles, respectively, and often caused patients to end up worse off than they were prior to treatment. Given these conditions, the common people opted to patronize the village apothecary, who was typically a local grocer selling ineffectual herbal remedies.

Protected by an imposing guild system, the citadel of medicine was finally cracked by Paracelsus, a rogue physician of the sixteenth century. Paracelsus was a self-taught medicine man who instructed his own students at the University of Basal in a local dialect instead of Latin, and actually burned copies of books on the traditional principles of medicine. Teaching only from his own experience as a doctor who had treated hundreds of patients, he enraged his fellow professors by freely disseminating the safeguarded wisdom of his profession among the common man. This not only violated the Hippocratic oath, in which the Doctor of Physick swore to guard his professional knowledge, but it also eventually proved detrimental to Paracelsus' career.

In 1528, Paracelsus was thrown out from the University, but the damage to medical tradition had already been done. The works of Paracelsus were published after his death, and among other things they completely altered the European notion of disease, overturning the then-popular opinion that disease was caused by unbalanced "humors" within a patient's body. But this was just the beginning of the far-reaching impact Paracelsus had on Western medicine.

It can be inferred from the passage that the Hippocratic oath stated in part that
- ○ doctors would not question traditional medical knowledge
- ○ patients were not able to prosecute negligent doctors
- ○ doctors were not to share medical information with nonprofessionals
- ○ disease was caused by unbalanced humors

Time

? Help

← Prev

→ Next

Reading

Early studies of anatomy were hampered by the authorities' disapproval of dissections, and by the lack of refrigeration. By the 1500s in Europe the collected knowledge about the human body had been codified and was the exclusive domain of the Doctors of Physick, a group of scholars who went to great lengths to prevent medical information from spreading. To this end, the Doctors stored their knowledge in obscure languages such as Greek, Latin, and Arabic. The Doctors, by not allowing the works of anatomy to be translated into common tongues, remained invincible to intellectual assaults by laymen. Not only did Doctors of Physick refuse to supplement the bodily lore they learned at the university with practical observations, but they also charged ludicrous amounts to treat their patients.

The doctors generally prescribed two different treatments for disease, blood lettings for those with physical disorders, and point-branding for those in need of psychiatric care. The treatments involved using leeches and needles, respectively, and often caused patients to end up worse off than they were prior to treatment. Given these conditions, the common people opted to patronize the village apothecary, who was typically a local grocer selling ineffectual herbal remedies.

Protected by an imposing guild system, the citadel of medicine was finally cracked by Paracelsus, a rogue physician of the sixteenth century. Paracelsus was a self-taught medicine man who instructed his own students at the University of Basal in a local dialect instead of Latin, and actually burned copies of books on the traditional principles of medicine. Teaching only from his own experience as a doctor who had treated hundreds of patients, he enraged his fellow professors by freely disseminating the safeguarded wisdom of his profession among the common man. This not only violated the Hippocratic oath, in which the Doctor of Physick swore to guard his professional knowledge, but it also eventually proved detrimental to Paracelsus' career.

In 1528, Paracelsus was **thrown out** from the University, but the damage to medical tradition had already been done. The works of Paracelsus were published after his death, and among other things they completely altered the European notion of disease, overturning the then-popular opinion that disease was caused by unbalanced "humors" within a patient's body. But this was just the beginning of the far-reaching impact Paracelsus had on Western medicine.

Look at the highlighted word in the text. Click on the answer choice that is closest in meaning to the phrase **thrown out**.

- ○ graduated
- ○ dismissed
- ○ evicted
- ○ evacuated

Time

Reading

When finished reading the passage, click on the icon below

The earliest scientific experiments explaining the nature of light were proposed around the end of the seventeenth century. Isaac Newton, who had discovered the visible spectrum in 1666, held that light was composed of tiny particles, or corpuscles, emitted by luminous bodies. For more than one hundred years, his corpuscular theory was favored mostly due to his great prestige and partly because not enough evidence existed to provide an adequate alternative theory.

Finally, two young scientists, Thomas Young and A. J. Fresnel, boldly published results of experiments on the diffraction of light that could only be interpreted in terms of wave theory. The wave theory was further supported by James Maxwell and Todd Sattler, who showed that the electric and magnetic fields were propagated together and that their speeds should be identical to the speed of light. It then became clear that visible light is a form of electromagnetic radiation and constituted only a small part of the entire electromagnetic spectrum.

At one time, however, light was thought to be infinite, that is, transmitted instantaneously from its source to an observer. To establish the contrary, it took a scientist named Olaus Roemer and the moons of Jupiter. In the spring of 1675 when Roemer first began observing the moons, he noticed that they appeared each night at the exact same time. In the succeeding months, when Jupiter and the Earth were furthest apart in their orbits, Jupiter's moons appeared about sixteen minutes later. Roemer correctly assumed the sixteen minute delay represented the time for the light to travel across Earth's elliptical orbit and, although a bit off on his final calculation, he will still be credited as being the first to speculate that light traveled at a finite rate.

Proceed

Time

? Help

← Prev

→ Next

Reading

Beginning

The earliest scientific experiments explaining the nature of light were proposed around the end of the seventeenth century. Isaac Newton, who had discovered the visible spectrum in 1666, held that light was composed of tiny particles, or corpuscles, emitted by luminous bodies. For more than one hundred years, his corpuscular theory was favored mostly due to his great prestige and partly because not enough evidence existed to provide an adequate alternative theory.

Finally, two young scientists, Thomas Young and A. J. Fresnel, boldly published results of experiments on the diffraction of light that could only be interpreted in terms of wave theory. The wave theory was further supported by James Maxwell and Todd Sattler, who showed that the electric and magnetic fields were propagated together and that their speeds should be identical to the speed of light. It then became clear that visible light is a form of electromagnetic radiation and constituted only a small part of the entire electromagnetic spectrum.

At one time, however, light was thought to be infinite, that is, transmitted instantaneously from its source to an observer. To establish the contrary, it took a scientist named Olaus Roemer and the moons of Jupiter. In the spring of 1675 when Roemer first began observing the moons, he noticed that they appeared each night at the exact same time. In the succeeding months, when Jupiter and the Earth were furthest apart in their orbits, Jupiter's moons appeared about sixteen minutes later. Roemer correctly assumed the sixteen minute delay represented the time for the light to travel across Earth's elliptical orbit and, although a bit off on his final calculation, he will still be credited as being the first to speculate that light traveled at a finite rate.

What does the passage mainly discuss?

○ The reason why Isaac Newton's theory on light was refuted

○ How radiation is responsible for light travel

○ The relationship between light and the manner in which it travels

○ Historical experiments on light and its properties

Time

?
Help

←
Prev

→
Next

Beginning

The earliest scientific experiments explaining the nature of light were proposed around the end of the seventeenth century. Isaac Newton, who had discovered the visible spectrum in 1666, **held** that light was composed of tiny particles, or corpuscles, emitted by luminous bodies. For more than one hundred years, his corpuscular theory was favored mostly due to his great prestige and partly because not enough evidence existed to provide an adequate alternative theory.

Finally, two young scientists, Thomas Young and A. J. Fresnel, boldly published results of experiments on the diffraction of light that could only be interpreted in terms of wave theory. The wave theory was further supported by James Maxwell and Todd Sattler, who showed that the electric and magnetic fields were propagated together and that their speeds should be identical to the speed of light. It then became clear that visible light is a form of electromagnetic radiation and constituted only a small part of the entire electromagnetic spectrum.

At one time, however, light was thought to be infinite, that is, transmitted instantaneously from its source to an observer. To establish the contrary, it took a scientist named Olaus Roemer and the moons of Jupiter. In the spring of 1675 when Roemer first began observing the moons, he noticed that they appeared each night at the exact same time. In the succeeding months, when Jupiter and the Earth were furthest apart in their orbits, Jupiter's moons appeared about sixteen minutes later. Roemer correctly assumed the sixteen minute delay represented the time for the light to travel across Earth's elliptical orbit and, although a bit off on his final calculation, he will still be credited as being the first to speculate that light traveled at a finite rate.

Look at the highlighted word in the text. Click on the answer choice that is closest in meaning to the word **held**.

○ lifted
○ believed
○ carried
○ enforced

Time

Help Prev Next

Reading

Beginning

The earliest scientific experiments explaining the nature of light were proposed around the end of the seventeenth century. Isaac Newton, who had discovered the visible spectrum in 1666, held that light was composed of tiny particles, or corpuscles, emitted by luminous bodies. For more than one hundred years, his corpuscular theory was favored mostly due to his great prestige and partly because not enough evidence existed to provide an adequate alternative theory.

Finally, two young scientists, Thomas Young and A. J. Fresnel, boldly published results of experiments on the diffraction of light that could only be interpreted in terms of wave theory. The wave theory was further supported by James Maxwell and Todd Sattler, who showed that the electric and magnetic fields were propagated together and that their speeds should be identical to the speed of light. It then became clear that visible light is a form of electromagnetic radiation and constituted only a small part of the entire electromagnetic spectrum.

At one time, however, light was thought to be infinite, that is, transmitted instantaneously from its source to an observer. To establish the contrary, it took a scientist named Olaus Roemer and the moons of Jupiter. In the spring of 1675 when Roemer first began observing the moons, he noticed that they appeared each night at the exact same time. In the succeeding months, when Jupiter and the Earth were furthest apart in their orbits, Jupiter's moons appeared about sixteen minutes later. Roemer correctly assumed the sixteen minute delay represented the time for the light to travel across Earth's elliptical orbit and, although a bit off on his final calculation, he will still be credited as being the first to speculate that light traveled at a finite rate.

According to the passage, what is the main reason Newton's corpuscular theory was so popular?

○ His law of mechanics was substantial proof of his claims.

○ He seldom published any of his previous experiments.

○ He had considerable influence in the scientific world.

○ His theories were validated by other scientists.

Time

? Help | ← Prev | → Next

Beginning

The earliest scientific experiments explaining the nature of light were proposed around the end of the seventeenth century. Isaac Newton, who had discovered the visible spectrum in 1666, held that light was composed of tiny particles, or corpuscles, emitted by luminous bodies. For more than one hundred years, his corpuscular theory was favored mostly due to his great prestige and partly because not enough evidence existed to provide an adequate alternative theory.

Finally, two young scientists, Thomas Young and A. J. Fresnel, boldly published results of experiments on the diffraction of light that could only be interpreted in terms of wave theory. The wave theory was further supported by James Maxwell and Todd Sattler, who showed that the electric and magnetic fields were propagated together and that their speeds should be identical to the speed of light. It then became clear that visible light is a form of electromagnetic radiation and constituted only a small part of the entire electromagnetic spectrum.

At one time, however, light was thought to be infinite, that is, transmitted instantaneously from its source to an observer. To establish the contrary, it took a scientist named Olaus Roemer and the moons of Jupiter. In the spring of 1675 when Roemer first began observing the moons, he noticed that they appeared each night at the exact same time. In the succeeding months, when Jupiter and the Earth were furthest apart in their orbits, Jupiter's moons appeared about sixteen minutes later. Roemer correctly assumed the sixteen minute delay represented the time for the light to travel across Earth's elliptical orbit and, although a bit off on his final calculation, he will still be credited as being the first to speculate that light traveled at a finite rate.

What can be inferred regarding the scientists Young and Fresnel?

○ Publishing their results on light diffraction took a lot of courage.

○ Their past scientific experience helped in their experiments.

○ They misinterpreted Newton's past theories.

○ The wave theory had been previously proven.

Time

Help Prev Next

Reading

Beginning

The earliest scientific experiments explaining the nature of light were proposed around the end of the seventeenth century. Isaac Newton, who had discovered the visible spectrum in 1666, held that light was composed of tiny particles, or corpuscles, emitted by luminous bodies. For more than one hundred years, his corpuscular theory was favored mostly due to his great prestige and partly because not enough evidence existed to provide an adequate alternative theory.

Finally, two young scientists, Thomas Young and A. J. Fresnel, boldly published results of experiments on the diffraction of light that could only be interpreted in terms of wave theory. The wave theory was further supported by James Maxwell and Todd Sattler, who showed that the electric and magnetic fields were propagated together and that `their` speeds should be identical to the speed of light. It then became clear that visible light is a form of electromagnetic radiation and constituted only a small part of the entire electromagnetic spectrum.

At one time, however, light was thought to be infinite, that is, transmitted instantaneously from its source to an observer. To establish the contrary, it took a scientist named Olaus Roemer and the moons of Jupiter. In the spring of 1675 when Roemer first began observing the moons, he noticed that they appeared each night at the exact same time. In the succeeding months, when Jupiter and the Earth were furthest apart in their orbits, Jupiter's moons appeared about sixteen minutes later. Roemer correctly assumed the sixteen minute delay represented the time for the light to travel across Earth's elliptical orbit and, although a bit off on his final calculation, he will still be credited as being the first to speculate that light traveled at a finite rate.

Look at the highlighted word in the passage. Click on the word or phrase in the bold text that `their` refers to.

Time

? Help | ← Prev | → Next

Beginning

➡The earliest scientific experiments explaining the nature of light were proposed around the end of the seventeenth century. Isaac Newton, who had discovered the visible spectrum in 1666, held that light was composed of tiny particles, or corpuscles, emitted by luminous bodies. For more than one hundred years, his corpuscular theory was favored mostly due to his great prestige and partly because not enough evidence existed to provide an adequate alternative theory.

➡Finally, two young scientists, Thomas Young and A. J. Fresnel, boldly published results of experiments on the diffraction of light that could only be interpreted in terms of wave theory. The wave theory was further supported by James Maxwell and Todd Sattler, who showed that the electric and magnetic fields were propagated together and that their speeds should be identical to the speed of light. It then became clear that visible light is a form of electromagnetic radiation and constituted only a small part of the entire electromagnetic spectrum.

At one time, however, light was thought to be infinite, that is, transmitted instantaneously from its source to an observer. To establish the contrary, it took a scientist named Olaus Roemer and the moons of Jupiter. In the spring of 1675 when Roemer first began observing the moons, he noticed that they appeared each night at the exact same time. In the succeeding months, when Jupiter and the Earth were furthest apart in their orbits, Jupiter's moons appeared about sixteen minutes later. Roemer correctly assumed the sixteen minute delay represented the time for the light to travel across Earth's elliptical orbit and, although a bit off on his final calculation, he will still be credited as being the first to speculate that light traveled at a finite rate.

What is the relationship between the first two paragraphs of the passage?

○ The second paragraph refutes the theory mentioned in the first paragraph.

○ Each paragraph describes the scientific basis for the speed of light.

○ The second paragraph defines the theory explained in the first paragraph.

○ Each paragraph describes a different approach to measuring light waves.

Time

Reading

Beginning

The earliest scientific experiments explaining the nature of light were proposed around the end of the seventeenth century. Isaac Newton, who had discovered the visible spectrum in 1666, held that light was composed of tiny particles, or corpuscles, emitted by luminous bodies. For more than one hundred years, his corpuscular theory was favored mostly due to his great prestige and partly because not enough evidence existed to provide an adequate alternative theory.

Finally, two young scientists, Thomas Young and A. J. Fresnel, boldly published results of experiments on the diffraction of light that could only be interpreted in terms of wave theory. The wave theory was further supported by James Maxwell and Todd Sattler, who showed that the electric and magnetic fields were propagated together and that their speeds should be identical to the speed of light. It then became clear that visible light is a form of electromagnetic radiation and constituted only a small part of the entire electromagnetic spectrum.

At one time, however, light was thought to be infinite, that is, transmitted instantaneously from its source to an observer. To establish the contrary, it took a scientist named Olaus Roemer and the moons of Jupiter. In the spring of 1675 when Roemer first began observing the moons, he noticed that they appeared each night at the exact same time. In the **succeeding** months, when Jupiter and the Earth were furthest apart in their orbits, Jupiter's moons appeared about sixteen minutes later. Roemer correctly assumed the sixteen minute delay represented the time for the light to travel across Earth's elliptical orbit and, although a bit off on his final calculation, he will still be credited as being the first to speculate that light traveled at a finite rate.

Look at the highlighted word in the passage. Click on the answer choice that is closest in meaning to the word **succeeding**.

- ○ prevailing
- ○ following
- ○ achieving
- ○ warmer

Time

? Help | ← Prev | → Next

Beginning

The earliest scientific experiments explaining the nature of light were proposed around the end of the seventeenth century. Isaac Newton, who had discovered the visible spectrum in 1666, held that light was composed of tiny particles, or corpuscles, emitted by luminous bodies. For more than one hundred years, his corpuscular theory was favored mostly due to his great prestige and partly because not enough evidence existed to provide an adequate alternative theory.

Finally, two young scientists, Thomas Young and A. J. Fresnel, boldly published results of experiments on the diffraction of light that could only be interpreted in terms of wave theory. The wave theory was further supported by James Maxwell and Todd Sattler, who showed that the electric and magnetic fields were propagated together and that their speeds should be identical to the speed of light. It then became clear that visible light is a form of electromagnetic radiation and constituted only a small part of the entire electromagnetic spectrum.

At one time, however, light was thought to be infinite, that is, transmitted instantaneously from its source to an observer. To establish the contrary, it took a scientist named Olaus Roemer and the moons of Jupiter. In the spring of 1675 when Roemer first began observing the moons, he noticed that they appeared each night at the exact same time. In the succeeding months, when Jupiter and the Earth were furthest apart in their orbits, Jupiter's moons appeared about sixteen minutes later. Roemer correctly assumed the sixteen minute delay represented the time for the light to travel across Earth's elliptical orbit and, although **a bit off** on his final calculation, he will still be credited as being the first to speculate that light traveled at a finite rate.

Look at the highlighted phrase in the text. What does the author mean by **a bit off.**

○ Roemer was perceived as eccentric.

○ Few people believed his speed-of-light theory.

○ The elliptical orbit was slightly different than it is now.

○ The final calculations weren't exactly accurate.

Time

Reading

Beginning

The earliest scientific experiments explaining the nature of light were proposed around the end of the seventeenth century. Isaac Newton, who had discovered the visible spectrum in 1666, held that light was composed of tiny particles, or corpuscles, emitted by luminous bodies. For more than one hundred years, his corpuscular theory was favored mostly due to his great prestige and partly because not enough evidence existed to provide an adequate alternative theory.

Finally, two young scientists, Thomas Young and A. J. Fresnel, boldly published results of experiments on the diffraction of light that could only be interpreted in terms of wave theory. The wave theory was further supported by James Maxwell and Todd Sattler, who showed that the electric and magnetic fields were propagated together and that their speeds should be identical to the speed of light. It then became clear that visible light is a form of electromagnetic radiation and constituted only a small part of the entire electromagnetic spectrum.

At one time, however, light was thought to be infinite, that is, transmitted instantaneously from its source to an observer. To establish the contrary, it took a scientist named Olaus Roemer and the moons of Jupiter. In the spring of 1675 when Roemer first began observing the moons, he noticed that they appeared each night at the exact same time. In the succeeding months, when Jupiter and the Earth were furthest apart in their orbits, Jupiter's moons appeared about sixteen minutes later. Roemer correctly assumed the sixteen minute delay represented the time for the light to travel across Earth's elliptical orbit and, although a bit off on his final calculation, he will still be credited as being the first to speculate that light traveled at a finite rate.

According to the passage, all of the following are true about light EXCEPT

- ○ it is finite
- ○ It is a form of electromagnetic radiation
- ○ it travels in waves
- ○ it is diffused by transparent objects

Time

? Help

← Prev

→ Next

Beginning

The earliest scientific experiments explaining the nature of light were proposed around the end of the seventeenth century. Isaac Newton, who had discovered the visible spectrum in 1666, held that light was composed of tiny particles, or corpuscles, emitted by luminous bodies. ■ For more than one hundred years, his corpuscular theory was favored mostly due to his great prestige and partly because not enough evidence existed to provide an adequate alternative theory.

Finally, two young scientists, Thomas Young and A. J. Fresnel, boldly published results of experiments on the diffraction of light that could only be interpreted in terms of wave theory. ■The wave theory was further supported by James Maxwell and Todd Sattler, who showed that the electric and magnetic fields were propagated together and that their speeds should be identical to the speed of light. It then became clear that visible light is a form of electromagnetic radiation and constituted only a small part of the entire electromagnetic spectrum. ■

At one time, however, light was thought to be infinite, that is, transmitted instantaneously from its source to an observer. ■To establish the contrary, it took a scientist named Olaus Roemer and the moons of Jupiter. ■In the spring of 1675 when Roemer first began observing the moons, he noticed that they appeared each night at the exact same time. In the succeeding months, when Jupiter and the Earth were furthest apart in their orbits, Jupiter's moons appeared about sixteen minutes later. Roemer correctly assumed the sixteen minute delay represented the time for the light to travel across Earth's elliptical orbit and, although a bit off on his final calculation, he will still be credited as being the first to speculate that light traveled at a finite rate. ■

The following sentence can be added to the passage.

By combining the corpuscular theory with the law of mechanics, Newton was able to explain many optical phenomena.

Where would it best fit in the passage? Click on the square ■ to add the sentence to the passage.

Time

Reading

Beginning

When finished reading the passage, click on the icon below

Flourishing in Italy from the sixteenth to the eighteenth centuries, *commedia dell'arte* is a unique style of comedy employing masked characters. Its influence on European drama could be seen in French pantomime and the English harlequinade. Even today, many modern stage movements and sets can be traced back to this post-Renaissance form of entertainment.

Commedia dell'arte, unlike the literary comedy of the Renaissance which placed an emphasis on written scripts, was a theater on improvisation. Actors in the *commedia* assumed the role of one of many stock characters and portrayed it throughout their careers. These actors exaggerated the stereotypes of doctors, merchants, lawyers, and other unpopular occupations present in Italian society at the time. They also poked fun at the different regions of Italy by speaking in exaggerated accents. The actors kept notebooks, called *zibaldone*, in which they kept monologues, dialogues, and tag lines which their characters regularly rehearsed with. Although the scenes they performed were improvised, *commedia dell'arte* actors gradually developed a set of routine scenes and situations which could be altered from one performance to the other.

Unfortunately, what was responsible for the *commedia dell'arte's* popularity was also ultimately responsible for its demise. The improvisational had turned stale by the end of the eighteenth century as the middle class tired of the dull slapstick and vulgar comedy found in the *commedia*. Some of this progressive shift away form the *commedia* had to do with a conservative revolution which occurred both in society and the theater. Audiences had tired of filthy jokes and poorly developed plots with no morals and no order. The improvised form, which had been a fresh and innovative break from traditional passion plays, had begun to fray soon after it became an established structure of Italian theater. The result was a transformation of the *commedia dell'arte* from an improvised show to a scripted form with less stereotypical characters and a moral. The new *commedia* plays limited the improvisational element to such an extent that the performances resembled melodramas more than comedies.

Proceed

Time

? Help

← Prev

→ Next

Reading

Beginning

➤ Flourishing in Italy from the sixteenth to the eighteenth centuries, *commedia dell'arte* is a unique style of comedy employing masked characters. Its influence on European drama could be seen in French pantomime and the English harlequinade. Even today, many modern stage movements and sets can be traced back to this post Renaissance form of entertainment.

Commedia dell'arte, unlike the literary comedy of the Renaissance which placed an emphasis on written scripts, was a theater on improvisation. Actors in the *commedia* assumed the role of one of many stock characters and portrayed it throughout their careers. These actors exaggerated the stereotypes of doctors, merchants, lawyers, and other unpopular occupations present in Italian society at the time. They also poked fun at the different regions of Italy by speaking in exaggerated accents. The actors kept notebooks, called *zibaldone*, in which they kept monologues, dialogues, and tag lines which their characters regularly rehearsed with. Although the scenes they performed were improvised, *commedia dell'arte* actors gradually developed a set of routine scenes and situations which could be altered from one performance to the other.

Unfortunately, what was responsible for the *commedia dell'arte's* popularity was also ultimately responsible for its demise. The improvisational had turned stale by the end of the eighteenth century as the middle class tired of the dull slapstick and vulgar comedy found in the *commedia*. Some of this progressive shift away form the *commedia* had to do with a conservative revolution which occurred both in society and the theater. Audiences had tired of filthy jokes and poorly developed plots with no morals and no order. The improvised form, which had been a fresh and innovative break from traditional passion plays, had begun to fray soon after it became an established structure of Italian theater. The result was a transformation of the *commedia dell'arte* from an improvised show to a scripted form with less stereotypical characters and a moral. The new *commedia* plays limited the improvisational element to such an extent that the performances resembled melodramas more than comedies.

According to the first paragraph, which of the following categories of the modern theatre is influenced by the *commedia dell'arte*?

○ Stage movements
○ Costume styles
○ Salaries
○ Scripts

Time

Reading

Beginning

Flourishing in Italy from the sixteenth to the eighteenth centuries, *commedia dell'arte* is a unique style of comedy employing masked characters. Its influence on European drama could be seen in French pantomime and the English harlequinade. Even today, many modern stage movements and sets can be traced back to this post-Renaissance form of entertainment.

Commedia dell'arte, unlike the literary comedy of the Renaissance which placed an emphasis on written scripts, was a theater on improvisation. Actors in the *commedia* assumed the role of one of many stock characters and portrayed it throughout their careers. These actors exaggerated the stereotypes of doctors, merchants, lawyers, and other unpopular occupations present in Italian society at the time. They also poked fun at the different regions of Italy by speaking in exaggerated accents. The actors kept notebooks, called *zibaldone*, in which they kept monologues, dialogues, and tag lines which their characters regularly rehearsed with. Although the scenes they performed were improvised, *commedia dell'arte* actors gradually developed a set of routine scenes and situations which could be altered from one performance to the other.

Unfortunately, what was responsible for the *commedia dell'arte's* popularity was also ultimately responsible for its demise. The improvisational had turned stale by the end of the eighteenth century as the middle class tired of the dull slapstick and vulgar comedy found in the *commedia*. Some of this progressive shift away form the *commedia* had to do with a conservative revolution which occurred both in society and the theater. Audiences had tired of filthy jokes and poorly developed plots with no morals and no order. The improvised form, which had been a fresh and innovative break from traditional passion plays, had begun to fray soon after it became an established structure of Italian theater. The result was a transformation of the *commedia dell'arte* from an improvised show to a scripted form with less stereotypical characters and a moral. The new *commedia* plays limited the improvisational element to such an extent that the performances resembled melodramas more than comedies.

How did *commedia dell'arte* differ from Renaissance comedy?
- ⟡ Members of Renaissance comedy were doctors and lawyers.
- ⟡ *Commedia dell'arte* was performed outdoors.
- ⟡ Renaissance comedy was scripted.
- ⟡ The actors of Renaissance comedy weren't paid.

Time

? Help

← Prev

→ Next

Reading

Beginning

Flourishing in Italy from the sixteenth to the eighteenth centuries, *commedia dell'arte* is a unique style of comedy employing masked characters. Its influence on European drama could be seen in French pantomime and the English harlequinade. Even today, many modern stage movements and sets can be traced back to this post-Renaissance form of entertainment.

→*Commedia dell'arte*, unlike the literary comedy of the Renaissance which placed an emphasis on written scripts, was a theater on improvisation. Actors in the *commedia* assumed the role of one of many stock characters and portrayed it throughout their careers. These actors exaggerated the stereotypes of doctors, merchants, lawyers, and other unpopular occupations present in Italian society at the time. They also poked fun at the different regions of Italy by speaking in exaggerated accents. The actors kept notebooks, called *zibaldone*, in which they kept monologues, dialogues, and tag lines which their characters regularly rehearsed with. Although the scenes they performed were improvised, *commedia dell'arte* actors gradually developed a set of routine scenes and situations which could be altered from one performance to the other.

Unfortunately, what was responsible for the *commedia dell'arte's* popularity was also ultimately responsible for its demise. The improvisational had turned stale by the end of the eighteenth century as the middle class tired of the dull slapstick and vulgar comedy found in the *commedia*. Some of this progressive shift away form the *commedia* had to do with a conservative revolution which occurred both in society and the theater. Audiences had tired of filthy jokes and poorly developed plots with no morals and no order. The improvised form, which had been a fresh and innovative break from traditional passion plays, had begun to fray soon after it became an established structure of Italian theater. The result was a transformation of the *commedia dell'arte* from an improvised show to a scripted form with less stereotypical characters and a moral. The new *commedia* plays limited the improvisational element to such an extent that the performances resembled melodramas more than comedies.

What is the main point of the second paragraph?
- ○ Improvisation was the key to the success of the *commedia dell'arte*.
- ○ The social elite regarded the *commedia dell'arte* as ridiculous.
- ○ The *commedia dell'arte* was the most effective way to influence lawyers.
- ○ The *commedia dell'arte* was performed throughout Italy.

Time

Reading

Beginning

Flourishing in Italy from the sixteenth to the eighteenth centuries, *commedia dell'arte* is a unique style of comedy employing masked characters. Its influence on European drama could be seen in French pantomime and the English harlequinade. Even today, many modern stage movements and sets can be traced back to this post-Renaissance form of entertainment.

Commedia dell'arte, unlike the literary comedy of the Renaissance which placed an emphasis on written scripts, was a theater on improvisation. Actors in the *commedia* assumed the role of one of many stock characters and portrayed it throughout their careers. **These actors exaggerated the stereotypes of doctors, merchants, lawyers, and other unpopular occupations present in Italian society at the time. They also poked fun at the different regions of Italy by speaking in exaggerated accents.** The actors kept notebooks, called *zibaldone*, in which they kept monologues, dialogues, and tag lines which their characters regularly rehearsed with. Although the scenes they performed were improvised, *commedia dell'arte* actors gradually developed a set of routine scenes and situations which could be altered from one performance to the other.

Unfortunately, what was responsible for the *commedia dell'arte's* popularity was also ultimately responsible for its demise. The improvisational had turned stale by the end of the eighteenth century as the middle class tired of the dull slapstick and vulgar comedy found in the *commedia*. Some of this progressive shift away form the *commedia* had to do with a conservative revolution which occurred both in society and the theater. Audiences had tired of filthy jokes and poorly developed plots with no morals and no order. The improvised form, which had been a fresh and innovative break from traditional passion plays, had begun to fray soon after it became an established structure of Italian theater. The result was a transformation of the *commedia dell'arte* from an improvised show to a scripted form with less stereotypical characters and a moral. The new *commedia* plays limited the improvisational element to such an extent that the performances resembled melodramas more than comedies.

Look at the highlighted word in the passage. Click on the word or phrase in the bold text that the word **they** refers to.

Time

Help Prev Next

Flourishing in Italy from the sixteenth to the eighteenth centuries, *commedia dell'arte* is a unique style of comedy employing masked characters. Its influence on European drama could be seen in French pantomime and the English harlequinade. Even today, many modern stage movements and sets can be traced back to this post-Renaissance form of entertainment.

Commedia dell'arte, unlike the literary comedy of the Renaissance which placed an emphasis on written scripts, was a theater on improvisation. Actors in the *commedia* assumed the role of one of many stock characters and portrayed it throughout their careers. These actors exaggerated the stereotypes of doctors, merchants, lawyers, and other unpopular occupations present in Italian society at the time. They also poked fun at the different regions of Italy by speaking in exaggerated accents. The actors kept notebooks, called *zibaldone*, in which they kept monologues, dialogues, and tag lines which their characters regularly rehearsed with. Although the scenes they performed were improvised, *commedia dell'arte* actors gradually developed a set of routine scenes and situations which could be altered from one performance to the other.

Unfortunately, what was responsible for the *commedia dell'arte's* popularity was also ultimately responsible for its demise. The improvisational had turned stale by the end of the eighteenth century as the middle class tired of the dull slapstick and vulgar comedy found in the *commedia*. Some of this progressive shift away form the *commedia* had to do with a conservative revolution which occurred both in society and the theater. Audiences had tired of filthy jokes and poorly developed plots with no morals and no order. The improvised form, which had been a fresh and innovative break from traditional passion plays, had begun to fray soon after it became an established structure of Italian theater. The result was a transformation of the *commedia dell'arte* from an improvised show to a scripted form with less stereotypical characters and a moral. The new *commedia* plays limited the improvisational element to such an extent that the performances resembled melodramas more than comedies.

The author implies that *zibaldones*
- ○ were read aloud during performances
- ○ helped the performers develop their characters
- ○ relaxed the audience members
- ○ were much sought after by Renaissance actors

Time

Help Prev Next

Reading

Beginning

Flourishing in Italy from the sixteenth to the eighteenth centuries, *commedia dell'arte* is a unique style of comedy employing masked characters. Its influence on European drama could be seen in French pantomime and the English harlequinade. Even today, many modern stage movements and sets can be traced back to this post-Renaissance form of entertainment.

Commedia dell'arte, unlike the literary comedy of the Renaissance which placed an emphasis on written scripts, was a theater on improvisation. Actors in the *commedia* assumed the role of one of many stock characters and portrayed it throughout their careers. These actors exaggerated the stereotypes of doctors, merchants, lawyers, and other unpopular occupations present in Italian society at the time. They also poked fun at the different regions of Italy by speaking in exaggerated accents. The actors kept notebooks, called *zibaldone*, in which they kept monologues, dialogues, and tag lines which their characters regularly rehearsed with. Although the scenes they performed were improvised, *commedia dell'arte* actors gradually developed a set of routine scenes and situations which could be altered from one performance to the other.

Unfortunately, what was responsible for the *commedia dell'arte's* popularity was also ultimately responsible for its demise. The improvisational had turned stale by the end of the eighteenth century as the middle class tired of the dull slapstick and vulgar comedy found in the *commedia*. Some of this progressive shift away form the *commedia* had to do with a conservative revolution which occurred both in society and the theater. Audiences had tired of filthy jokes and poorly developed plots with no morals and no order. The improvised form, which had been a fresh and innovative break from traditional passion plays, had begun to fray soon after it became an established structure of Italian theater. The result was a transformation of the *commedia dell'arte* from an improvised show to a scripted form with less stereotypical characters and a moral. The new *commedia* plays **limited** the improvisational element to such an extent that the performances resembled melodramas more than comedies.

Look at the highlighted word in the passage. Click on the answer choice that is closest in meaning to the word **limited**.

- ○ combined
- ○ damaged
- ○ restricted
- ○ discouraged

Time

? Help

← Prev

→ Next

Beginning

Flourishing in Italy from the sixteenth to the eighteenth centuries, *commedia dell'arte* is a unique style of comedy employing masked characters. Its influence on European drama could be seen in French pantomime and the English harlequinade. Even today, many modern stage movements and sets can be traced back to this post-Renaissance form of entertainment.

Commedia dell'arte, unlike the literary comedy of the Renaissance which placed an emphasis on written scripts, was a theater on improvisation. Actors in the *commedia* assumed the role of one of many stock characters and portrayed it throughout their careers. These actors exaggerated the stereotypes of doctors, merchants, lawyers, and other unpopular occupations present in Italian society at the time. They also poked fun at the different regions of Italy by speaking in exaggerated accents. The actors kept notebooks, called *zibaldone*, in which they kept monologues, dialogues, and tag lines which their characters regularly rehearsed with. Although the scenes they performed were improvised, *commedia dell'arte* actors gradually developed a set of routine scenes and situations which could be altered from one performance to the other.

Unfortunately, what was responsible for the *commedia dell'arte's* popularity was also ultimately responsible for its demise. The improvisational had turned stale by the end of the eighteenth century as the middle class tired of the dull slapstick and vulgar comedy found in the *commedia*. Some of this progressive shift away form the *commedia* had to do with a conservative revolution which occurred both in society and the theater. Audiences had tired of filthy jokes and poorly developed plots with no morals and no order. The improvised form, which had been a fresh and innovative break from traditional passion plays, had begun to fray soon after it became an established structure of Italian theater. The result was a transformation of the *commedia dell'arte* from an improvised show to a scripted form with less stereotypical characters and a moral. The new *commedia* plays limited the improvisational element to such an extent that the performances resembled melodramas more than comedies.

Look at the highlighted word in the passage. Click on the word or phrase in the bold text that is closest in meaning to stale.

Time

Help   Prev   Next

Reading

Beginning

Flourishing in Italy from the sixteenth to the eighteenth centuries, *commedia dell'arte* is a unique style of comedy employing masked characters. Its influence on European drama could be seen in French pantomime and the English harlequinade. Even today, many modern stage movements and sets can be traced back to this post-Renaissance form of entertainment.

Commedia dell'arte, unlike the literary comedy of the Renaissance which placed an emphasis on written scripts, was a theater on improvisation. Actors in the *commedia* assumed the role of one of many stock characters and portrayed it throughout their careers. These actors exaggerated the stereotypes of doctors, merchants, lawyers, and other unpopular occupations present in Italian society at the time. They also poked fun at the different regions of Italy by speaking in exaggerated accents. The actors kept notebooks, called *zibaldone*, in which they kept monologues, dialogues, and tag lines which their characters regularly rehearsed with. Although the scenes they performed were improvised, *commedia dell'arte* actors gradually developed a set of routine scenes and situations which could be altered from one performance to the other.

Unfortunately, what was responsible for the *commedia dell'arte's* popularity was also ultimately responsible for its demise. The improvisational had turned stale by the end of the eighteenth century as the middle class tired of the dull slapstick and vulgar comedy found in the *commedia*. Some of this **progressive** shift away form the *commedia* had to do with a conservative revolution which occurred both in society and the theater. Audiences had tired of filthy jokes and poorly developed plots with no morals and no order. The improvised form, which had been a fresh and innovative break from traditional passion plays, had begun to fray soon after it became an established structure of Italian theater. The result was a transformation of the *commedia dell'arte* from an improvised show to a scripted form with less stereotypical characters and a moral. The new *commedia* plays limited the improvisational element to such an extent that the performances resembled melodramas more than comedies.

Look at the highlighted word in the text. Click on the answer choice that is closest in meaning to the word **progressive**.

○ gradual
○ awful
○ eternal
○ modern

Time

? Help | ← Prev | → Next

Beginning

Flourishing in Italy from the sixteenth to the eighteenth centuries, *commedia dell'arte* is a unique style of comedy employing masked characters. Its influence on European drama could be seen in French pantomime and the English harlequinade. Even today, many modern stage movements and sets can be traced back to this post-Renaissance form of entertainment.

Commedia dell'arte, unlike the literary comedy of the Renaissance which placed an emphasis on written scripts, was a theater on improvisation. Actors in the *commedia* assumed the role of one of many stock characters and portrayed it throughout their careers. These actors exaggerated the stereotypes of doctors, merchants, lawyers, and other unpopular occupations present in Italian society at the time. They also poked fun at the different regions of Italy by speaking in exaggerated accents. The actors kept notebooks, called *zibaldone*, in which they kept monologues, dialogues, and tag lines which their characters regularly rehearsed with. Although the scenes they performed were improvised, *commedia dell'arte* actors gradually developed a set of routine scenes and situations which could be altered from one performance to the other.

➜ Unfortunately, what was responsible for the *commedia dell'arte's* popularity was also ultimately responsible for its demise. The improvisational had turned stale by the end of the eighteenth century as the middle class tired of the dull slapstick and vulgar comedy found in the *commedia*. Some of this progressive shift away form the *commedia* had to do with a conservative revolution which occurred both in society and the theater. Audiences had tired of filthy jokes and poorly developed plots with no morals and no order. The improvised form, which had been a fresh and innovative break from traditional passion plays, had begun to fray soon after it became an established structure of Italian theater. The result was a transformation of the *commedia dell'arte* from an improvised show to a scripted form with less stereotypical characters and a moral. The new *commedia* plays limited the improvisational element to such an extent that the performances resembled melodramas more than comedies.

According to the third paragraph, all of the following are reasons *commedia dell'arte* decreased in popularity EXCEPT

○ people became more conservative

○ plot lines were too complicated

○ the audience tired of vulgar comedy

○ improvisational theater became routine

Time

Reading

Beginning

Flourishing in Italy from the sixteenth to the eighteenth centuries, *commedia dell'arte* is a unique style of comedy employing masked characters. Its influence on European drama could be seen in French pantomime and the English harlequinade. Even today, many modern stage movements and sets can be traced back to this post-Renaissance form of entertainment.

Commedia dell'arte, unlike the literary comedy of the Renaissance which placed an emphasis on written scripts, was a theater on improvisation. Actors in the *commedia* assumed the role of one of many stock characters and portrayed it throughout their careers. These actors exaggerated the stereotypes of doctors, merchants, lawyers, and other unpopular occupations present in Italian society at the time. They also poked fun at the different regions of Italy by speaking in exaggerated accents. The actors kept notebooks, called *zibaldone*, in which they kept monologues, dialogues, and tag lines which their characters regularly rehearsed with. Although the scenes they performed were improvised, *commedia dell'arte* actors gradually developed a set of routine scenes and situations which could be altered from one performance to the other.

Unfortunately, what was responsible for the *commedia dell'arte's* popularity was also ultimately responsible for its demise. The improvisational had turned stale by the end of the eighteenth century as the middle class tired of the dull slapstick and vulgar comedy found in the *commedia*. Some of this progressive shift away form the *commedia* had to do with a conservative revolution which occurred both in society and the theater. Audiences had tired of filthy jokes and poorly developed plots with no morals and no order. The improvised form, which had been a fresh and innovative break from traditional passion plays, had begun to fray soon after it became an established structure of Italian theater. The result was a transformation of the *commedia dell'arte* from an improvised show to a scripted form with less stereotypical characters and a moral. The new *commedia* plays limited the improvisational element to such an extent that the performances resembled melodramas more than comedies.

According to the passage, what was the result of the transformation of *commedia dell'arte*?

○ The performances were considerably shorter.

○ Audience members missed the comedy element.

○ The cast rehearsed scripted melodramas.

○ *Commedia dell'arte* became subsidized by the government.

Time

Help   Prev   Next

Beginning

Flourishing in Italy from the sixteenth to the eighteenth centuries, *commedia dell'arte* is a unique style of comedy employing masked characters. ■Its influence on European drama could be seen in French pantomime and the English harlequinade. Even today, many modern stage movements and sets can be traced back to this post-Renaissance form of entertainment. ■

Commedia dell'arte, unlike the literary comedy of the Renaissance which placed an emphasis on written scripts, was a theater on improvisation. ■Actors in the *commedia* assumed the role of one of many stock characters and portrayed it throughout their careers. These actors exaggerated the stereotypes of doctors, merchants, lawyers, and other unpopular occupations present in Italian society at the time. ■They also poked fun at the different regions of Italy by speaking in exaggerated accents. The actors kept notebooks, called *zibaldone*, in which they kept monologues, dialogues, and tag lines which their characters regularly rehearsed with. Although the scenes they performed were improvised, *commedia dell'arte* actors gradually developed a set of routine scenes and situations which could be altered from one performance to the other. ■

Unfortunately, what was responsible for the *commedia dell'arte's* popularity was also ultimately responsible for its demise. The improvisational had turned stale by the end of the eighteenth century as the middle class tired of the dull slapstick and vulgar comedy found in the *commedia*. ■Some of this progressive shift away form the *commedia* had to do with a conservative revolution which occurred both in society and the theater. Audiences had tired of filthy jokes and poorly developed plots with no morals and no order. The improvised form, which had been a fresh and innovative break from traditional passion plays, had begun to fray soon after it became an established structure of Italian theater. ■The result was a transformation of the *commedia dell'arte* from an improvised show to a scripted form with less stereotypical characters and a moral. The new *commedia* plays limited the improvisational element to such an extent that the performances resembled melodramas more than comedies. ■

The following sentence can be added to the passage.

These predictable scenes combined with the improvisation helped account for its extraordinary popularity.

Where would it best fit in the passage? Click on the square ■ to add the sentence to the paragraph.

Time

Help   Prev   Next

Reading

Beginning

When finished reading the passage, click on the icon below

For many years, doctors have championed the view that cholesterol is a dangerous substance. When consumed in large quantities, cholesterol tends to build up as excess residue in the arteries and veins of the body. This buildup tends to constrict and limit the flow of blood through the body. In turn, this means that the heart must beat more forcefully if it is to circulate the same amount of blood. Because the heart is pumping harder, the risk of high blood pressure increases. Eventually, high blood pressure, resulting from excessive cholesterol, can lead to heart disease and other physical problems.

But, when consumed in moderation, cholesterol is actually one of the most important substances in the body. It provides suppleness to the outer walls of cells, thus making these walls stronger. Cholesterol also aids in the digestive process, since it is the main ingredient in stomach bile. Finally, cholesterol forms the basis of several important hormones, namely testosterone and estrogen, which are necessary for proper human growth and development. It is somewhat ironic that without cholesterol, a person's body would not be able to function correctly.

Recently, scientists have discovered that cholesterol has a fourth function. Cholesterol controls a protein necessary for the development of embryos. Without cholesterol, a fertilized egg would be unable to develop into a child. Cholesterol guides specialized proteins and in turn tells them when and where to form the physical parts of the body. During initial development of the human body, cholesterol guides proteins which form bones, the spinal chord, large internal organs, and skin. Later, cholesterol helps in the formation of individual fingers and toes.

This information is proving useful in treating certain diseases. Smith-Lemli-Opitz syndrome (SLOS) is a condition in which babies are born lacking the ability to manufacture cholesterol. Such babies typically suffer from a variety of physical and developmental defects. Recent discoveries about cholesterol may help to prevent developmental problems such as SLOS. Scientists hope that if cholesterol were to be administered early enough in the development process it would prevent SLOS from occurring. Although SLOS is fairly rare, incidents have increased in recent years as health-conscious women with very low levels of cholesterol are deciding to have children.

Proceed

Time

? Help

← Prev

→ Next

Beginning

For many years, doctors have championed the view that cholesterol is a dangerous substance. When consumed in large quantities, cholesterol tends to build up as excess residue in the arteries and veins of the body. This buildup tends to constrict and limit the flow of blood through the body. In turn, this means that the heart must beat more forcefully if it is to circulate the same amount of blood. Because the heart is pumping harder, the risk of high blood pressure increases. Eventually, high blood pressure, resulting from excessive cholesterol, can lead to heart disease and other physical problems.

But, when consumed in moderation, cholesterol is actually one of the most important substances in the body. It provides suppleness to the outer walls of cells, thus making these walls stronger. Cholesterol also aids in the digestive process, since it is the main ingredient in stomach bile. Finally, cholesterol forms the basis of several important hormones, namely testosterone and estrogen, which are necessary for proper human growth and development. It is somewhat ironic that without cholesterol, a person's body would not be able to function correctly.

Recently, scientists have discovered that cholesterol has a fourth function. Cholesterol controls a protein necessary for the development of embryos. Without cholesterol, a fertilized egg would be unable to develop into a child. Cholesterol guides specialized proteins and in turn tells them when and where to form the physical parts of the body. During initial development of the human body, cholesterol guides proteins which form bones, the spinal chord, large internal organs, and skin. Later, cholesterol helps in the formation of individual fingers and toes.

This information is proving useful in treating certain diseases. Smith-Lemli-Opitz syndrome (SLOS) is a condition in which babies are born lacking the ability to manufacture cholesterol. Such babies typically suffer from a variety of physical and developmental defects. Recent discoveries about cholesterol may help to prevent developmental problems such as SLOS. Scientists hope that if cholesterol were to be administered early enough in the development process it would prevent SLOS from occurring. Although SLOS is fairly rare, incidents have increased in recent years as health-conscious women with very low levels of cholesterol are deciding to have children.

Time

What is the main point of the passage?
- ○ The impacts of cholesterol on the development of babies
- ○ The different functions of cholesterol in humans and animals
- ○ The benefits of cholesterol to the human body
- ○ The methods used by doctors to lower cholesterol levels

?
Help   **Prev**   **Next**

Reading

Beginning

For many years, doctors have **championed** the view that cholesterol is a dangerous substance. When consumed in large quantities, cholesterol tends to build up as excess residue in the arteries and veins of the body. This buildup tends to constrict and limit the flow of blood through the body. In turn, this means that the heart must beat more forcefully if it is to circulate the same amount of blood. Because the heart is pumping harder, the risk of high blood pressure increases. Eventually, high blood pressure, resulting from excessive cholesterol, can lead to heart disease and other physical problems.

But, when consumed in moderation, cholesterol is actually one of the most important substances in the body. It provides suppleness to the outer walls of cells, thus making these walls stronger. Cholesterol also aids in the digestive process, since it is the main ingredient in stomach bile. Finally, cholesterol forms the basis of several important hormones, namely testosterone and estrogen, which are necessary for proper human growth and development. It is somewhat ironic that without cholesterol, a person's body would not be able to function correctly.

Recently, scientists have discovered that cholesterol has a fourth function. Cholesterol controls a protein necessary for the development of embryos. Without cholesterol, a fertilized egg would be unable to develop into a child. Cholesterol guides specialized proteins and in turn tells them when and where to form the physical parts of the body. During initial development of the human body, cholesterol guides proteins which form bones, the spinal chord, large internal organs, and skin. Later, cholesterol helps in the formation of individual fingers and toes.

This information is proving useful in treating certain diseases. Smith-Lemli-Opitz syndrome (SLOS) is a condition in which babies are born lacking the ability to manufacture cholesterol. Such babies typically suffer from a variety of physical and developmental defects. Recent discoveries about cholesterol may help to prevent developmental problems such as SLOS. Scientists hope that if cholesterol were to be administered early enough in the development process it would prevent SLOS from occurring. Although SLOS is fairly rare, incidents have increased in recent years as health-conscious women with very low levels of cholesterol are deciding to have children.

Look at the highlighted word in the text. Click on the answer choice that is closest in meaning to the word **championed**.

○ supported
○ combated
○ tolerated
○ defeated

Time

Help Prev Next

Beginning

For many years, doctors have championed the view that cholesterol is a dangerous substance. When consumed in large quantities, cholesterol tends to build up as excess residue in the arteries and veins of the body. **This buildup tends to constrict and limit the flow of blood through the body. In turn, this means that the heart must beat more forcefully if it is to circulate the same amount of blood.** Because the heart is pumping harder, the risk of high blood pressure increases. Eventually, high blood pressure, resulting from excessive cholesterol, can lead to heart disease and other physical problems.

But, when consumed in moderation, cholesterol is actually one of the most important substances in the body. It provides suppleness to the outer walls of cells, thus making these walls stronger. Cholesterol also aids in the digestive process, since it is the main ingredient in stomach bile. Finally, cholesterol forms the basis of several important hormones, namely testosterone and estrogen, which are necessary for proper human growth and development. It is somewhat ironic that without cholesterol, a person's body would not be able to function correctly.

Recently, scientists have discovered that cholesterol has a fourth function. Cholesterol controls a protein necessary for the development of embryos. Without cholesterol, a fertilized egg would be unable to develop into a child. Cholesterol guides specialized proteins and in turn tells them when and where to form the physical parts of the body. During initial development of the human body, cholesterol guides proteins which form bones, the spinal chord, large internal organs, and skin. Later, cholesterol helps in the formation of individual fingers and toes.

This information is proving useful in treating certain diseases. Smith-Lemli-Opitz syndrome (SLOS) is a condition in which babies are born lacking the ability to manufacture cholesterol. Such babies typically suffer from a variety of physical and developmental defects. Recent discoveries about cholesterol may help to prevent developmental problems such as SLOS. Scientists hope that if cholesterol were to be administered early enough in the development process it would prevent SLOS from occurring. Although SLOS is fairly rare, incidents have increased in recent years as health-conscious women with very low levels of cholesterol are deciding to have children.

Look at the highlighted word in the passage. Click on the word or phrase in the bold text that **it** refers to.

Time

? Help | **← Prev** | **→ Next**

Reading

Beginning

For many years, doctors have championed the view that cholesterol is a dangerous substance. When consumed in large quantities, cholesterol tends to build up as excess residue in the arteries and veins of the body. This buildup tends to constrict and limit the flow of blood through the body. In turn, this means that the heart must beat more forcefully if it is to circulate the same amount of blood. Because the heart is pumping harder, the risk of high blood pressure increases. Eventually, high blood pressure, resulting from excessive cholesterol, can lead to heart disease and other physical problems.

But, when consumed in moderation, cholesterol is actually one of the most important substances in the body. It provides suppleness to the outer walls of cells, thus making these walls stronger. Cholesterol also aids in the digestive process, since it is the main ingredient in stomach bile. Finally, cholesterol forms the basis of several important hormones, namely testosterone and estrogen, which are necessary for proper human growth and development. It is somewhat ironic that without cholesterol, a person's body would not be able to function correctly.

Recently, scientists have discovered that cholesterol has a fourth function. Cholesterol controls a protein necessary for the development of embryos. Without cholesterol, a fertilized egg would be unable to develop into a child. Cholesterol guides specialized proteins and in turn tells them when and where to form the physical parts of the body. During initial development of the human body, cholesterol guides proteins which form bones, the spinal chord, large internal organs, and skin. Later, cholesterol helps in the formation of individual fingers and toes.

This information is proving useful in treating certain diseases. Smith-Lemli-Opitz syndrome (SLOS) is a condition in which babies are born lacking the ability to manufacture cholesterol. Such babies typically suffer from a variety of physical and developmental defects. Recent discoveries about cholesterol may help to prevent developmental problems such as SLOS. Scientists hope that if cholesterol were to be administered early enough in the development process it would prevent SLOS from occurring. Although SLOS is fairly rare, incidents have increased in recent years as health-conscious women with very low levels of cholesterol are deciding to have children.

According to the passage, which of the following can be inferred about blocked veins and arteries?

○ They store useful cholesterol residue until the body processes it.

○ They naturally grow stronger with age.

○ They increase the chance of high blood pressure.

○ They produce cholesterol-fighting chemicals.

Time   Help   Prev   Next

Reading

Beginning

For many years, doctors have championed the view that cholesterol is a dangerous substance. When consumed in large quantities, cholesterol tends to build up as excess residue in the arteries and veins of the body. This buildup tends to constrict and limit the flow of blood through the body. In turn, this means that the heart must beat more forcefully if it is to circulate the same amount of blood. Because the heart is pumping harder, the risk of high blood pressure increases. Eventually, high blood pressure, resulting from excessive cholesterol, can lead to heart disease and other physical problems.

➡ But, when consumed in moderation, cholesterol is actually one of the most important substances in the body. It provides suppleness to the outer walls of cells, thus making these walls stronger. Cholesterol also aids in the digestive process, since it is the main ingredient in stomach bile. Finally, cholesterol forms the basis of several important hormones, namely testosterone and estrogen, which are necessary for proper human growth and development. It is somewhat ironic that without cholesterol, a person's body would not be able to function correctly.

Recently, scientists have discovered that cholesterol has a fourth function. Cholesterol controls a protein necessary for the development of embryos. Without cholesterol, a fertilized egg would be unable to develop into a child. Cholesterol guides specialized proteins and in turn tells them when and where to form the physical parts of the body. During initial development of the human body, cholesterol guides proteins which form bones, the spinal chord, large internal organs, and skin. Later, cholesterol helps in the formation of individual fingers and toes.

This information is proving useful in treating certain diseases. Smith-Lemli-Opitz syndrome (SLOS) is a condition in which babies are born lacking the ability to manufacture cholesterol. Such babies typically suffer from a variety of physical and developmental defects. Recent discoveries about cholesterol may help to prevent developmental problems such as SLOS. Scientists hope that if cholesterol were to be administered early enough in the development process it would prevent SLOS from occurring. Although SLOS is fairly rare, incidents have increased in recent years as health-conscious women with very low levels of cholesterol are deciding to have children.

Click on the sentence in paragraph 2 that gives an example of the role cholesterol plays in food consumption.

Time

? Help   ← Prev   → Next

Reading

Beginning

For many years, doctors have championed the view that cholesterol is a dangerous substance. When consumed in large quantities, cholesterol tends to build up as excess residue in the arteries and veins of the body. This buildup tends to constrict and limit the flow of blood through the body. In turn, this means that the heart must beat more forcefully if it is to circulate the same amount of blood. Because the heart is pumping harder, the risk of high blood pressure increases. Eventually, high blood pressure, resulting from excessive cholesterol, can lead to heart disease and other physical problems.

But, when consumed in moderation, cholesterol is actually one of the most important substances in the body. It provides suppleness to the outer walls of cells, thus making these walls stronger. Cholesterol also aids in the digestive process, since it is the main ingredient in stomach bile. Finally, cholesterol forms the basis of several important hormones, namely testosterone and estrogen, which are necessary for proper human growth and development. It is somewhat **ironic** that without cholesterol, a person's body would not be able to function correctly.

Recently, scientists have discovered that cholesterol has a fourth function. Cholesterol controls a protein necessary for the development of embryos. Without cholesterol, a fertilized egg would be unable to develop into a child. Cholesterol guides specialized proteins and in turn tells them when and where to form the physical parts of the body. During initial development of the human body, cholesterol guides proteins which form bones, the spinal chord, large internal organs, and skin. Later, cholesterol helps in the formation of individual fingers and toes.

This information is proving useful in treating certain diseases. Smith-Lemli-Opitz syndrome (SLOS) is a condition in which babies are born lacking the ability to manufacture cholesterol. Such babies typically suffer from a variety of physical and developmental defects. Recent discoveries about cholesterol may help to prevent developmental problems such as SLOS. Scientists hope that if cholesterol were to be administered early enough in the development process it would prevent SLOS from occurring. Although SLOS is fairly rare, incidents have increased in recent years as health-conscious women with very low levels of cholesterol are deciding to have children.

Look at the highlighted word in the text. Click on the answer choice that is closest in meaning to the word **ironic**.

○ useless
○ paradoxical
○ biological
○ coincidental

Time

? Help

← Prev

→ Next

Reading

Beginning

For many years, doctors have championed the view that cholesterol is a dangerous substance. When consumed in large quantities, cholesterol tends to build up as excess residue in the arteries and veins of the body. This buildup tends to constrict and limit the flow of blood through the body. In turn, this means that the heart must beat more forcefully if it is to circulate the same amount of blood. Because the heart is pumping harder, the risk of high blood pressure increases. Eventually, high blood pressure, resulting from excessive cholesterol, can lead to heart disease and other physical problems.

But, when consumed in moderation, cholesterol is actually one of the most important substances in the body. It provides suppleness to the outer walls of cells, thus making these walls stronger. Cholesterol also aids in the digestive process, since it is the main ingredient in stomach bile. Finally, cholesterol forms the basis of several important hormones, namely testosterone and estrogen, which are necessary for proper human growth and development. It is somewhat ironic that without cholesterol, a person's body would not be able to function correctly.

Recently, scientists have discovered that cholesterol has a fourth function. Cholesterol controls a protein necessary for the development of embryos. Without cholesterol, a fertilized egg would be unable to develop into a child. Cholesterol guides specialized proteins and in turn tells them when and where to form the physical parts of the body. During **initial** development of the human body, cholesterol guides proteins which form bones, the spinal chord, large internal organs, and skin. Later, cholesterol helps in the formation of individual fingers and toes.

This information is proving useful in treating certain diseases. Smith-Lemli-Opitz syndrome (SLOS) is a condition in which babies are born lacking the ability to manufacture cholesterol. Such babies typically suffer from a variety of physical and developmental defects. Recent discoveries about cholesterol may help to prevent developmental problems such as SLOS. Scientists hope that if cholesterol were to be administered early enough in the development process it would prevent SLOS from occurring. Although SLOS is fairly rare, incidents have increased in recent years as health-conscious women with very low levels of cholesterol are deciding to have children.

Look at the highlighted word in the text. Click on the answer choice that is closest in meaning to the word **initial**.

○ early
○ crucial
○ complex
○ aging

Time

? Help

← Prev

→ Next

Reading

Beginning

For many years, doctors have championed the view that cholesterol is a dangerous substance. When consumed in large quantities, cholesterol tends to build up as excess residue in the arteries and veins of the body. This buildup tends to constrict and limit the flow of blood through the body. In turn, this means that the heart must beat more forcefully if it is to circulate the same amount of blood. Because the heart is pumping harder, the risk of high blood pressure increases. Eventually, high blood pressure, resulting from excessive cholesterol, can lead to heart disease and other physical problems.

But, when consumed in moderation, cholesterol is actually one of the most important substances in the body. It provides suppleness to the outer walls of cells, thus making these walls stronger. Cholesterol also aids in the digestive process, since it is the main ingredient in stomach bile. Finally, cholesterol forms the basis of several important hormones, namely testosterone and estrogen, which are necessary for proper human growth and development. It is somewhat ironic that without cholesterol, a person's body would not be able to function correctly.

Recently, scientists have discovered that cholesterol has a fourth function. Cholesterol controls a protein necessary for the development of embryos. Without cholesterol, a fertilized egg would be unable to develop into a child. Cholesterol guides specialized proteins and in turn tells them when and where to form the physical parts of the body. During initial development of the human body, cholesterol guides proteins which form bones, the spinal chord, large internal organs, and skin. Later, cholesterol helps in the formation of individual fingers and toes.

This information is proving useful in treating certain diseases. Smith-Lemli-Opitz syndrome (SLOS) is a condition in which babies are born lacking the ability to manufacture cholesterol. Such babies typically suffer from a variety of physical and developmental defects. Recent discoveries about cholesterol may help to prevent developmental problems such as SLOS. Scientists hope that if cholesterol were to be administered early enough in the development process it would prevent SLOS from occurring. Although SLOS is fairly rare, incidents have increased in recent years as health-conscious women with very low levels of cholesterol are deciding to have children.

It can be inferred from the passage that embryonic skin
- ○ covers the veins and arteries
- ○ builds up inside the heart muscle
- ○ forms before the fingers and toes
- ○ produces cholesterol in its cells

Time

? Help

← Prev

→ Next

Reading

Reading

40 of 49

Beginning

For many years, doctors have championed the view that cholesterol is a dangerous substance. When consumed in large quantities, cholesterol tends to build up as excess residue in the arteries and veins of the body. This buildup tends to constrict and limit the flow of blood through the body. In turn, this means that the heart must beat more forcefully if it is to circulate the same amount of blood. Because the heart is pumping harder, the risk of high blood pressure increases. Eventually, high blood pressure, resulting from excessive cholesterol, can lead to heart disease and other physical problems.

But, when consumed in moderation, cholesterol is actually one of the most important substances in the body. It provides suppleness to the outer walls of cells, thus making these walls stronger. Cholesterol also aids in the digestive process, since it is the main ingredient in stomach bile. Finally, cholesterol forms the basis of several important hormones, namely testosterone and estrogen, which are necessary for proper human growth and development. It is somewhat ironic that without cholesterol, a person's body would not be able to function correctly.

Recently, scientists have discovered that cholesterol has a fourth function. Cholesterol controls a protein necessary for the development of embryos. Without cholesterol, a fertilized egg would be unable to develop into a child. Cholesterol guides specialized proteins and in turn tells them when and where to form the physical parts of the body. During initial development of the human body, cholesterol guides proteins which form bones, the spinal chord, large internal organs, and skin. Later, cholesterol helps in the formation of individual fingers and toes.

This information is proving useful in treating certain diseases. Smith-Lemli-Opitz syndrome (SLOS) is a condition in which babies are born lacking the ability to manufacture cholesterol. Such babies typically suffer from a variety of physical and developmental defects. Recent discoveries about cholesterol may help to prevent developmental problems such as SLOS. Scientists hope that if cholesterol were to be administered early enough in the development process it would prevent SLOS from occurring. Although SLOS is fairly rare, incidents have increased in recent years as health-conscious women with very low levels of cholesterol are deciding to have children.

Time

According to the passage, children born with Smith-Lemli-Opitz syndrome
- ○ are treated with the hormones estrogen and testoterone
- ○ are unable to produce healthy levels of cholesterol
- ○ have difficulty digesting foods rich in cholesterol
- ○ need diets of cholesterol-free foods

Help Prev Next

DIAGNOSTIC EXAM ◆ 523

Reading

Beginning

For many years, doctors have championed the view that cholesterol is a dangerous substance. When consumed in large quantities, cholesterol tends to build up as excess residue in the arteries and veins of the body. This buildup tends to constrict and limit the flow of blood through the body. In turn, this means that the heart must beat more forcefully if it is to circulate the same amount of blood. Because the heart is pumping harder, the risk of high blood pressure increases. Eventually, high blood pressure, resulting from excessive cholesterol, can lead to heart disease and other physical problems.

But, when consumed in moderation, cholesterol is actually one of the most important substances in the body. It provides suppleness to the outer walls of cells, thus making these walls stronger. Cholesterol also aids in the digestive process, since it is the main ingredient in stomach bile. Finally, cholesterol forms the basis of several important hormones, namely testosterone and estrogen, which are necessary for proper human growth and development. It is somewhat ironic that without cholesterol, a person's body would not be able to function correctly.

Recently, scientists have discovered that cholesterol has a fourth function. Cholesterol controls a protein necessary for the development of embryos. Without cholesterol, a fertilized egg would be unable to develop into a child. Cholesterol guides specialized proteins and in turn tells them when and where to form the physical parts of the body. During initial development of the human body, cholesterol guides proteins which form bones, the spinal chord, large internal organs, and skin. Later, cholesterol helps in the formation of individual fingers and toes.

This information is proving useful in treating certain diseases. Smith-Lemli-Opitz syndrome (SLOS) is a condition in which babies are born lacking the ability to manufacture cholesterol. Such babies typically suffer from a variety of physical and developmental defects. Recent discoveries about cholesterol may help to prevent developmental problems such as SLOS. Scientists hope that if cholesterol were to be administered early enough in the development process it would prevent SLOS from occurring. Although SLOS is fairly rare, incidents have increased in recent years as health-conscious women with very low levels of cholesterol are deciding to have children.

All of the following are mentioned as functions of cholesterol EXCEPT
- ○ it makes cell walls stronger
- ○ it aids in the circulation of blood
- ○ it aids in human development
- ○ it guides the creation of bones and organs

Time

? Help ← Prev → Next

When
finished
reading the
passage,
click on the
icon below

James Watson, Francis Crick, and Maurice Wilkins are the Nobel prize–winning molecular biologists credited with the discovery of the double helix shape of DNA. DNA, the enzymes that make up the chromosomes and therefore the cells of the body, are linked together in two parallel strands of billions of enzymes which coil around one another. This pattern resembles curled train rails intertwined and twisted around each other to form an overlapping and spiraled strand of genetic information. This discovery is one of the most significant in the entire field of molecular biology.

Some recent investigations have uncovered evidence that Watson, Crick, and Wilkins were not the sole specialists researching the properties of DNA. A British scientist, Rosalind Franklin, may have contributed to crucial experimental work which led to the discovery of the DNA strand. Franklin spent the first half of her professional career in England where she researched how rodents responded to interbreeding. She later relocated to France soon after the Second World War. Under the guidance of French crystallographer Jaques Mering, who is credited with the first mapping of crystal scaffolding, she learned to design complex models of various chemical compositons. In addition, she perfected a technique for diffracting X-rays. After returning to England in 1951, she began conducting experiments in molecular genetics at King's College, Cambridge University under the critical supervision of James Randal.

At Cambridge, Franklin ingeniously combined her knowledge of X-ray diffraction with chemical and crystal mapping to successfully photograph a rough image of a single strand of DNA. Unfortunately, the equipment she used was substandard and it exposed her to dangerous X-rays. In 1956, Franklin learned she had cancer and died two years later. Some scientists now speculate that the overexposure to dangerous X-rays during the course of her work was actually the cause of her cancer. Subsequently, Franklin's compiled notes were given over to Watson, Crick, and Wilkins who then went on to perfect nucleic acid research. When the three scientists finally did recieve the Nobel prize, they gave no credit to Franklin for the crucial work she performed which led to the discovery of the double helix shape of DNA.

Proceed

Time

?
Help

← Prev

→ Next

Reading

Beginning

James Watson, Francis Crick, and Maurice Wilkins are the Nobel prize–winning molecular biologists credited with the discovery of the double helix shape of DNA. DNA, the enzymes that make up the chromosomes and therefore the cells of the body, are linked together in two parallel strands of billions of enzymes which coil around one another. This pattern resembles curled train rails intertwined and twisted around each other to form an overlapping and spiraled strand of genetic information. This discovery is one of the most significant in the entire field of molecular biology.

Some recent investigations have uncovered evidence that Watson, Crick, and Wilkins were not the sole specialists researching the properties of DNA. A British scientist, Rosalind Franklin, may have contributed to crucial experimental work which led to the discovery of the DNA strand. Franklin spent the first half of her professional career in England where she researched how rodents responded to interbreeding. She later relocated to France soon after the Second World War. Under the guidance of French crystallographer Jaques Mering, who is credited with the first mapping of crystal scaffolding, she learned to design complex models of various chemical compositons. In addition, she perfected a technique for diffracting X-rays. After returning to England in 1951, she began conducting experiments in molecular genetics at King's College, Cambridge University under the critical supervision of James Randal.

At Cambridge, Franklin ingeniously combined her knowledge of X-ray diffraction with chemical and crystal mapping to successfully photograph a rough image of a single strand of DNA. Unfortunately, the equipment she used was substandard and it exposed her to dangerous X-rays. In 1956, Franklin learned she had cancer and died two years later. Some scientists now speculate that the overexposure to dangerous X-rays during the course of her work was actually the cause of her cancer. Subsequently, Franklin's compiled notes were given over to Watson, Crick, and Wilkins who then went on to perfect nucleic acid research. When the three scientists finally did recieve the Nobel prize, they gave no credit to Franklin for the crucial work she performed which led to the discovery of the double helix shape of DNA.

What is the main idea of the passage?

○ How Rosalind Franklin was instrumental in the discovery of the shape of DNA

○ Whether Watson, Crick, and Wilkins were students of the physicist Rosalind Franklin

○ How the double helix shape of the DNA molecule radically altered genetics

○ The dangers of using potentially substandard X-ray equipment

Time

? Help

← Prev

→ Next

Beginning

James Watson, Francis Crick, and Maurice Wilkins are the Nobel prize–winning molecular biologists credited with the discovery of the double helix shape of DNA. DNA, the enzymes that make up the chromosomes and therefore the cells of the body, are linked together in two parallel strands of billions of enzymes which coil around one another. This pattern resembles curled train rails intertwined and twisted around each other to form an overlapping and spiraled strand of genetic information. This discovery is one of the most significant in the entire field of molecular biology.

Some recent investigations have uncovered evidence that Watson, Crick, and Wilkins were not the sole specialists researching the properties of DNA. A British scientist, Rosalind Franklin, may have contributed to crucial experimental work which led to the discovery of the DNA strand. Franklin spent the first half of her professional career in England where she researched how rodents responded to interbreeding. She later relocated to France soon after the Second World War. Under the guidance of French crystallographer Jaques Mering, who is credited with the first mapping of crystal scaffolding, she learned to design complex models of various chemical compositons. In addition, she perfected a technique for diffracting X-rays. After returning to England in 1951, she began conducting experiments in molecular genetics at King's College, Cambridge University under the critical supervision of James Randal.

At Cambridge, Franklin ingeniously combined her knowledge of X-ray diffraction with chemical and crystal mapping to successfully photograph a rough image of a single strand of DNA. Unfortunately, the equipment she used was substandard and it exposed her to dangerous X-rays. In 1956, Franklin learned she had cancer and died two years later. Some scientists now speculate that the overexposure to dangerous X-rays during the course of her work was actually the cause of her cancer. Subsequently, Franklin's compiled notes were given over to Watson, Crick, and Wilkins who then went on to perfect nucleic acid research. When the three scientists finally did recieve the Nobel prize, they gave no credit to Franklin for the crucial work she performed which led to the discovery of the double helix shape of DNA.

Click on the drawing below that most closely resembles the object described in the text.

Time

Help Prev Next

Reading

Beginning

James Watson, Francis Crick, and Maurice Wilkins are the Nobel prize–winning molecular biologists credited with the discovery of the double helix shape of DNA. DNA, the enzymes that make up the chromosomes and therefore the cells of the body, are linked together in two parallel strands of billions of enzymes which coil around one another. This pattern resembles curled train rails intertwined and twisted around each other to form an overlapping and spiraled strand of genetic information. This discovery is one of the most significant in the entire field of molecular biology.

Some recent investigations have uncovered evidence that Watson, Crick, and Wilkins were not the **sole** specialists researching the properties of DNA. A British scientist, Rosalind Franklin, may have contributed to crucial experimental work which led to the discovery of the DNA strand. Franklin spent the first half of her professional career in England where she researched how rodents responded to interbreeding. She later relocated to France soon after the Second World War. Under the guidance of French crystallographer Jaques Mering, who is credited with the first mapping of crystal scaffolding, she learned to design complex models of various chemical compositons. In addition, she perfected a technique for diffracting X-rays. After returning to England in 1951, she began conducting experiments in molecular genetics at King's College, Cambridge University under the critical supervision of James Randal.

At Cambridge, Franklin ingeniously combined her knowledge of X-ray diffraction with chemical and crystal mapping to successfully photograph a rough image of a single strand of DNA. Unfortunately, the equipment she used was substandard and it exposed her to dangerous X-rays. In 1956, Franklin learned she had cancer and died two years later. Some scientists now speculate that the overexposure to dangerous X-rays during the course of her work was actually the cause of her cancer. Subsequently, Franklin's compiled notes were given over to Watson, Crick, and Wilkins who then went on to perfect nucleic acid research. When the three scientists finally did recieve the Nobel prize, they gave no credit to Franklin for the crucial work she performed which led to the discovery of the double helix shape of DNA.

Look at the highlighted word in the text. Click on the answer choice that is closest in meaning to the word **sole**.

○ original
○ last
○ few
○ only

Time

Beginning

James Watson, Francis Crick, and Maurice Wilkins are the Nobel prize–winning molecular biologists credited with the discovery of the double helix shape of DNA. DNA, the enzymes that make up the chromosomes and therefore the cells of the body, are linked together in two parallel strands of billions of enzymes which coil around one another. This pattern resembles curled train rails intertwined and twisted around each other to form an overlapping and spiraled strand of genetic information. This discovery is one of the most significant in the entire field of molecular biology.

Some recent investigations have uncovered evidence that Watson, Crick, and Wilkins were not the sole specialists researching the properties of DNA. A British scientist, Rosalind Franklin, may have contributed to crucial experimental work which led to the discovery of the DNA strand. Franklin spent the first half of her professional career in England where she researched how rodents responded to interbreeding. She later relocated to France soon after the Second World War. Under the guidance of French crystallographer Jaques Mering, who is credited with the first mapping of crystal scaffolding, she learned to design complex models of various chemical compositons. In addition, she perfected a technique for diffracting X-rays. After returning to England in 1951, she began conducting experiments in molecular genetics at King's College, Cambridge University under the critical supervision of James Randal.

At Cambridge, Franklin ingeniously combined her knowledge of X-ray diffraction with chemical and crystal mapping to successfully photograph a rough image of a single strand of DNA. Unfortunately, the equipment she used was substandard and it exposed her to dangerous X-rays. In 1956, Franklin learned she had cancer and died two years later. Some scientists now speculate that the overexposure to dangerous X-rays during the course of her work was actually the cause of her cancer. Subsequently, Franklin's compiled notes were given over to Watson, Crick, and Wilkins who then went on to perfect nucleic acid research. When the three scientists finally did recieve the Nobel prize, they gave no credit to Franklin for the crucial work she performed which led to the discovery of the double helix shape of DNA.

It can be inferred from the passage that before World War II, Franklin

○ was uninterested in the genetical science
○ immigrated to the United States
○ worked in England
○ changed her course of study at Cambridge

Time

Reading

Beginning

James Watson, Francis Crick, and Maurice Wilkins are the Nobel prize–winning molecular biologists credited with the discovery of the double helix shape of DNA. DNA, the enzymes that make up the chromosomes and therefore the cells of the body, are linked together in two parallel strands of billions of enzymes which coil around one another. This pattern resembles curled train rails intertwined and twisted around each other to form an overlapping and spiraled strand of genetic information. This discovery is one of the most significant in the entire field of molecular biology.

Some recent investigations have uncovered evidence that Watson, Crick, and Wilkins were not the sole specialists researching the properties of DNA. A British scientist, Rosalind Franklin, may have contributed to crucial experimental work which led to the discovery of the DNA strand. Franklin spent the first half of her professional career in England where she researched how rodents responded to interbreeding. She later relocated to France soon after the Second World War. Under the guidance of French crystallographer Jaques Mering, who is credited with the first mapping of crystal scaffolding, she learned to design complex models of various chemical compositons. In addition, she perfected a technique for diffracting X-rays. After returning to England in 1951, she began conducting experiments in molecular genetics at King's College, Cambridge University under the critical supervision of James Randal.

At Cambridge, Franklin ingeniously combined her knowledge of X-ray diffraction with chemical and crystal mapping to successfully photograph a rough image of a single strand of DNA. Unfortunately, the equipment she used was substandard and it exposed her to dangerous X-rays. In 1956, Franklin learned she had cancer and died two years later. Some scientists now speculate that the overexposure to dangerous X-rays during the course of her work was actually the cause of her cancer. Subsequently, Franklin's compiled notes were given over to Watson, Crick, and Wilkins who then went on to perfect nucleic acid research. When the three scientists finally did recieve the Nobel prize, they gave no credit to Franklin for the crucial work she performed which led to the discovery of the double helix shape of DNA.

Look at the highlighted word in the passage. Click on the word or phrase in the bold text that it refers to.

Time

? Help

← Prev

→ Next

Beginning

James Watson, Francis Crick, and Maurice Wilkins are the Nobel prize–winning molecular biologists credited with the discovery of the double helix shape of DNA. DNA, the enzymes that make up the chromosomes and therefore the cells of the body, are linked together in two parallel strands of billions of enzymes which coil around one another. This pattern resembles curled train rails intertwined and twisted around each other to form an overlapping and spiraled strand of genetic information. This discovery is one of the most significant in the entire field of molecular biology.

Some recent investigations have uncovered evidence that Watson, Crick, and Wilkins were not the sole specialists researching the properties of DNA. A British scientist, Rosalind Franklin, may have contributed to crucial experimental work which led to the discovery of the DNA strand. Franklin spent the first half of her professional career in England where she researched how rodents responded to interbreeding. She later relocated to France soon after the Second World War. Under the guidance of French crystallographer Jaques Mering, who is credited with the first mapping of crystal scaffolding, she learned to design complex models of various chemical compositons. In addition, she perfected a technique for diffracting X-rays. After returning to England in 1951, she began conducting experiments in molecular genetics at King's College, Cambridge University under the critical supervision of James Randal.

At Cambridge, Franklin ingeniously combined her knowledge of X-ray diffraction with chemical and crystal mapping to successfully photograph a rough image of a single strand of DNA. Unfortunately, the equipment she used was substandard and it exposed her to dangerous X-rays. In 1956, Franklin learned she had cancer and died two years later. Some scientists now speculate that the overexposure to dangerous X-rays during the course of her work was actually the cause of her cancer. Subsequently, Franklin's compiled notes were given over to Watson, Crick, and Wilkins who then went on to perfect nucleic acid research. When the three scientists finally did recieve the Nobel prize, they gave no credit to Franklin for the crucial work she performed which led to the discovery of the double helix shape of DNA.

According to the passage, to what do scientists attribute Franklin's cancer?

○ Radiation from World War II
○ Faulty and inadequate equipment
○ Genetic inheritance
○ Overexposure to dangerous chemicals

Time   Help   Prev   Next

Reading

Beginning

James Watson, Francis Crick, and Maurice Wilkins are the Nobel prize–winning molecular biologists credited with the discovery of the double helix shape of DNA. DNA, the enzymes that make up the chromosomes and therefore the cells of the body, are linked together in two parallel strands of billions of enzymes which coil around one another. This pattern resembles curled train rails intertwined and twisted around each other to form an overlapping and spiraled strand of genetic information. This discovery is one of the most significant in the entire field of molecular biology.

Some recent investigations have uncovered evidence that Watson, Crick, and Wilkins were not the sole specialists researching the properties of DNA. A British scientist, Rosalind Franklin, may have contributed to crucial experimental work which led to the discovery of the DNA strand. Franklin spent the first half of her professional career in England where she researched how rodents responded to interbreeding. She later relocated to France soon after the Second World War. Under the guidance of French crystallographer Jaques Mering, who is credited with the first mapping of crystal scaffolding, she learned to design complex models of various chemical compositons. In addition, she perfected a technique for diffracting X-rays. After returning to England in 1951, she began conducting experiments in molecular genetics at King's College, Cambridge University under the critical supervision of James Randal.

At Cambridge, Franklin ingeniously combined her knowledge of X-ray diffraction with chemical and crystal mapping to successfully photograph a rough image of a single strand of DNA. Unfortunately, the equipment she used was substandard and it exposed her to dangerous X-rays. In 1956, Franklin learned she had cancer and died two years later. Some scientists now speculate that the overexposure to dangerous X-rays during the course of her work was actually the cause of her cancer. Subsequently, Franklin's compiled notes were **given over to** Watson, Crick, and Wilkins who then went on to perfect nucleic acid research. When the three scientists finally did recieve the Nobel prize, they gave no credit to Franklin for the crucial work she performed which led to the discovery of the double helix shape of DNA.

Look at the highlighted phrase in the text. What does the author imply by saying that Franklin's notes, were **given over to** Watson, Crick, and Wilkins?

○ Watson, Crick, and Wilkins continued Franklin's research.

○ Watson, Crick, and Wilkins stole Franklin's research.

○ Watson, Crick, and Wilkins presented Franklin's research to other scientists.

○ Watson, Crick, and Wilkins devoted themselves to Franklin's research.

Time

? Help ← Prev → Next

Beginning

James Watson, Francis Crick, and Maurice Wilkins are the Nobel prize–winning molecular biologists credited with the discovery of the double helix shape of DNA. DNA, the enzymes that make up the chromosomes and therefore the cells of the body, are linked together in two parallel strands of billions of enzymes which coil around one another. This pattern resembles curled train rails intertwined and twisted around each other to form an overlapping and spiraled strand of genetic information. This discovery is one of the most significant in the entire field of molecular biology.

Some recent investigations have uncovered evidence that Watson, Crick, and Wilkins were not the sole specialists researching the properties of DNA. A British scientist, Rosalind Franklin, may have contributed to crucial experimental work which led to the discovery of the DNA strand. Franklin spent the first half of her professional career in England where she researched how rodents responded to interbreeding. She later relocated to France soon after the Second World War. Under the guidance of French crystallographer Jaques Mering, who is credited with the first mapping of crystal scaffolding, she learned to design complex models of various chemical compositons. In addition, she perfected a technique for diffracting X-rays. After returning to England in 1951, she began conducting experiments in molecular genetics at King's College, Cambridge University under the critical supervision of James Randal.

At Cambridge, Franklin ingeniously combined her knowledge of X-ray diffraction with chemical and crystal mapping to successfully photograph a rough image of a single strand of DNA. Unfortunately, the equipment she used was substandard and it exposed her to dangerous X-rays. In 1956, Franklin learned she had cancer and died two years later. Some scientists now speculate that the overexposure to dangerous X-rays during the course of her work was actually the cause of her cancer. Subsequently, Franklin's compiled notes were given over to Watson, Crick, and Wilkins who then went on to perfect nucleic acid research. When the three scientists finally did recieve the Nobel prize, they gave no credit to Franklin for the crucial work she performed which led to the discovery of the double helix shape of DNA.

In what order does the author discuss Franklin's accomplishments in the passage?
- ○ From the most prominent to the least prominent
- ○ In the order in which they occurred
- ○ According to the scientific journal in which they were published
- ○ The most recent to the earliest

Time

? Help

← Prev

→ Next

Writing

Writing

- Read the essay questions carefully.
- Think before you write. Making notes may help to organize your essay.
- It is important to write only on the topic you are given.
- Check your work. Allow a few minutes before the time is up to read over your essay and make changes.
- In the actual test you must stop writing at the end of 30 minutes. If you continue to write, it will be considered cheating.
- If you finish your essay before 30 minutes, click on Next and then on Confirm Answer.
- When you are ready to continue, click on the Dismiss Directions icon.

When finished reading directions click on the icon below

Dismiss Directions

Time

Help

Answer Confirm

Next

Writing

Read the question below and type your response in the box.

Do you agree or disagree with the following statement?
The best education comes from experience, not from a book.
Use reasons and specific examples to support your opinion.

Cut

Paste

Undo

Time

? Help

Answer Confirm

→ Next

Writing

_____

_____

_____

_____

_____

_____

_____

_____

_____

_____

_____

_____

_____

_____

_____

_____

_____

_____

_____

_____

_____

_____

Answer Key

LISTENING SECTION

1. Take some time before deciding.

2. She's not responsible for the lost notecards.

3. He probably isn't interested in seeing the play.

4. She forgot about their plans to play racquetball.

5. She's too tired to travel.

6. The work on the laser center should be completed soon.

7. He still hasn't decided on a topic.

8. See if the game was canceled.

9. David will not go to the movie.

10. He would prefer to take a taxi.

11. She feels that the room is already too cold.

12. Pete lent her his notes.

13. The twentieth-century painting collection is also small.

14. The journalism classes helped her with her new position.

15. He doesn't have the right skills for debate.

16. The disk could be among some other disks.

17. To clarify a previous lecture on banking

18. To give an example of earlier methods of acquiring goods

19. It was dangerous to carry. It was too heavy.

20. They issued receipts.

21. Dangers facing the Earth's trees

22. Farming, Shelter

23. To give an example of the serious threat natural disasters are to trees

24. Most severe threat = Humans

    Severe threat = Natural disasters

    Least severe threat = Insects and disease

25. Hunting and gathering = Tribal method

    Southern colonial = Manor method

    Pompeii = Brazier method

26. Outdoor kitchens wouldn't increase the indoor temperature.

27. Bathing, Sewing

28. They are used for more than just food preparation.

29. To inform the students of the side effects of smoking

30. To seal peace treaties among tribes

31. The infants are born earlier than expected.

32. Recent studies on the dangers of second-hand smoke

33. Heart rate, Circulation

34. They need more to bring about the same effects.

35. The survival techniques of moths

36. Moths are active during the night.

37. They are knobby and feathery.

38. Leaves, Sticks

39. The correct order is:

    The caterpillars weave a communal silk tent.

    A predator threatens the larvae.

    Thousands of larvae begin to wiggle and squirm.

    The larvae release a highly offensive smell.

40. Its legs detach from its body.

41. How various joints differ from each other

42. Ball and socket joint = Shoulder

    Hinge joint = Elbow

    Pivot joint = Neck

43. It allows the greatest range of movement.

44. Ball and socket

45. Picture C

46. It becomes painful and movement is limited.

47. It is replaced by newer information.

48. Associate the name with something ridiculous or absurd.

49. How well the material was stored in the association stage

50. Age, Disuse

Structure Section

1. most plentiful element
2. organization
3. it useful
4. which they
5. included
6. they need
7. attract
8. language native
9. how to go
10. although
11. but account
12. thereby making
13. necessary
14. ranch
15. There are about
16. are children
17. a such
18. were of no use
19. incorporates
20. prevent

Reading Section

1. The overthrow of established medical tradition
2. prevent
3. They kept the common people from understanding medicine.
4. ridiculous
5. needles
6. often were of no help to their patients
7. chose
8. He educated himself about medicine.
9. doctors were not to share medical information with nonprofessionals

10. dismissed

11. Historical experiments on light and its properties

12. believed

13. He had considerable influence in the scientific world.

14. Publishing their results on light diffraction took a lot of courage.

15. electric and magnetic fields

16. The second paragraph refutes the theory mentioned in the first paragraph.

17. following

18. The final calculations weren't exactly accurate.

19. it is diffused by transparent objects

20. The sentence should be added at the first black square.

21. Stage movements

22. Renaissance comedy was scripted.

23. Improvisation was the key to the success of the *commedia dell'arte.*

24. actors

25. helped the performers develop their characters

26. restricted

27. dull

28. gradual

29. plot lines were too complicated

30. The cast rehearsed scripted melodramas.

31. The sentence should be added to the end of paragraph 2.

32. The benefits of cholesterol to the human body

33. supported

34. heart

35. They increase the chance of high blood pressure.

36. Cholesterol also aids in the digestive process, since it is the main ingredient in stomach bile.

37. paradoxical

38. early

39. forms before the fingers and toes

40. are unable to produce healthy levels of cholesterol

41. it aids in the circulation of blood

42. How Rosalind Franklin was instrumental in the discovery of the shape of DNA

43. Drawing A

44. only

45. worked in England

46. equipment

47. overexposure to dangerous chemicals

48. Watson, Crick, and Wilkins continued Franklin's research.

49. In the order in which they were occurred

10

How to Score Your Test

HOW TO SCORE YOUR TEST

Calculating your score on the TOEFL CBT is quite a process. However, you can follow the steps below to find your estimated score. Remember that your 30-minute essay is one-half of your total Structure score. Although we know that ETS grades your essay on a scale of 1 to 6, we don't know their exact grading criteria and how they incorporate it into the final Structure score. Therefore, it is impossible to incorporate your Writing score into your final score.

To calculate your estimated score on the diagnostic test, you must first determine how many questions you answered correctly. Fill in the number of correctly answered questions for each section in the spaces below.

Listening section 1: Number correct _____

Structure section 2: Number correct _____

Reading section 3: Number correct _____

Now, find the corresponding raw score range on the Converted Score Range in Chart 1. For example, if you answered 31 questions correctly in a section, your raw score range would be 30–32. After you find the right raw score range for each section, find the converted score range that corresponds to it by moving across that row to the column for the appropriate section. If you answered 31 questions correctly in the Listening Section 1, you would receive a converted score range of 49–51. Convert your scores for all three sections using Chart 1.

CONVERTED SCORE RANGES—CHART 1			
Raw Score Range	Listening Section 1	Structure Section 2	Reading Section 3
48–50	64–68		66–68
45–47	61–63		62–65
42–44	58–60		58–61
39–41	56–57		55–57
36–38	53–55		52–54
33–35	50–51		49–51
30–32	49–51		47–48
27–29	48–49		45–46
24–26	46–47		43–44
21–23	44–45		41–42
18–20	42–43	58–68	39–40
15–17	40–42	50–56	36–38
12–14	37–39	44–49	33–35
9–11	33–36	39–43	29–32
6–8	30–32	32–38	26–28
3–5	28–29	24–30	23–25
0–2	25–27	20–22	20–22

SAMPLE CONVERSION

Look at a sample conversion. Below is the number of questions one student answered correctly on The Princeton Review Diagnostic Exam:

Listening section 1: 28   Converted raw score range for section 1: 48–49

Structure section 2: 15   Converted raw score range for section 2: 50–56

Reading section 3: 38   Converted raw score range for section 3: 52–54

1. Add together the first number in each of the converted score range. In the sample above, 48 + 50 + 52 = 150.

2. Next, add the last number in each of the converted score range. In the sample above, 49 + 56 + 54 = 159.

3. Multiply each number by 10/3. Round down to the nearest whole number. This will give you a converted score range. For our sample scores: 150 × 10/3 = 500. 159 × 10/3 = 530. The converted score range is 500–530.

4. Now find the halfway point between your score range. In this case, the halfway point between 500–530 is 515. 515 is now your pre-score.

5. Find your pre-score in the left column of Comparison Chart 2 below. Our pre-score, 515, falls between the range 499–520. Move directly to the right to find the final score range. In this case, 174–190.

6. Find the halfway point between 174–190, which is 182. 182 is your final score.

COMPARISON CHART 2	
Pre-score	**Final score range**
661–677	228–300
641–661	272–287
621–640	261–271
601–620	251–260
581–600	238–250
561–580	221–237
541–560	208–220
521–540	191–207
499–520	174–190
481–498	158–173
461–480	141–157
441–460	124–140
421–440	111–123
400–420	98–110
381–399	82–97
361–380	71–81
341–360	61–70
321–340	48–60
310–320	40–47

YOUR TURN

Number correct for

     Section 1: _____

     Section 2: _____

     Section 3: _____

     Converted score range for section 1 (refer to chart 1): _____

     Converted score range for section 2 (refer to chart 1): _____

     Converted score range for section 3 (refer to chart 1): _____

ADD first number in each of converted score range sections.

     1. _____ + _____ + _____ = _____

ADD second number in each of converted score range sections.

     2. _____ + _____ + _____ = _____

MULTIPLY your respective results.

     3. _____ $\times \dfrac{10}{3}$ = _____

          _____ $\times \dfrac{10}{3}$ = _____

     4. Find the halfway point of your score range _____.

     5. Find your pre-score in the left column of Comparison Chart 2 and move directly to the right to find your final score range. Final score range _____.

     6. Find the halfway point of your final score range. Final score _____.

Appendix

TRANSCRIPTIONS OF THE LISTENING SECTION

Track 2

Question 1 (pages 75–76)
M: "Check this out! I just found this incredibly interesting-looking book buried up in the reserved periodical room."
W: "You know what, Paul? If I were you, I wouldn't waste time looking around the library. We barely have three hours to get our paper written, typed, and handed in."

Question 2 (pages 77–78)
M: "So, it's all set. We're meeting in front of the movie theatre down by that new laundromat in twenty minutes. Will you be there?"
W: "Just as soon as I finish this chapter."

Question 3 (pages 79–80)
M: "I haven't seen Jim at one of our group meetings in ages. What was his excuse this time?"
W: "Supposedly, he has a big midterm exam to study for."

Question 4 (pages 81–82)
W: "I just spoke to my travel agent and I'm afraid the only available flight leaves the Saturday of your concert."
M: "Can't you put the trip off until the following week?"

Question 5 (pages 83–84)
M: "Congratulations! I hear that you beat out fifty other applicants to win the scholarship you applied for. Does it cover your tuition?"
W: "I wish! It barely covers the cost of my books and supplies."

Question 6 (pages 85–86)
W: "Say, Bob, did you take those videotapes back to the library? They're due back today."
M: "Actually, Ellen was heading in that direction, so I just got her to do it."

Question 7 (pages 87–88)
W: "Thank goodness that algebra exam is over. Did you notice Lara? She didn't even touch her calculator."

M: "How she can figure out those types of problems in her head is beyond me."

Question 8 (pages 89–90)
M: "Listen, you've got to help me figure out what I'm going to wear to Fred's graduation party."
W: "Oh, so you are going?"

Question 9 (pages 91–92)
M: "I can't believe it! Professor Blake gave me a C on my biology test."
W: "Next time, perhaps you should consider studying without the television on."

Question 10 (pages 93–94)
M: "What are the chances that my term paper will be done by this Friday?"
W: "Well, if you give me the weekend, I can have it ready for you by Monday."

Question 11 (pages 95–96)
M: "Look, there's John. Do you think he passed his calculus final?"
W: "Judging from his expression, I'd say he did."

Question 12 (pages 97–98)
M: "I don't want to miss my appointment with the dean tomorrow. Do you think I should ask my roommate to wake me up?"
W: "It couldn't hurt."

Question 13 (pages 99–100)
W: "I've been working on this essay all night, and I still haven't written a word."
M: "Stick with it a little longer."

Question 14 (pages 101–102)
M: "Have you heard the latest about Jeff?"
W: "Just that he is graduating early."
M: "Not only that, but he was awarded a full scholarship for his doctoral studies."
W: "Sounds like he really has got it made."

Question 15 (pages 103–104)
W: "I'm off to my workout at the gym over at the recreation center."
M: "You've been spending a lot of time over there recently."
W: "Well, to tell you the truth, ever since I took up aerobics, I've been feeling a lot more energetic."
M: "What did I tell you?"

TRACK 3

Drill 1 (pages 121–127)

(pages 122–123) Listen to a conversation between a student and a chemistry professor.

M: "Good morning, Jill. How is everything?"

W: "Well, good and bad, actually. First, I just want to let you know that I decided to accept your offer to work as your teaching assistant in chemistry this coming semester."

M: "Jill, that's great."

W: "I'm really excited to be working with you. Are you still involved in the electrochemistry research? I was hoping to maybe help you coauthor at least part of the final publication."

M: "Actually, I am. I can't wait to fill you in on the details. Fortunately, the dean came through on the research grant that I had applied for last spring. Without that grant, I doubt if the project would've ever gotten off the ground. I'm really going to need you to conduct all the experiments and record the data."

W: "Well, the main reason I wanted to speak with you is about this letter I just received from the registrar, informing me that I was unable to register for classes. And, if I can't register for classes, I can't work as your research assistant. I must admit I was a little shocked to find all this out."

M: "OK, let me take a look at this letter. Wow, this is a surprise. According to this, Jill, you are on academic probation, and until you clear it up, it looks as if you won't be allowed to register."

W: "Something is drastically wrong. I can't be on academic probation. I have a 3.8 grade point average."

M: "You're correct about that, but academic probation isn't just limited to grade point average. There could be a whole range of issues that qualify someone for academic probation. The reference number given is 8525, which is the telephone extension to the librarian's office."

W: "You've got to be kidding! I know what this is about, and it's unfair! A library book was stolen out of my car last semester, and the library has been trying to get me to pay for it. I refused on the fact that it wasn't my fault. In fact, I've even spoken to them, and they assured me that they would look into it. They can't keep me from registering over a thirty-dollar book."

M: "Actually, I'm afraid they can. All outstanding bills must be paid before a student is eligible to register for the next semester. If you want to contest, you'll have to speak with the registrar."

W: "Listen, I need to take care of this before this weekend. I'm going to be out of town for my sister's wedding, and won't be back until the day before classes begin. I would rather not have all this hassle on the first day of classes. Know what I mean?"

M: "Well, if you want to clear things up, why don't you just run over to the library and pay for the book—better to pay thirty dollars on a book than register late for classes. If you wait, you might not be able to get some of the courses you need."

W: "I guess I don't really have any other choice in the matter now, do I?"

TRACK 4

Drill 2 (pages 129–135)

(pages 130–131) Listen to the following discussion about the history of smoking.

Professor: "Today's class focuses on perhaps one of the most controversial topics of the medical world: smoking. Now, smoking has been in practice for longer than most of you think. Any ideas as to where smoking originated? Pat."

W [Student 1, Pat]: "Didn't the Native American Indian tribes smoke?"

P: "Right, but not all of them. Usually, they were the tribes of the southeast region of what is now known as the United States. In addition, the tribes didn't smoke in the same sense that people smoke today. In fact, for the Native Americans, smoking was a way that members of the same tribe, or leaders from different tribes, sealed an agreement, treaty, or pact. It was regarded as a ritual so sacred that it was performed only in the most solemn of ceremonies."

M [Student 2]: "I learned in my French class that the pipe they used to smoke was called a calumet, which is actually the French word for 'reed.'"

P: "That's correct. The calumet, or peace pipe, as it is referred to in English, usually consisted of a long, feathered stem or reed and a bowl at the end that held the tobacco. These pipes were considered as treasured objects to the tribe, because it was believed that smoking them opened a direct channel with the animate powers of the universe. It was believed that those who smoked from the ornate peace pipes could actually absorb some of these animate powers."

W: "Did everyone have a chance to smoke from these peace pipes?"

P: "Not actually. Only the representatives of the tribes were allowed to smoke. Normally, after the tobacco harvest, those leaders who were involved in the negotiations would assemble in the living quarters of one of the parties. The peace pipe was smoked only after all verbal agreements were reached."

M: "Who harvested the tobacco?"

P: "It was considered a matriarchal duty to plant, grow, cultivate, and harvest the tobacco. In fact, not only were the locations of the tobacco fields kept confidential, but they were also closely guarded to ensure an abundant harvest. High crop yields were believed to mean the upcoming year would be especially prosperous."

TRACK 5

Drill 3 (pages 137–144)

(pages 138–139) Listen to a nutrition professor lecture on the topic of weight.

Professor: "Today, I would like to focus on just one of the many health problems young college students much like yourselves face on a day-to-day basis: weight loss and weight gain. Now, as you are all aware, weight loss occurs when calorie intake is lower than calorie expenditure, whereas weight gain is just the opposite. There are both involuntary and deliberate reasons as to why a person might gain or lose weight. The former could be depression, parasite, or chronic illness; the latter might be dieting or a change in the level of physical activity. In any event, a healthy adult should take his weight seriously and avoid both rapid loss and gain.

"Recently, there has been published research that claims that body weight can be directly linked to personality traits. Medical experts group body types into three different categories: ectomorphic, mesomorphic, and endomorphic. The ectomorphic body type has a thin physique, with light bones and underdeveloped muscles. The mesomorphic body type resembles that of an athlete—strong, well-developed bones, and well-built muscles. The endomorphic body type tends to have a heavy physique, possibly overweight with poorly developed bones and muscles. After conducting hundreds of interviews and countless surveys, psychologists matched each body type with a general personality category. For example, the physically thinner, ectomorphic body types tended to be more sensitive, self-conscious, introspective, and generally quiet people. At the opposite end, the physically heavier, endomorphic body types were sociable, easygoing, relaxed, and pleasure-loving. Meanwhile, the more athletic, mesomorphic body types were aggressive, ready for action with an inkling for adventure, and more prone to interact with strangers. Now, although the personality characteristics did actually follow the three different body types, there were inconsistencies in data. This controversial theory has led certain psychologists and medical experts to disagree over the validity of such research. Opponents warn against associating personality traits with physical appearance simply because during the average life span, people's looks greatly change without much alteration in temperament.

"In any event, whatever your current body weight is, be aware of extreme fluctuation. If you lose or gain weight without deliberately attempting to do so, take the matter seriously, especially if other symptoms suggest the possibility of illness. If you do not weigh yourself regularly, there are other signs that may indicate irregular weight trends: your appearance noticeably changes, or your clothing becomes lose or tight around the waist. All rapid weight deviation from the norm should always be immediately investigated by a medical expert."

TRACK 6
Drill 4 (pages 145–153)

(pages 146–147) Listen to a lecture on the social structure of ants in a biology class.

Professor: "Ants are truly a fascinating species. Unfortunately, few people take notice of these toiling laborers except to either step on them or brush them off their picnic lunch. However, ants are very complex creatures, and I guarantee you the more you learn, the more fascinated you will become with these insects. Perhaps the most interesting thing about ants is their method of social organization.

"Any colony you examine, whether existing in miles of tunnels under the soil or in the cavity of dead logs, is quite cosmopolitan and has a very rigid caste system. By caste, I mean that every ant has a specific role to play and duty to carry out. Most of the time, a colony will be broken down into three castes. The first of these castes include the queens, which have wings and are solely responsible for reproduction. The second class is composed of infertile females called workers. In addition to gathering food for the nest, the workers also double as soldiers, fighting and even sacrificing their own lives to protect the queen. The third caste of ant society includes the males. The male class is responsible for fertilizing the queen, but, more importantly, they build and maintain the infrastructure in which they all reside. Surprisingly, even though the three classes of ants exist in any given colony, one is not considered more valuable than the other. Each role is essential for the survival of succeeding generations.

"Under this highly structured caste system, ant communities have the potential to rapidly grow in size to over a half a million members. Therefore, it is imperative that the ants readily split to form a new community. The process is quite complex. First, the mature generation of queens and males leave on a mating flight. After their job of fertilizing the queen, all the males die. Once the queen is impregnated, they each return to earth where they establish a new colony. The queen then excavates an egg chamber, and proceeds to lay eggs for the rest of her life. All fertilized and unfertilized eggs become females and males, respectively.

"As a group, ants actually benefit humans. First, their ability to tunnel not only mixes the soil, but also exposes it to the air, and thereby prevents it from becoming barren. Second, as they feed on small insects, they consequently eliminate many pests that would otherwise attack and destroy acres of crops. Now that you have had at least a little introduction on ants, let's take a closer look at an ant farm to see exactly how they live."

TRACK 7
[The Princeton Review TOEFL CBT Diagnostic Exam: Listening (Part A)]

Question 1 (pages 385–386)
M: "Tina, would you like to participate in this psychology experiment I have to do for class?"
W: "Why don't I get back to you later."

Question 2 (pages 387–388)
M: "Did anyone see my note cards? I left them on my desk, and now they're gone."
W: "Don't look at me."

Question 3 (pages 389–390)
M: "I couldn't get tickets to homecoming, but I did get some seats for the school play. Would you object to a change in plans?"
W: "Not at all, but John might."

Question 4 (pages 391–392)
M: "Hey, what happened? I thought we were supposed to play racquetball over in the new athletic center this morning."
W: "Would you believe it completely slipped my mind."

Question 5 (pages 393–394)

M: "Ralph and I are considering heading to Florida for spring vacation; that is, if we can afford it."

W: "Really? I'm staying put. Midterm exams really wiped me out."

Question 6 (pages 395–396)

W: "Have they even begun to finish the new addition to the laser center yet?"

M: "The word on campus is that they're hoping to wrap up construction by the summer semester."

Question 7 (pages 397–398)

W: "Do you have any idea as to what subject you're going to focus on for the final project?"

M: "I've been brainstorming, but, unfortunately, I haven't come up with anything yet."

Question 8 (pages 399–400)

M: "My boss really came through on these football tickets. We have to remember to send him a thank you card."

W: "You know, since it's raining, shouldn't we find out if it's been called off?"

Question 9 (pages 401–402)

M: "We still need one more person to get a group discount to the campus movie. If we ask David, do you think he'll come?"

W: "It couldn't hurt to ask. I do know that he's got a final tomorrow, so he'll probably end up studying."

Question 10 (pages 403–404)

W: "With these new fares, the university bus will be even cheaper than before."

M: "The bus is always so packed, though. I think we'd be better off with a taxi."

Question 11 (pages 405–406)

M: "Do you mind if I crack open this window a bit?"

W: "I'd rather you didn't. It's not as warm in here as it feels."

Question 12 (pages 407–408)

M: "You've been out sick for quite a while. Any idea how you are going to catch up?"

W: "Well, I asked the professor for several make-up exams, and I got Pete to lend me his notes."

M: "Pete, really? Usually, he won't let anyone near his notes."

W: "I know, but I just didn't take 'no' for an answer."

Question 13 (pages 409–410)

W: "Our new university museum has the smallest twentieth-century sculpture collection of any museum in the area."

M: "Not to mention paintings."

Question 14 (pages 411–412)

M: "How's everything going with the new position as campus editor? I know that you were dreading the start of the semester."

W: "Well, to tell you the truth, it's turning out to be quite easier than I originally expected."

M: "What did I tell you? With all those journalism classes you were taking, I knew you would have no trouble."

W: "Yeah, little did I know how much they would actually pay off."

Question 15 (pages 413–414)
M: "It's hard for me to believe that you are now president of the campus debate team. How you can stand up and defend some obscure topic is beyond me."

W: "It doesn't surprise me that you feel that way considering that speech was never one of your strengths."

Question 16 (pages 415–416)
M: "You haven't seen my disc around, have you? It was black with a green label. I'm afraid that I left it in the drive over in the computer center."

W: "Did you check that bunch of discs stacked on the shelf?"

[The Princeton Review TOEFL CBT Diagnostic Exam: Listening (Part B)]

Questions 17–20 (pages 418–423)
(pages 418–419) Listen to a class discussion on the origins of banking.

Professor: "Since yesterday's brief introduction on the origin of banking confused some of you, today I would like to review a little bit about this concept. Banking, as we know it today, began as a convenience for those individuals who didn't know what to do with their money. Centuries ago, countries lacked the technology to issue paper money. Any ideas as to what might have been used instead? Joan?"

W [Student 1, Joan]: "I imagine that those cultures that didn't have paper money traded goods for other goods."

P: "Correct. The system of exchanging one good for another of equal value is called bartering. Bartering was quite common in primitive societies—exchanging unessential items, such as art or other cultural objects, for essential items, such as food and shelter. However, what was considered valuable in one society could be deemed worthless in another. Therefore, a more consistent method of payment was needed. Paul, can you give one example of something that might have had cross-cultural value?"

M [Student 2, Paul]: "How about gold? It's been valued since prehistoric times, and, due to its durability, malleability, and beauty, it could have functioned as a type of money in various cultures."

P: "That's right. Gold is a perfect example. As societies gradually grew more stable, gold replaced the bartering system. However, what do you think might have been some problems with using gold as money? Yes, Joan?"

W: "Well, besides the obvious safety problem of carrying around gold, I imagine it was really heavy and inconvenient."

P: "Right you are. Not only was hauling around all your gold a risk in earlier, less law-abiding societies, but it was extremely burdensome, especially if they had a lot of it to carry for a long distance. As a result, people started to leave their gold with gold specialists for safekeeping. Every time a person left their gold with these so-called goldsmiths, a receipt concerning the weight, size, purity, and total value was issued to the individual who owned the gold."

W: "So, if a person gave a goldsmith five hundred ounces of gold, he would issue receipts for five hundred ounces."

P: "That's right, but what's important is that soon these receipts slowly came to be regarded as a form of paper money. Instead of running to the goldsmith's to withdraw gold and then returning to the store to pay for materials, the people simply handed these receipts over to the merchant. Once they became the property of the merchant, he could give them out to other customers for change."

M: "So, what did the goldsmiths do with the gold in the meantime?"

P: "Well, goldsmiths cleverly realized that they could lend out this gold and earn interest on the loans."

W: "So, now goldsmiths weren't just keepers of the gold, they became bankers."

M: "And by making loans, they created money."

P: "Now you have it."

Questions 21–24 (pages 424–429)

(pages 424–425) Listen to a biology professor discuss the importance of trees.

Professor: "Of course, you all know the importance of oxygen to our survival, but I wonder if any one of you can tell me exactly what produces the oxygen we depend on for life. Claire?"

W [Student 1, Claire]: "I would have to say 'plants.'"

P: "Correct. However, more specifically, it is the trees that dot our landscapes that provide the largest portion of our oxygen supply. Through the process of photosynthesis, trees take the carbon monoxide from the surrounding air, and, in return, create a sizable amount of oxygen. Recently, there has been great debate as to what is responsible for the dwindling number of trees. Any ideas?"

M [Student 2]: "It seems to me that the greatest threat to trees is, ironically, humans."

P: "True enough. Humans pose the most significant threat to the survival of the world wide tree population by cutting them down to create shelter, energy, and cultivable land. But, we are not the only force that threatens the survival of these mighty members of the plant kingdom. Trees, which are among the oldest and largest organisms on the planet, face many other dangers."

W: "What about natural disasters? I suppose they could destroy trees as well."

P: "Actually, natural disasters, such as floods, lightning, tornadoes, and volcanic eruptions, can destroy hundreds of square miles of old-growth forest in a matter of minutes. In fact, so severe are some of the natural disasters that special teams of experts dedicate their careers to predicting them in order to prevent old-growth trees from destruction. Even so, natural disasters still destroy fewer acres of trees than humans. Yes, Samuel?"

M [Student 2, Samuel]: "Aren't we overlooking diseases and insects? I know that my hometown lost hundreds of elm trees to a disease."

P: "Surprisingly, disease-causing fungi and insects pose the least threat to trees. Even though they tend to be confined to local areas and may be quickly treated with pesticides, they have been known to eradicate an entire population of a specific type of tree within one or two growing seasons."

Questions 25–28 (pages 430–435)

(pages 430–431) Listen to a discussion on the historical development of the kitchen.

Professor: "Today, I would like to begin our class by speaking about the historical development of what may very well be one of the most utilized rooms in our living environments: the kitchen. In hunting and gathering societies, food was always cooked outside in the open air on fires. This type of cooking, known as the Tribal method, was not only extremely advantageous for ancient nomads that were continually on the move, but the food preparation itself was easier to accomplish due to the communal effort. However, once society became less transient, cooking moved indoors. Can anyone think of some advantages or disadvantages to cooking food indoors? Phil."

M [Student 1, Phil]: "Well, one obvious advantage would be that food could be prepared during severe weather conditions, such as rain or wind."

W [Student 2]: "But, wouldn't there be a problem with ventilation? I can just imagine that smoke might pose some sort of a health risk."

P: "Well, excavations at the ancient city of Pompeii revealed that they used a method of cooking, now known as the Brazier method, where food was prepared in a sort of metal basket filled with burning charcoal. While this indeed decreased the dependency on suitable weather, it also created the ventilation problem that Bernice referred to. Any ideas how one could solve this dilemma?"

W [Student 2, Bernice]: "How about building a separate room that's not connected to the common living area?"

P: "Right. Once architecture became more refined, this method of food preparation was known as the Manor method, and was most common in the southern areas during colonial America. Any guesses as to why this technique was normally found in the south?"

M: "I suppose it had something to do with the heat."

P: "Simply. Cooking raised the temperature in the household to unbearable degrees. Therefore, with the cooking performed in a completely separate area, residents could enjoy a cool environment in which to dwell. A question, Bernice?"

W: "Yes. I know I use my kitchen for a lot more than just making something to eat. I study and hang out with friends. Didn't other cultures do the same?"

P: "Actually, yes. Unlike their neighbors in the south, large farmhouses in northern colonial America constructed huge kitchens directly attached to the common living area. This served to warm the house during the winter, and provide enough space to accommodate such activities as sewing, weaving, harness mending, and bathing."

M: "I'm sure their kitchens looked nothing like mine does now."

P: "Nowadays, the typical kitchen is filled with timesaving gadgets for food preparation, such as microwaves, food processors, and coffeemakers. Even cleanup time has been drastically reduced with such handy appliances as garbage disposals, trash compactors, and dishwashers. In fact, one could safely conclude that modern-day life finds kitchens becoming less of a place for food preparation and more of a hub for family life."

Questions 29–34 (pages 436–443)

(pages 436–437) Listen to the following lecture in a physiology class about the effects of smoking.

Professor: "Before we examine the physiological effects of nicotine, I'd like to talk about some of the issues associated with smoking. Today, it's an accepted scientific fact that smoking tobacco has widespread negative effects on the human body. It hasn't always been this way, though. Historically, smoking was used to seal peace treaties among native North American tribes. Later, in Europe, smoking was considered a pleasant social custom, and was even believed to be healthy. That's right. Even here in the United States, physicians were still prescribing tobacco for nervousness or indigestion until the early part of this century. Today, however, medical research shows that the relaxing effect of nicotine is actually caused by a reduction in the amount of oxygen supplied to the brain. And, while the action of nicotine on the stomach may help with digestion, it can also contribute to the formation of ulcers.

"Smoking is extremely harmful to the fetus during pregnancy. Infants of women who smoke tend to be born prematurely, and almost always have a lower birth weight and higher infant mortality rate. Furthermore, studies conclude that children whose parents smoke have a wide variety of health problems ranging from asthma to a general weakening of the immune system. But, children are not the only ones to suffer from secondhand smoke. In fact, research has proven that anybody in the near vicinity of a smoker is at an increased risk of developing tobacco-related disorders. These recent studies have led to an explosion in antismoking legislation that is creating smokeless environments in such public spaces as government buildings, office buildings, restaurants, and train stations.

"Nicotine is the chemical found in tobacco that causes addiction to smoking. It acts primarily on the autonomic nervous system. The autonomic nervous system controls the involuntary body activities, such as heart rate, digestion, breathing, and circulation, to name a few. For habitual smokers, nicotine stimulates the central nervous system, and, consequently, reduces fatigue, increases alertness, and improves concentration. Regular tobacco smoking results in a tolerance so great that a higher intake is needed to bring about the same effect. Eventually, the organs become poisoned and cease to function correctly as the dependency on nicotine increases. That's why quitting smoking is so tough. The withdrawal symptoms are so physically demanding that most smokers would rather just take their chances at not developing serious disease than suffering through the drowsiness, headaches, fatigue, and irritation."

Questions 35–40 (pages 444–451)

(pages 444–445) Listen to a lecture on moths.

Professor: "You've probably all become aware in the last month of the beautiful butterflies seen fluttering about on campus. That's because butterflies tend to be diurnal, that is, hunting, migrating, and mating during the day. Moths, on the other hand, are less likely to be seen due to their nocturnal activity. But, even though they receive much less adoration than butterflies, moths surprisingly outnumber them in both diversity and number of species. But, how can you tell the difference between a butterfly and a moth? Simply examine their antennae. The butterfly's antennae are smooth whereas the moth's are knobby and feathery.

"Moths are able to dwell in almost any unimaginable climate, from the wet, tropical rain forests to arid deserts. Their survival techniques are among the most adaptable known. Most commonly, moths camouflage themselves, either imitating a leaf or stick, to blend into their surrounding environment. A select group of moths resemble poisonous insects, such as killer wasps and bees. One type of Southeast Asian moth actually has huge eye-like markings on its hind wings that frightens potential foes away and ensures the moth's survival. Although moths are generally harmless and pose little threat to their predators, one species has been observed to spit formic acid at the eyes of its enemies. The tiger moth secretes a fluid with such a highly offensive odor that predators are quickly turned away.

"But, the survival techniques of moths are not limited to the adults. During the pupal stage of development, the moth larvae also employ diverse survival techniques. The Eastern tent caterpillars, for example, weave a communal silk tent in which hundreds or thousands of larvae pupate. If threatened by a predator, such as a bird or frog, the larvae all begin to wiggle and squirm about simultaneously, thus intimidating and frightening away the predator with their collective movement. If this fails to deter the predator, they then give off an extremely noxious mix of hydrogen cyanide and benzaldehyde. This smell alone is enough to convince any enemy to look for its dinner elsewhere. Perhaps the most impressive survival technique of moth larvae is demonstrated by the monkey moth. If the colorful monkey moth caterpillars attacked, it allows the predator to remove its detachable legs of its exoskeleton. The legs immediately begin to regenerate, and are fully regrown in a matter of hours.

"The spectacular abilities to adapt to adverse conditions in both the larval and adult stages reveal the reasons why the moth exists today. Besides being a crucial link in the food chain, moths provide biologists with living examples of evolution in action."

Questions 41–46 (pages 452–459)

(pages 452–453) Listen to a professor lecture on the different types of joints.

Professor: "Now, I know that most of you are healthy individuals who participate in some sort of physical activity on a weekly basis. Some of you jog, others bicycle, throw frisbee, or rollerblade. But did you ever stop to think that none of this would be possible if our bodies lacked the ability to bend? This ability is made possible by joints. A joint is any junction where two or more bones connect, and are either movable or immovable. A movable joint is surrounded by various tissue to ensure smooth and painless movement. One of the most common types of movable joints found in almost all mammals is called a hinge joint. It allows bending and straightening with little other movement. Can anybody here give me an example of a simple hinge joint? Tony."

M [Student 1, Tony]: "Well, I guess my elbow or knee is an example of a hinge joint. But, what about my hip? Is that also considered a hinge joint?"

P: "Actually, no. The hip, as well as the shoulder, is a perfect example of a ball-and-socket joint. The ball-and-socket joint allows the greatest range of movement, and therefore is the most anatomically complex. It is formed when the rounded end of one bone fits snugly into the hollow, or socket, of another bone. The ball-and-socket joint is a type of joint characteristically found in more evolved creatures, such as apes and us, humans. Can anyone think of another type of joint?"

W [Student 2]: "Well, I know that as I rollerblade, I have to turn my head constantly to make sure I don't crash into anyone. But, the neck doesn't seem to be an example of either a hinge joint or a ball-and-socket joint."

P: "Good example, Louise. The neck is actually a type of pivot joint. Pivot joints permit rotary movement, like turning the head from side to side."

M: "You mentioned earlier that joints are surrounded by different tissues that reduce pain and ensure easy movement. Could you explain that a little more?"

P: "Sure. Joints are held together with ligaments, and cushioned by either liquid or cartilage. The joints that are lubricated and nourished with liquid are called synovial joints. The knuckles on the fingers are an excellent example of a synovial joint. The fluid is held in place by what is known as a bursa sac. Cartilaginous joints are padded with a tough smooth tissue that lines the surfaces of joints and provides an almost frictionless layer over the bony parts of the joint. If this cartilaginous joint becomes worn or damaged, joint movement may be painful or severely restricted."

Questions 47–50 (pages 460–465)

(pages 460–461) Listen to a professor lecture on the process of memory.

Professor: "A popular saying goes, 'An elephant never forgets,' but how about people? Have you ever forgotten the name of someone you just met at a party? Sure, we all have. This is because our memories are complex processes. Some psychologists have conducted research projects on hundreds of volunteers, and, as a result, have divided memory into three stages: registration, long-term memory, and recall.

"In the initial stage, registration, information is perceived and understood, like when you first hear a name or an address. This information is then retained in the short-term memory system. Unfortunately, the short-term memory is limited in the amount of material it can store at one time. And, unless refreshed by constant repetition, the new contents are lost within minutes when replaced by even newer information. To solve this dilemma, the information needs to be transferred to the second stage, long-term memory.

"In the second stage, the remembering of the new information is most easily accomplished by using what the research team labeled association. Associating the new information with the visual imagery evoked by it gives the individual a crutch on which he can rely to remember. For example, let's say you're at a party and you've just met a woman named Lily. To remember her name, visualize it in connection to the lily flower. Picture her with a big basket of lilies, or wearing a hat with a lily on it, or even sitting inside a giant lily. The more ridiculous and absurd the image, the easier it will be to remember it.

"The third stage, recall, is when the information stored in an unconscious level is then deliberately brought into the conscious mind. However, this final stage primarily depends on how well the material was stored in stage two. Of course, there are other disturbances that may affect the recall stage—age, for example. The older a person gets, the less new information he can recall. Disuse is another example. Here, forgetting occurs because stored information is not used, and, therefore, is lost. Memory loss can also be physiological. If a person receives an injury to the head, he may experience what is known as amnesia, the failure to remember certain or even all events preceding the accident.

"Of course, many self-help books on how to improve your memory have been published, and many other mnemonic methods have been tried and tested. Let's take a closer look at some of the more widely accepted approaches to memory enhancement. Perhaps you may even incorporate some of them into your study habits as you prepare for the upcoming finals."